SET YOUR VOICE FREE

SET YOUR VOICE FREE

How to Get the Singing or Speaking Voice You Want

Expanded Edition

ROGER LOVE
with DONNA FRAZIER

LITTLE, BROWN AND COMPANY

New York   Boston   London

Little, Brown and Company
Hachette Book Group
1290 Avenue of the Americas, New York, NY 10104
littlebrown.com

First edition: October 1999
Expanded edition: December 2016

Little, Brown and Company is a division of Hachette Book Group, Inc. The Little, Brown name and logo are trademarks of Hachette Book Group, Inc.

The publisher is not responsible for websites (or their content) that are not owned by the publisher.

The Hachette Speakers Bureau provides a wide range of authors for speaking events. To find out more, go to hachettespeakersbureau.com or call (866) 376-6591.

ISBN 978-0-316-31126-7
LCCN 2016953125

10 9 8 7 6 5 4 3 2 1

LSC-C

Printed in the United States of America

This book is dedicated to

MIYOKO, MADISON, AND COLIN,

for teaching me what unconditional love

feels and sounds like.

Contents

Preface to the Expanded Edition   ix

CHAPTER 1   Your Best Voice   3

CHAPTER 2   How Do I Sound?   18

CHAPTER 3   Breathing   34

CHAPTER 4   The Miracle of Middle Voice   51

CHAPTER 5   How to Practice   70

CHAPTER 6   Staking Claim to Middle   83

CHAPTER 7   Making Your Speaking Voice Sing   97

CHAPTER 8   Songs without Fear   113

CHAPTER 9   The Care and Feeding of Great Voices   130

CHAPTER 10   Essential Extras for Singers   150

CHAPTER 11   Standing Out in a World Shaped
              by *American Idol*   172

CHAPTER 12   Going Big When You Sing   185

CHAPTER 13   Creating Your Own Material:
              Yes You Can   198

CHAPTER 14   Essential Extras for Speakers   207

CHAPTER 15   The New World of Presentation   227

CONTENTS

CHAPTER 16 Secrets of the Internet Stars 239

CHAPTER 17 Breakthrough Techniques for Stuttering
and Spasmodic Dysphonia 253

CHAPTER 18 The Healing Power of Voice 262

Epilogue 271

Appendix 273

Acknowledgments 283

Index 285

A Note About the Author 299

Preface to the
Expanded Edition

WELCOME TO the new, expanded edition of *Set Your Voice Free*.

The world has changed massively since this book first appeared in 1999, and shifts in technology, the music industry, and our understanding of the true power of the voice have opened amazing new possibilities for people who know how to control the way they sound.

Today, any of us can potentially reach millions of people almost instantly, and start the process of getting our audience to trust us, believe us, like us, and connect with us. Based on what people hear as soon as we begin to sing or speak, they decide whether they want to listen to our music, hand us money, be moved by our message, or fall in love with us and what we have to offer.

Your new SoundCloud track, your Kickstarter campaign, your TED Talk, your audition, your big break—all that opportunity hinges on the power of your voice. Scientists tell us that we have *one second* to make the vocal impression that determines the way we're received, and in the time since this book first appeared, I've developed new techniques to help you ensure that your voice carries the precise sounds that will make people want to stay with you, rather than immediately tuning you out.

By using the classic exercises and the new material in this book, you'll be able to showcase the best of yourself—your talents, your passion, your originality, your authenticity. The techniques at the heart of the book are the ones I've been refining for decades in my work with artists such as John Mayer and Gwen Stefani, as well as with actors such as Reese Witherspoon and Jeff Bridges, who didn't consider themselves to be singers before they worked with me, and these techniques will give your voice the power and resonance you've always wanted.

If all you do is focus on these techniques, you'll be way ahead of almost every other singer or speaker competing for the attention of your audience. But I hope you'll take advantage of the additional exercises and advice you'll find in this edition to go beyond simply sounding good. I'd like to plant the seed of the idea that you can use your voice to become a master influencer. The most profound discovery I've made in the past fifteen years is this: If you know how to control the pitch, pace, tone, volume, and melody of your voice—the elements that form the core of this book—you can consciously use them to guide the emotions of your listeners and magnify the impact of every communication you have.

The link between music and emotion has always been clear to us—a song can make us weep or rage or dance for joy—but we rarely carry the power of music into the way we speak. By marrying music and speech, I can help you become a much better singer and speaker at the same time. I'll show you how the best communicators use the intimate, musical power of sound to control people's perceptions of them and move their listeners to action. That's what real influence is, and I'll give you the tools to develop it.

New Tools for Singers

It's odd to think about, but when this book originally appeared, there was no *American Idol* or *America's Got Talent* or *The Voice*. *Idol* debuted in 2002, *AGT* in 2006, and *The Voice* didn't sing out in America until 2011. When the book came out, not even 50 percent of Americans were using the Internet regularly. iPhones weren't even a glimmer in someone's imagination. That time looks almost like the Dark Ages.

But I was busy on the front lines of the transformation of the music industry into a place where reality singing competitions, music-centered programs like *Glee*, audio streaming, and live performance became the new kingmakers. So in new chapters of this edition geared to singers, I'll share what I learned.

◆ I'll give you a firsthand look at what it takes to live through the whirlwind of a show like *Glee*, or an Eminem or Gwen Stefani tour, managing the demands of performing on insane schedules and keeping your voice in top shape. When it's time to hit the stage, where the profits are made in today's music industry, you need to be able to count on your voice. You can't just hide in the studio and order takeout. I'll show you how the hardest-working people I know do what they need to do, put shows together, and make sure their voices *keep working for them.*

◆ I'll show you how stars such as Joaquin Phoenix and Reese Witherspoon, who weren't singers before they worked with me, prepare for singing roles with techniques that will help you get ready for any demanding new role that's at the outer limits of your comfort zone.

◆ I'll tell you exactly what you'll need to do to stand out in an audition or a reality competition, and keep impressing the judges and audiences who are your gateway to opportunity.

◆ I'll also show you how to master the art of being truly original — by writing your own material, even if you "can't" or "aren't musical." If you want control of your career, especially today, that's the step you've got to take, and I'll guide you through getting started, and making the most of your unique vision.

New Tools for Speakers

Because of the work I do with voice and emotion, I've become known as an influence expert and vocal strategist, and students pay thousands of dollars a day to learn what I know. I'll introduce you to the basics of what I teach them and show you the next steps you can take to turn your voice into the vehicle that connects you in an intimate, powerful, and persuasive way with your listeners.

We live in a world now that's all about the *elevator pitch.* How fast and efficiently can you tell a group of strangers about yourself or a passion project? How fast can you move them emotionally and get them to take action in favor of you and your project or idea?

◆ I'll show you the four key emotions you need to evoke in your audiences to make them like and believe you, and I'll show you exactly how to create the sounds you need to deliver those emotions convincingly. With this foundation, you can begin to infuse your speaking style with a new layer of connection and feeling.

Then I'll give you a close-up look at how the masters do it, focusing on two of my students who happen to be among the most influential people on the Internet.

♦ My student Bethany Mota, a young woman barely out of her teens, has parlayed a love of fashion and a magnetic presentation style into a YouTube channel with 10.3 million subscribers, her own fashion line, and a fledgling singing career. I'll break down the elements that make her so believable and make her fans so ready to follow her anywhere.

♦ My student Brendon Burchard, who was primarily known as a motivational speaker, woke up one morning and decided to shoot some YouTube videos. Almost overnight he became one of the Top 100 Most Followed Public Figures on Facebook. His weekly YouTube show is the most-viewed direct-to-camera personal development series in YouTube history. His motivational podcast, *The Charged Life*, debuted at #1 on iTunes across all categories in the United States and several other countries, and his blog posts rank as the most liked and shared in the history of the motivational genre. All of this success started with an idea, a dream, and, most of all, a voice to carry his message to the public. I'll show you how he creates that powerful presence.

Special Help for People with Speech Disorders

Finally, in a new chapter, I'll share techniques I've developed to help individuals with speech disorders for which effective treatments have been hard to find: stuttering and a condition called spasmodic dysphonia, in which the voice becomes choked off, making it almost impossible to speak. There's no cure for these conditions, but by starting with basic vocal technique and tweaking the tools in my teaching toolbox, I've been able to offer relief to many of the people who come to see me.

What I Believe about the Power of the Voice

I think the public has a different kind of respect for the voice than it did back in 1999. Singing competitions and videos that go viral have changed the landscape for singers, offering them new opportunities, feeding their dreams, and opening the public's imagination to the possibilities of where our voices can take us.

The revolution came when *The Voice* asked its judges to do blind auditions, in which they faced away from the contestants who were performing for them. The voice alone did the selling, and if a short, chubby barista had a voice like Amy Winehouse, we and the judges were ready to fall in love. All of us realized that no matter what you look like, no matter what your age or background, if you can create the right sounds, people will see the beauty, kindness, intelligence, and uniqueness in you. We were ready to see all that based entirely on the voices we heard.

That is the power of the voice, your voice. And with this new edition, I hope you'll find every reason to discover it, and Set Your Voice Free.

SET YOUR VOICE FREE

· I ·

Your Best Voice

OUR VOICE is an intimate part of you. A breath of air travels through your body, taking on the colors of your thoughts and emotions, and when it re-emerges it's filled with your essence. Something that intimate should be as strong, sweet, pure, seductive, funny, and commanding as you are. But words like *strong, warm, sexy,* and *powerful* may not be the ones that pop into mind when you listen to the voice you've recorded on your outgoing message, or the one you made of yourself plodding through a chorus of "Happy Birthday."

In fact, when I ask most people to describe their own speaking voices, the typical list is full of brutal assessments: thin, harsh, gravelly, hoarse, weak, nasal, tinny. And when it comes to singing, they couldn't be tougher on themselves: "I'm no Beyoncé, that's for sure." "Can't carry a tune in a bucket." "Tone deaf." "Fingernails on a blackboard." "I don't sing. Can't sing. Don't ask."

I believe that many of us are trapped in voices that don't begin to convey who we really are. We think we're shy, but actually we feel beaten down by the way other people have reacted—or failed to react—when they've listened to us. In our minds, James Earl Jones or Scarlett Johansson is speaking our thoughts, but too often what comes out of our mouths is anything but. Maybe your voice is hoarse or strained; maybe it's more like Pee Wee Herman's. Maybe you're soft-spoken, like a librarian, but you're ready to unleash the vocal exotic dancer. You'd be surprised at how often the voice just doesn't convey our passions, our convictions, our affection, or our intentions. And you'll be amazed to see what happens when you learn how to let it.

A Powerful New Tool

I'd like to show you how to find your true voice, the voice that is as rich and full and beautiful and exciting as you are. I've spent more than three decades developing specific techniques for enriching every voice and helping speakers and singers solve the problems, both common and rare, that stand between them and the voices they were born to have. The tools I'll share with you in this book and the audio exercises and examples on the book's new website (www.setyourvoicefreebook.com) are the same ones I've used with clients such as John Mayer, Gwen Stefani, Maroon 5, Selena Gomez, the Beach Boys, Def Leppard, Chicago, Matchbox Twenty, the Jacksons, Earth Wind & Fire, Wilson Phillips, and Phish; as well as actors such as Angelina Jolie, Keira Knightley, Rooney Mara, Jeff Bridges, Reese Witherspoon, Joaquin Phoenix, and Jennifer Lawrence; and speakers such as Tony Robbins, Brendon Burchard, and John Gray (Men Are from Mars, Women Are from Venus). These are people who depend on their voices—and will do anything they can to protect and develop them. Often, when they call, they need help fast. So, as you'll see, the lessons in this book are designed to show dramatic results in minutes, days, and weeks—not years. Many of my clients can afford to go anywhere they want and to study any technique ever devised, but they come to me because I have developed the most specific, effective exercises that exist for opening up the voice to all its possibilities. They know that in one lesson I can give them access to parts of their voices they've never been able to reach and that they might not have known existed.

Let me give you a few examples of just how powerful this technique is:

♦ John Mayer called me, stressed because he had run into a problem as he was recording the song "Say," which was to be the theme song for a Jack Nicholson movie called *The Bucket List*. The verses fell into a great vocal spot for him, but the choruses sat in a less-than-comfortable part of his range, and he couldn't get a good take of the song.

I flew to New York the next day, and headed to the studio, where I asked John to sing what he had. I realized, as I listened and watched, that his Adam's apple was going up when he tried to sing the chorus, making it impossible for him to hit his high notes. I gave him exercises that would lower his Adam's apple, the same ones I'll tell you about later in this book, and the results speak for themselves. We finished the song during my visit, and it made it into the film, playing over the end credits. But it had a bigger life than that: "Say" became a huge Top 40 radio hit and went on to win the Grammy Award for Best Pop Male Performance in 2008. All of this started with a song, a great artist — and the vocal techniques that let him deliver his best work on deadline.

◆ A highly successful prime-time TV star (to protect his privacy, I'll call him Larry) developed a throat infection. He lost his voice and went to an ear, nose, and throat specialist, who advised complete vocal rest for several weeks. Larry took that news like a death sentence — the entire show would have to come to a halt while he recovered, and the network was pressuring him to meet deadlines for new shows that were scheduled to be taped. But because he was a pro and a perfectionist, he followed doctor's orders and spent his weeks in silence, communicating only with a pencil and a pad of paper.

At the end of this time, Larry was almost afraid to talk. He was terrified to find out what he'd sound like when he opened his mouth again. And he was also afraid that the voice that had let him down once would do it again. Larry didn't even recognize the sounds he was making when he began to speak. His voice didn't have the thickness and power he remembered. It sounded almost wispy — and it didn't sound like *him*. He was agitated, and extremely nervous, when he arrived at my studio.

After less than an hour of vocal exercises, Larry's voice had regained its resonance, and we'd actually built on the strengths of his old voice to give it more power. Larry was back on the air two days later—receiving rave reviews for the greater amount of character and personality that came through when he spoke. His newfound vocal prowess gave him so much confidence, it translated effortlessly into a positive change that radiated through both his personal and his professional life.

I've found that by using singing exercises to help people improve the way they speak, I can make bigger leaps much more quickly than even a speech pathologist might. That's because singing helps you bypass the logical, skeptical left side of the brain. Instead, when you take a chance and sing sounds for me, you tap into the creative, playful right side of the brain—the side that's ready to believe you can fly.

◆ Finally, I'd like to tell you the story of someone you've never heard of. He's never won a Grammy or appeared on TV, but I consider my work with him to be among my proudest achievements. Owen, a young college student, wanted to sing. He had an exuberant personality, and you couldn't help but be happy to be around him, but when he tried to sing along with the radio, people would cringe. All his life, people had told him he was tone deaf, and to hear him, you might have said so too.

Owen's was one of the most difficult cases I've ever encountered. When he tried to sing anything higher than his regular speaking voice, he could hardly make a sound. His face would turn bright red, and only a tiny wisp of sound would come out. His larynx, the housing for the vocal cords, was so high that it was blocking his throat, and he was holding his stomach muscles so tightly that it was as if he were holding his breath the whole time he was trying to sing. I showed him a very simple set of low-larynx exercises—the same ones I'll show you—and in thirty seconds his larynx moved to a normal position, the back part of his throat opened up, and the pressure in his head and throat disappeared.

Next I taught him some simple breathing exercises, and suddenly he wasn't holding his breath while trying to sing. Those two simple techniques allowed him to experience the freedom of letting his voice travel unrestricted out of his body. Now I had to get him on pitch. Here we were starting from ground zero. When I hit a note on the piano and asked him to repeat it, he'd blast out a pitch that was way off in left field. People waiting for their lessons would hear his attempts through the door and comment on them after he left. "Why does that guy want to take singing lessons?" they'd ask. "You're stealing his money."

But Owen persisted. It took him a while to realize that when he was hitting a wrong note he could steer his way back to the right one—while he was singing. Like a lot of people, he had the tendency to stop, or worse, plow on in the wrong direction, when his sound went sour. We worked on simple pitch-correcting exercises for several weeks, and a month later people were standing with their ears pressed to the door to hear the fabulous singer who was practicing with me. It was Owen. Once his throat was open and he'd learned to correct his pitches, he could open his voice to all the life that was in his heart and let his true personality come through. The result was incredibly moving.

Great speaking and singing is not about being the best. It's about being unique. It's about expressing who you are and what's particularly special about you. If you learn to use your own instrument with confidence, people will open their ears to you and recognize what sets you apart from everyone else. Whether you're singing a lullaby to your baby, saying a prayer, making a toast, spontaneously bursting into song, or giving the presentation that can make or break your career, your voice will reveal what you most genuinely want to convey. That's the best kind of success there is. It's my pleasure, and my mission, to help you find it.

Voice Lessons? They're Not about Talent

People tend to be afraid of the term *voice lessons* because it makes them think of being locked up in a room with a stuffy old guy who has a metronome ticking in the background, a perfectionist who will crack the whip over something as natural as the sound that comes out of their mouths. "Who needs voice lessons?" we ask ourselves, certain that the answer doesn't include us. "I know how to talk, and I can't sing, so what's the point? Lessons are for people with *talent!*"

But using your voice well isn't always about having special gifts, or performing or being the star of your church or family or community production. At the deepest level, the reason we need to develop the voice is to allow it to be as expressive and flexible as possible, because when you do that, you're setting your voice, and *yourself*, free.

What Your Voice Says about You

The sounds coming out of your mouth set up a whole range of expectations about how you'll behave, how accessible you are, what your sense of humor is like, and how high your energy level is—to name just a few of the qualities we encode in our voices. Think of the times you've "met" someone over the phone and created a whole visual picture of him or her, just from the vocal personality that slides into your ear. (Ever set up a meeting by phone with someone you were sure was "tall, dark, and distinguished," only to find yourself shocked to be shaking hands a couple days later with the nerdy-looking little guy who owns the great voice? That mental image-making, based solely on sound, is the power of speech and the literal vibrations, positive or negative, that precede us.)

We absorb the information packed into a voice almost intuitively. I have spent many years detailing exactly how we telegraph information through sound, independent of the words we use. Whether you realize it or not, your voice hits a lot of pitches as you speak. A friend and student of mine, who happens to be a former rocket scientist, took an interest in the relationship between voice and occupation. For several months, as he traveled the world on business, he carried a small musical keyboard. He'd pull it out during conversations, and he'd use it to figure out what the other person's voice was doing, musically, as he or she spoke. (As we'll see throughout this book, there's a short, easy leap between speaking and singing.) Our voices, at their most expressive points, swoop around, rather than confining themselves to a monotone, and with a little practice, you can hear the various pitches you hit while you're speaking. (You can try this by sitting down at the keyboard and saying the word *hello* with a lot of enthusiasm, as though you're greeting someone you're surprised and very happy to meet. If you hold the *o* as though you're chanting it, you might be able to pick out the note that you're speaking/singing by touching the keys on the keyboard until you find the note that matches the one you're making.)

My friend became adept at listening to the pitches (the familiar "do, re, mi, fa, sol, la, ti, do" that we've all learned to sing) that people were hitting as they spoke, and he became interested in the intervals between those pitches. Were they making tiny steps with their voices, or were they striding (or flying) up and down? My friend collected information about hundreds of voices, noting the exact intervals the speaker used and the speaker's occupation.

Among his findings: Musicians and singers, not surprisingly, used the widest range of notes. In the course of a conversation, they'd use many thirds (moving from *do* to *mi*), fourths (*do* up to *fa*), and fifths (from *do* to *sol*). Engineers used mostly thirds and tended to stay within that small range. And bankers used only seconds (*do-re*), which are very limiting and almost monotonous. After a while my friend had no trouble guessing what a person did for a living, based simply on the intervals used in speech. He also identified the odd, dissonant intervals (minor seconds and flatted fifths) that cause us instantly to back off from someone we think might be emotionally off—the wackos and crazies we sometimes come across.

Does your way of speaking mirror the patterns of other people in your profession? Probably. The colors of your voice might be different, but you might still be using the same intervals that everyone around you does. And actually, you don't have to walk around with a keyboard to figure that out. Our voices so clearly reflect our personalities, our souls, our mind-sets, and our characters that our vocal habits hand our dossier to everyone we meet. That may be wonderful, but it may also be as confining as a pair of pants that's two sizes too small.

The factor that's most important here is that you have some choice in the way you use your voice. If you have access to a whole palette of color and hue when you speak and *choose* to toe the narrow banker's line and limit yourself to just a couple of musical tones, that's great. If it fits you, wear it with gusto. Or, choose a voice that gets you where you want to go. If you're an expansive, arm-waving salesperson whose voice covers a lot of territory, you might make a conscious decision to talk in an engineer's more limited cadence—because you're selling widgets to engineers and you want them to trust you as one of their own. The more awareness you bring to your voice and the more you know about its true capacities, the more choices you have about how you come across and the more you can use your voice to your advantage, rather than letting it (or misconceptions about it) limit you.

I've often noticed that singers, who you'd think would be continuously aware of their voices, put aside all their vocal prowess and insight when they step away from the microphone and into their "civilian" lives. One striking and familiar example of this phenomenon was Michael Jackson.

At the height of his career, when *Thriller* was on the charts and the moonwalking wonder was touring the world, Michael worked with my partner at our vocal studio, and frequently we'd have a chance to sit and talk. One afternoon I was looking out my office window and spotted Michael doing a triple twirl in the parking lot as he left his car. I was amazed at his energy—the man was a comet. But when he sat down in a chair across from me and began to speak, none of that energy seemed to be available. He whispered, as though he were afraid to let a sound come out. I had to strain to hear him, and he seemed tentative and shy—though I knew he had the power to fill a stadium with his presence.

A lot of singers, and many of the stars, seem to have two distinct energy levels, conveyed by their voices, that don't seem to intersect: onstage, where they give it a thousand percent, and offstage, when they switch into conservation mode. To many of them, "conservation" seems to mean whispering, or speaking with an airy voice. Are there other vocal choices for people who don't want to operate at a zillion watts in everyday life? Sure. But every day I hear them falling into the same traps the rest of us do, thinking that if they turn the vibrations and power in their voices all the way down in their off hours, they'll "fit in" better. In fact, though, they just seem to disappear.

So might their singing voices if they're not careful. Whispering and soft, airy speech happen to be murderous for the vocal cords. That alone is reason enough for me to encourage you to broaden your repertoire of "approachable" voices to include something a little easier on the pipes. A full 80 percent of all singers who develop physical problems with their vocal cords do so because of the way they *speak*, not the way they sing. If you're a singer, I urge you to pay attention to the way you talk and to all the information about speaking that you'll find in this book. Even if you're not interested in using your speaking voice more expressively, do it to safeguard against inadvertently damaging your ability to sing.

Whether you're interested in speaking or singing, I'd like to help you replace your unconscious habits with choices. Once you *can* set your singing voice soaring or speak with nuance, strength, and color, you may decide that you want to walk through a new sonic door now and then. Maybe you'll try on a new persona, or branch out from pensive melodies to show tunes or opera. Once you see the possibilities, it becomes tempting to sample a few.

The Truth about Your Voice

It's time someone leveled with you about what your voice can really do and what's reasonable to expect from your basic set of vocal equipment. I know old beliefs die hard, and what I'm about to tell you may sound counterintuitive (that is, impossible, silly, or fictitious), but the statements below are absolutely true.

◆ **The human voice is set up to speak or sing twenty-four hours a day without getting hoarse or strained or creating any physical problems.**

If yours can't, it's because you're doing something wrong.

SET YOUR VOICE FREE

- **The average (not the *exceptional*) person should be able to sing smoothly through two and a half octaves with no breaks, squawks, or squeals in his or her voice.**

It's a myth to think that high and low notes are for someone else, or that you're doomed to sound like a wet alley cat when you sing the national anthem. Training, perseverance, and the techniques I'll teach you can make every note of those octaves come to life.

- **Less than 2 percent of the population is tone deaf.**

Contrast that with the 40 or 50 percent of the people I meet who are sure that they "can't sing" because of some inherent defect. Actually, tone deafness is a relatively rare condition that results from damage to the ear, for instance from a high childhood fever. If you're truly tone deaf, you can't sing on pitch because you can't hear the pitch accurately to begin with. If you're one of those people who cringe at their own, or others', missed notes in talent shows or at karaoke bars, you're not tone deaf, you're just tone shy. I'm happy to report that your hearing is just fine, and even if you sing like an untrained Owen, the young man I spoke about earlier, we can fix the pitch problems. Allow me to introduce you to the voice you've been dreaming of.

Some Basic Equipment

You're probably wondering just what it'll take to start shifting your voice toward the part of the spectrum that you, and other people, might label beautiful—or even just strain-free. Actually, there are just three main requirements:

1. Stay in touch with your desire to improve your voice.
2. Be willing to play, and to fake it till you make it.
3. Be willing to put yourself first—even if it's just for a few minutes a day.

In your heart of hearts, what is it that makes you want to improve your voice? Maybe you have a fantasy—that you're singing in a community theater, or telling stories to kids at the library, or inspiring the troops at your workplace like Patton. As we start out, I hope you'll make a note to yourself that completes two fill-in-the-blank statements:

- I want to improve my voice because _____ _____.
- If my voice were as strong as I want it to be, I would _____ _____.

I hope you'll consider speaking those answers into the recorder app on your smartphone, or any other recording device you have, because I think you'll find it to be a valuable record of where you are and, eventually, of how far you've come. As you complete the statement, and later begin practicing with all the exercises, you'll need to silence the harsh critic who lives inside you, the voice that makes wet-blanket statements like "It sucks"; "It's embarrassing"; "It makes me sound stupid." It's fine to keep a critical ear, but don't be too hard on yourself at the beginning. Just gather information and use it.

The second statement is important because it's essential, as you begin, to put some of your desire into words. That's a way of keeping your eye on the prize. No one wants to take voice lessons for abstract reasons. It's always something personal. There may be a specific song you want to sing or a feeling of confidence and satisfaction you want to walk away with at the end of a meeting where you and your voice have done your best. Or you may have a feeling that's more like an intuition—that improving your voice will change your life in some way you haven't yet imagined.

This work may feel scary to you. It may even feel silly and out of character. But your desire is real, and powerful. And once you've spoken that desire, like a birthday wish or a mission statement, it can work for you. It'll help keep you motivated when you feel stuck and inspire you to keep exploring your vocal possibilities when you've realized that your voice has hundreds of colors, instead of just a couple.

How to Use This Book

Throughout the book, I'll direct you to specific audio samples that I've recorded and placed on a special website just for you. The address is: www.setyourvoicefreebook.com. You'll hear clear demonstrations of the sounds I'm referring to, and you may also be asked to make the sounds yourself. Don't skip that part! Imagining what you'd sound like doesn't count—you need to try copying what you hear. That's where the lights go on and the learning begins to happen in your body and mind.

What we'll be doing is as simple as follow the leader. I'll make sounds and you'll copy them. There's not a lot of complicated theory, just a wide variety of playful experiments. As you follow my voice through the exercises, you will be automatically placing your mouth, jaws, stomach, breath, and vocal cords in positions that make it nearly impossible, over time, to produce weak, strained, or "bad" sounds. *This is not an intellectual exercise.* All you have to do is be willing to let go of a little fear and self-doubt, and duplicate the sounds you hear. To work with me, you'll need to listen carefully, copy what you hear me doing, let yourself have a little fun, and give up the misconceptions and bad habits that have kept you stuck in an ill-fitting voice. You may not feel that you're doing everything right, so just fake it and have a little faith. Make the funny sounds. Giggle if you need to. There's no need to worry about looking dignified, because that's going to be impossible anyway. Just listen and repeat after me and you'll be fine.

The easiest way to ensure that you're getting the same benefit from this material as the students who come into my offices is to do what they do: set up a regular weekly voice lesson. When you're through reading this chapter, I'd like you to get out your calendar and block out some time for your private sessions with me. Plan one session of at least half an hour or forty-five minutes during the week for reading and listening to each chapter. Consider that to be lesson time, during which you'll learn about and experience different parts of your voice. I suggest that you take the lessons a week at a time to give yourself a chance to assimilate the material and let it "soak in."

I may ask you to practice simple exercises between the weekly sessions. Practice sets in motion a physical training process that reshapes the way you make sound. You're learning to control the voice-production muscles, and even a little regular practice will go a long way toward building the physical strength that will make your voice more powerful.

Please remember that you're doing this for yourself. You have a lot of demands on your time, and chances are you spend most of your time thinking about what you need to do for other people. You've got a to-do list that's full of pragmatic questions: How can I earn more money? How can I take care of my family? How can I squeeze in sleep and exercise and the job and the kids and the parents and romance and everyone who wants something from me? Maybe there doesn't seem to be a lot of room left for more dreamy items like: I want to be a singer. I want to speak better.

So, you'll have to be bold and just take the time to learn and to practice. My most successful students are the ones who can tell themselves: "I'm finally going to do this for myself, even though the choir director laughed when I mentioned wanting to be a soloist. Even though my friends think I'm nuts. Even though I've sung in a joke voice for years and pretended I didn't care that I sounded like a cartoon character. Making this change is my gift to me."

You're taking a risk, making this investment in yourself. You may well have to give up a lot of comfortable ideas about your limitations and what a person like you can dream of doing. But if the experience of my students over the years is any indication, it's a risk you'll be glad you took.

Do It for the Joy

Having a voice you can count on to reflect who you are and express the ideas, emotions, and soulfulness you have inside is a gift. And it's one of the wonderful secrets of my business that those who seek the voice they deserve find benefits they never expected. I'm not talking just about money or fame or even confidence — I'm talking about joy. Students who sing with me, whether their ultimate goal is to improve the way they speak or to ensure that their voices hold up on a year-long album tour, find that singing makes them feel better.

"When I'm done with a lesson," my client Bill told me, "I feel happy.

It must be something about making those sounds. It makes me feel a lot better than going to therapy—and it's a lot less expensive."

I hear comments like this all the time, so I wasn't surprised to see that science is beginning to pay attention to the effects of sounds on the body. It's long been known that sound is incredibly powerful (think of all the savage beasts that have been soothed by music), and that it lifts the soul (spend time singing or chanting in any house of worship and you'll see what I mean). And it doesn't feel like that much of a stretch to expect that it can work some kind of healing physical magic on the body. The results are still coming in, and I'll share some of them with you later. Meanwhile, try making some of the sounds I'll teach you—I'm almost certain that, like Bill, you'll feel the joy.

My Story

Working with the voice isn't just a job for me—it's a lifelong, life-changing passion. And the power of the voice isn't something I think of as an abstract concept. It's a vital force I've seen again and again in my life.

I've always loved to sing. Some of my earliest memories are of interrupting my parents' dinner parties just as the food was being served and singing my heart out until someone would pick me up, put me under his or her arm—still singing away—and place me in another room. From the time I was seven or eight, I begged for singing lessons, and though my mother believed I didn't need lessons until I was thirteen, nothing kept me from belting out songs at any opportunity.

I was a healthy, happy, active kid, but at the age of ten I developed osteomyelitis, a bone condition that required major surgery. I was in a wheelchair and attending a school for handicapped students for a year, then in a walking cast for six months. I couldn't exercise, couldn't walk, couldn't play as I used to—it was the biggest hardship of my life to that point. But I could sing, and I clung to my voice like a lifeline. I began giving concerts at lunchtime, and I realized that I could fill a gym when I sang a song. At twelve and a half I was an overweight, awkward kid trying to fit back into a regular school, and I used singing to rebuild my ego and my life. It was my first genuine lesson in balancing the good and the bad in life, and my journey to wholeness was made possible by the love I had for singing. To this day, in working with my clients, I believe that finding and developing the voice is an amazing tool for rebuilding self-worth.

At thirteen I finally got the singing lessons I'd longed for, and in a short time I was winning vocal competitions and performing as a baritone in operatic productions around Los Angeles. A couple of years later I also began teaching professionally. My voice teacher was offered a temporary out-of-town position, and he asked me to take over his studio and work with his clients, a roster that included the Beach Boys, Stevie Wonder, Earth Wind & Fire, Luther Vandross, the Jacksons, and many more of the biggest recording stars in the world.

I continued my training and established myself through competitions as the number one voice in the state. But at twenty, two years into my college career, my voice went through another change, and it was an enormous shock to me. Suddenly I was a tenor, and I couldn't perform the baritone repertoire I'd been working so long to perfect. I was dropped from the competitions I was used to dominating—my voice had betrayed me. I felt like a huge, in-transition loser.

That bend in the road led me to a world of vocal adventures I wouldn't trade for anything, and to the most rewarding work of my life, both teaching and performing. I've traveled the world and the country, performed with and shaped the vocal sounds of thousands of top artists, and written and recorded my own music. My voice has given me some of my greatest joys, but I'm also acutely sensitive to how it feels when, even temporarily, we can't count on this part of our self that's so closely tied to the breath of life.

Please believe me when I tell you that I know how you feel if you are frustrated, discouraged, hopeful, or filled with secret dreams for your voice. And I know the heights to which your voice can take you if you let it. Let's begin the journey now. I'd like to take you there.

· 2 ·

How Do I Sound?

W ITH YOUR goals and dreams firmly in mind, you're ready to
take what I know will be an eye- and ear-opening trip
toward your best voice. Let's start by addressing the questions that I
know are at the front of your mind, the very personal questions that
every student I meet, beginner or professional, wants answered:
What's really happening in my voice? If it's already damaged, can it
be fixed? And my favorites: On a scale of bad to excellent, how's my
voice? How good is my voice? How far can I go with it — really?

I try not to think in terms of "good" and "bad," and I'd like you to put
those judgments aside too. For one thing, I've learned that they're too
subjective to be useful. Over the years, I've asked some of the biggest
stars the same question: Putting ego aside, do you like the sound of
your voice? And I've never found one famous singer who bragged about
the way he or she sounded. Generally they admit to me that their voices
are full of flaws — and luckily, the public hasn't picked up on them yet.
People who aren't professional speakers or singers often think that once
you reach a certain level, you have great confidence, but the truth is,
the voice is always a work in progress, with higher levels to achieve. So
instead of good and bad, I'd like to shift our orientation to the two primary questions we'll be working with in this session:

- What is actually going on in my body when I make sounds?
- How does that translate into the qualities I hear in my voice?

With the diagnostic tests and exercises in this chapter, we'll get to know where your voice is at this moment. This will be our starting point for your vocal makeover. The idea is not to accentuate the negative but to get an honest sense of what you're doing, to get a clear picture of your vocal strengths, and to pinpoint your weak spots — so that we can fix them. Don't worry — in the course of this book, I'll give you concrete ways to solve every problem we highlight here.

How Your Voice Works

It will help a lot, as we begin, for you to have a basic idea of how your voice works. We all know that to play a violin you have to press down the strings on the neck with one hand and draw a bow over the lower part of the strings with the other. Playing an oboe involves blowing over a vibrating reed into a tube with holes we cover to create different tones. But the voice is often a mystery. For one thing, we can't really see our vocal apparatus, and there's no orchestral equivalent of the strange combination-wind-and-string instrument that resides in our throats and uses our whole bodies as a resonating, sound-shaping container. All we know is that we open our mouths and out comes our sound.

The relationships and dynamics that go into making music and words flow effortlessly from our throats are complex and fascinating. But for our purposes right now, you just need to know the bare-bones basics, which will help you visualize what's going on as you run through the exercises.

◆ You've got a stringed instrument that you blow through. Inside your neck, two passages run side by side. At the front is the one that carries air from the nose and mouth into the lungs. And at the back is the tube that carries food and liquid to the stomach. Resting at the top of the air passage is the cartilage box called the larynx, which contains the vocal cords. The pair of cords responsible for producing the sounds we make are strong, fibered bands of mucous membranes. They move apart and together and vibrate in response to the air we push through them, making this odd little voice box a bit like a violin that you need to blow through to manipulate its pitch, tone, and volume.

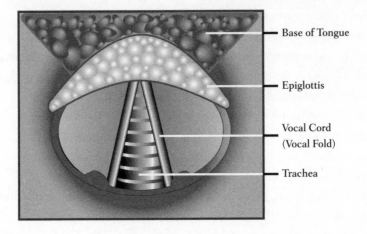

Base of Tongue

Epiglottis

Vocal Cord
(Vocal Fold)

Trachea

TOP VIEW OF VOCAL CORDS

The cords have a unique way of vibrating. Small amounts of air build up behind them, and when the pressure of that air becomes greater than the air pressure above the cords, the cords open to release the air, then close. This process happens an astonishing number of times, creating the cords' vibration. For example, when you sing the note A above middle C, the cords open and close 440 times a second to produce that frequency.

♦ The quality of your voice depends primarily on the way you position the cords and the amount of air you move through them, and great singing or speaking happens when the right amount of air meets the right amount of cord. Remember that phrase because it's the basis of just about everything we'll be doing together.

You'll find that I'll be explaining many of the sounds you make, particularly problematic sounds that cause you (and your listeners) discomfort, in terms of what's happening in the crucial relationship between the vocal cords and the air passing through them.

The Spoken You

Whether you're mainly concerned about your speaking or your singing, I'd like to look first at the speaking voice, because even if we're professional singers, we spend far more time talking than we do singing. We draw sharp distinctions between what's spoken and what's sung, but interestingly, our brains don't. To the brain, speaking and singing feel almost like the same thing. They use the same body parts, the same muscles, and when you sing, your brain simply thinks you're speaking but sustaining words an unusually long time and using more pitch variation. Speaking is the jumping-off point for larger leaps into song, so it's vital to be sure that this foundation is strong.

If you are primarily interested in singing, please don't skip the tests that focus on how you speak. As I've mentioned, one of the greatest dangers to the singing voice isn't singing but using your voice badly when you talk. By taking time to listen carefully to your speech habits, and correcting any problems, you are protecting your voice against some of its most insidious enemies.

Let a Recording Be Your Second Set of Ears

I strongly recommend that you get out your smartphone and record each of the tests and exercises we do here. Why record? The voice that other people hear doesn't sound like the one you hear when you speak and sing because you're feeling the vibrations in your tissues and bones and hearing sounds as they bounce around the "cave" of your body. Your own voice rings and vibrates inside you. But a listener hears only what emerges into the air, and that version of your voice may seem stripped down or flat compared with the richness you feel yourself producing. On top of that, sound traveling away from you actually sounds different from sound traveling toward you. Because of the gap between our inner perception and the listener's, it helps many students to give themselves an "objective" ear by recording some of the exercises they do.

Take out your phone or other convenient recording device and get ready to make part one of your progress recording. This will be an example of where you began and a powerful motivator along the way, allowing you to look back periodically and see how far you've come.

It will make your growth visible to you, and especially as you start out, it will be the easiest way for you to listen to your own voice and assess it.

The Overview

Please read the preceding passage aloud into your recorder.

As you read the paragraph, you may have noticed a number of things happening with your voice, if not at the beginning of your reading, then as you got closer to the end. Get out a pencil, and as you play the recording back, look through the following list and mark the items that you think apply to you. Did you

- Start strong but peter out by the end, feeling strained?
- Have to clear your throat frequently?
- Sound too soft?
- Notice that your voice felt too low, and gravelly, especially at the ends of sentences?
- Hear your voice breaking in spots?
- Sound nasal?
- Sound monotonous?
- Sound squeaky?
- Sound breathy?

Did you hear anything else that sticks out or bothers you?

I believe that people generally have a sense of what they don't like about their voices, but they may not be able to put it into technical terms. Don't worry—this is as technical as it gets. Look over the list and notice how many checks you made. It'll give us a sense of how you hear yourself now and where your problems might be.

Now let's take a deeper look by doing some specific tests for the most common vocal "flaws"—qualities in the voice that detract from its power by drawing attention to themselves rather than to what's being said. As you do the tests and exercises, have fun with the interesting sounds that pop up. Some of them may seem a little funny to you, but believe me, I have a specific reason for asking you to make each sound.

It's All in the Nose

There are a lot of misconceptions about how and why our voices sound nasal. Many people imagine that too much air being expelled is going into the nose, echoing around and giving their voices a nasal quality. And that's partly right. As you go higher in the range, a certain amount of air is supposed to be directed below the roof of your mouth, and a certain amount is supposed to go above the soft palate into the sinus area. (Anatomy lesson: Put the tip of your tongue right behind your front teeth and run it over the roof of your mouth. The hard section you feel in the front is the hard palate, and the softer area toward your throat is, you guessed it, the soft palate.)

Some nasal sounds come about when a speaker tightens the back of his or her throat, which keeps the air from freely flowing into the mouth. With that escape route from the body blocked, unnatural amounts of air are directed toward the nasal area. That produces the rather harsh, trebly nasal sound of the Nasal Professor. Listen to my demonstration on audio 2 on the website (www.setyourvoicefreebook. com). The sound is blatantly obvious here, but many people are painfully close to it without knowing.

Could that be you? Try this test. Begin to count slowly from one to ten. When you reach the number five, gently pinch your nostrils shut and keep counting. How do you sound on numbers six through ten? Did the sound drastically change?

It might surprise you to learn that there should be no severe change after you pinch your nose. Just listen to how I sound on audio 3. There's no huge shift when I reach the number six. Why? If you're speaking correctly, only a tiny amount of air goes into your nose. So when you pinch your nostrils, the amount of air you're restricting should barely affect the way you sound, though you may hear a slightly blocked sound on the numbers that contain *ns*—that's normal. If you noticed a drastic change, it's a sure indication that you've got too much air going toward the nasal area.

The Other Nasal Voice

There's another very common cause of the "too nasal" voice, and it's the opposite of what we just saw: too little air in the nose. Think of Sylvester Stallone as Rocky, with a low, blocked nasal sound that was most certainly the result of one too many run-ins with a boxing glove.

Listen to the demonstration on audio 4 on the website. Once again, my examples are extreme because I want you to recognize easily what I'm after. Unless you currently have a severe cold, your voice probably doesn't sound like this. But toward the light end of this nasal spectrum, you might recognize something of yourself.

It's entirely possible that you have mild, unwanted nasal tones in your voice and won't be aware of them until you hear your voice played back to you. So right now, go back to your recordings and listen specifically for the two nasal sounds I've demonstrated. If you're hearing them, you're not alone. Nasality is common because it's so easy to send too much or too little air into the nasal passages until your voice is completely aligned.

Once your voice becomes nasal, for whatever reason, it may get stuck in that nasal place. Why? One prominent reason is "sound memory." Your brain remembers what you sound like every day, and it's constantly reassessing what the qualities of "you" are. It hears the sounds you make and tries to duplicate them the next time you speak.

Say you spend a couple of weeks with a cold. The brain begins to associate that plugged-up sound with you and subtly prods you to hold on to that sound—even when you can breathe again. The cold ends but your voice stays nasal. Your brain is misguidedly telling you that this is what you sounded like yesterday, so this is what you should sound like today.

Fortunately, you can use the same sound memory to help lead you out of the problem. Practicing new ways of making sounds not only teaches you how to do it—it also tells the brain, repeatedly, this is how I sound. This is the voice I want, and when I get off track, this is the way to get back.

The Sound of Gravel

You may have noticed that as you were reading the text for your progress recording, the quality of your voice varied. Sometimes it felt smooth, and at others the smooth, mellifluous tones seemed to break up into particles that crackled like a creaky old door hinge. I describe this sound as gravelly, and to be sure we're on the same wavelength as we try to diagnose it, please listen to audio 5 on the website.

You'll notice that as I read, using my gravelly voice, I seem to fall into a consistent pattern. I start out strong at the beginning of a phrase, as full of fuel and power as a jet at takeoff. But as I go on, the sound seems to peter out and get harsh. This tonality can actually take on a dark, even sinister, edge. If I use it through the entire course of a sentence, it's about as appealing as the sound of paper being crumpled. It's problematic, too, because the process of producing it makes the vocal cords red and swollen.

What's happening here? It's fairly accurate to compare a voice at the beginning of a sentence with a car that's just had the gas tank filled. As you begin to read aloud or speak, you take a breath—the fuel of the voice—and the words ride out on a solid cushion of air. At that moment, the vocal cords are wonderfully content, vibrating beautifully and evenly. But just as a car sputters to a stop when it runs out of fuel, when you are speaking and run out of air, the cords continue to vibrate without their air "cushion," and as they do, they rub together aggressively. If you push on anyway, they become irritated, and the voice creaks to a stop.

Listen to the demonstration once more and imitate me. Close your lips, say *mmmmmmm,*...and feel vibration in back of your throat. Now read a couple of sentences on your own and see if you notice that same type of vibration as you reach the end of your breaths. Try it one more time, this time holding your hand about a half inch from your mouth. Pay attention to how much air you feel hitting your fingers. If your sentences end in that gravelly sound, you'll notice that almost no air is reaching your fingers. Read again and try to keep a consistent flow of air hitting the fingers; when the air stops or greatly diminishes — take another breath.

This incorrect use of the voice affects a large percentage of the population. Fortunately, it's one of the easiest problems to correct. Simple changes in how you breathe, which we'll cover in the next chapter, will give you almost immediate relief. Many people are reluctant to breathe more. We have a sense of urgency about getting words out, making us press on instead of pausing to refuel. But there's an acceptable middle ground, somewhere between panting and talking till we're blue in the face and gasping for air. We'll learn how and where to take in the right amount of air and what exactly to do with it.

The Breathy Voice: Sexy but Deadly

I always used to laugh when I called my friend Jeff at his office and got his answering machine. He'd gotten his secretary to record a short message in breathy, Marilyn Monroe–like tones, and when she said, "Jeff can't come to the phone right now," it was easy to imagine that the reason had something to do with what was going on in the bedroom instead of the boardroom.

I became interested in studying the effects of using the breathy side of the voice in junior high, when a friend and I decided to make a documentary at a religious retreat in the mountains. As I interviewed the monks, I was immediately aware of how calming their light, airy voices were. They spoke so softly that the sound of my camera often seemed to drown them out, but they still somehow commanded attention.

What is it about this kind of speaking that's so appealing? Maybe it's the vulnerability it seems to hint at. Perhaps we find it attractive because instead of asserting itself, it tends to invite us in. In more than a few instances, this quality seems useful and positive, and we choose it because we think it's the best way to convey certain qualities we want other people to sense. But some people end up breathy because of overcompensation. It's not unusual for a person who's been told that his or her voice is harsh, irritating, abrasive, or loud to swing far in the other direction and to tone it down with breathiness. The problem is, no matter how you arrive at this way of speaking, it's incredibly hard on your vocal cords.

Listen to the demonstration of this sound on audio 6. Now try reading a couple of sentences this way yourself. When you speak like this, only a small portion of the vocal cords is vibrating at all. So much air is pushing through them that much of their natural vibration stops. They begin to move out of the way and begrudgingly let too much air pass. The result is something like windburn. The vocal cords get dry, red, and irritated, and their natural lubrication all but disappears. The irritation makes them swell, a condition called edema, and if you don't step in to give them relief, it's possible that soon no sound will come out at all.

I'd like you to keep in mind that while you may find a breathy voice inviting, the lover or mystic who's flirting with laryngitis is less than appealing, and laryngitis is definitely on the menu if you don't find alternatives to this way of speaking. You think breathy is the only way to sound sexy, approachable, gentle, or romantic? That's just not the case. A healthy voice that has command of all the sound possibilities will eventually be more than enough to seduce anyone.

Attaaaaaack of the Brassy Voice

What would a band be without its horn section adding bright, concentrated sound? In the mix of vocal qualities, a little bit of brass provides a jolt of energy that can make you memorable. But when your voice is all brass, the effect can be just a wee bit...irritating.

What exactly do I mean by a brassy voice? Say the word *brassy*. Now say it again, this time holding the *aaa* sound. When you do that, you'll probably get a rendition that has too much extra buzz. Listen to audio 7 on the website and you'll hear my over-the-top demonstration of various brassy renditions that sound as though I'm hitting a buzzer when I speak. It's the sound of a bratty kid or a person who can't, or won't, soften her sharp edges.

Brassiness happens when your vocal cords are vibrating fully, like the long strings of a piano. Under the right circumstances, that kind of vibration is the basis of a wonderfully resonant tone. Here, however, there's not enough airflow to produce great resonance. Instead, your body is actually swallowing up the richness before it can come out.

Remember that there are two passages in your throat, one for air and one for food. When you swallow, one function of the larynx, the house of the vocal cords, is to rise, blocking the air passage so no food or liquid gets in your lungs. You can feel this happening if you put your finger on your chin and slide it backward down your throat until you get to the first bump, your Adam's apple, which is the front part of the larynx. As you swallow, you'll feel how it goes way above your finger and then back down. At certain times that "swallow, rise, block-the-throat" motion may be a lifesaver—none of us needs food in the windpipe—but when it happens at the wrong time, it cuts off the air passage and stops the production of great vocal sounds.

To find out if your larynx is rising too high, closing up your throat as you speak, try this. Put your index finger back on your Adam's apple and read the next few sentences aloud. If the larynx jumps substantially above your finger, as it did when you swallowed, that's too much movement. The larynx is allowed to move up and down between one-quarter and one-third of an inch as you speak, but any more than that places it in a blocking position.

A high larynx is one of the most common problems affecting speakers and singers, but it's very simple to get the larynx to its proper position with a series of low-larynx exercises. Let me give you a quick hint here of how easy it is to lower your larynx. Listen to audio 8 on the website. The exercise I'm doing here is specifically designed to move your larynx down. As you imitate my sounds, you should feel your Adam's apple move to a very low spot in your neck. You'll be happy to know that the larynx is one of the parts of the body that has great sense memory. Once it gets used to sitting in its normal position, it stays there, even if you aren't doing an exercise. And with the larynx in its normal, healthy speaking position, you will have effectively turned down the excess brassiness of your voice.

The Husky Voice

Less common than the qualities we've seen so far, but an occasional standout in the sea of troublesome vocal traits, is the guttural, raspy, Louis Armstrong sound. My demonstration of this sound is on audio 9 on the website. Grating and often unpleasant, it's produced when the forces that produced the breathy voice and the ones that produced the brassy voice come together. For this sound to happen, the larynx must rise and partially block the windpipe. At the same time, a tremendous amount of air must be pushed through the vocal cords, forcing them apart so that only their outer edges vibrate. As the excess air pushes through, it combines with phlegm and natural moisture and begins to rumble. This sound is a cord killer. When I demonstrate it for even a few seconds, I feel my throat start to hurt and the cords beginning to dry and swell.

But if it's your habitual sound, you probably don't even notice the constriction of your throat or the irritation in the cords. It's a sure bet, though, that you have a little trouble with hoarseness and occasionally lose your voice. If you hear even small traces of this quality in your voice when you listen to yourself, pay close attention to the sections of this book that deal with breathing, larynx work, and reducing phlegm. All of them will move you out of the vocal danger zone that the husky voice places you in.

Too High? Too Low?

It's always disconcerting to hear someone speaking a range that doesn't seem to suit the person—like a David Beckham with a high, childlike voice, for example. Our voices naturally want to fall into a particular pitch range as we speak, but often we've developed bad habits, or made unconscious choices, that force our voices into uncomfortable areas of the range, the equivalent of a shoe that doesn't really fit.

How do you know if you're too high or too low? First try this: Go to the lowest note you can comfortably hit with a certain amount of volume (your rendition of "Ol' Man River" might help you get there). From that place, say "Hello," holding out the *o* sound. If you're doing it right, you should hear and feel a low, rumbling voice coming out of your mouth. Recognize it? If this is anywhere near the normal sound and placement of your speaking voice, it's way too low. I'll show you how to reset it in a more comfortable, and natural, range.

Now listen to audio 10. You'll hear me repeating my first low hello and talking you through the following exercise. Put your four fingers (no thumb) on your stomach right below your sternum, the area at the top of the stomach where your ribs come together. As you say that drawn-out "helloooooo," press with your fingers in a rapid, pulsating motion that pushes your stomach in. As you do this, your voice should jump from the low pitch to a note that is much higher. Concentrate on the higher pitch and try to let go of the low one altogether.

Try again, and this time, when you get to the higher pitch, change the words. Say "Helloooooo. How are you todaaaaaaaaay." Keep pushing your stomach in with that pulsating rhythm. The pitch you are now hovering around is closer to the range where you should normally be speaking.

This is by no means a foolproof test but rather a way to give you a fast hint at a better pitch for your voice. You won't really have to worry about actively finding the right pitch area because, as we do the vocal warm-ups I'll show you in chapter 4, the right pitch will find you. Your voice will effortlessly fall into the correct pitch range for speaking.

At this point, don't worry about whether you're a soprano (the highest female voice) or a bass (the lowest male voice). If you're curious, I'll help you categorize your voice once you've worked on putting it in its most natural spot. For now, though, just try the exercise and see if you find your voice in an unaccustomed, but perhaps intriguing, new place.

Getting a Fix on Your Singing Voice

Singers, I know this is what you've been waiting for. Speakers, I'd really like you to stay with me and give this a try. Follow me through these exercises and you'll gain a wealth of vocal characteristics that will immediately and forever enrich your speaking voice. It's important for all of us to stop drawing a line between speaking and singing. Remember, your brain thinks they're almost the same thing, and I hope you'll regard the work we'll be doing next as sound exercises. They're simply vocal exercises attached to musical notes, and they'll help you, as nothing else can, to make your voice its most resonant and beautiful.

In a moment, when you listen to audio 11 (male) or audio 12 (female) on the website, please understand that I'm using this exercise to give you detailed information about where your voice is right now. Every student I work with starts here, and students often ask me why I choose such a difficult first test. The answer is that I hate wasting time. I want to cut right to the heart of the situation, with sounds that bring all good and bad immediately to the fore. The reason I've chosen the *ah* sound is that it opens up the back part of your throat and sends a lot of air to the vocal cords. It takes great skill to control that much air, and as you try to do it, you'll get a quick, vivid picture of the pluses and minuses in your voice.

When people come to my seminars and lectures, they're amazed to find that I can diagnose the full potential of their voices with just one exercise. I can tell people what type of voice lessons they've had, what kind of techniques they might have studied, whether they smoke, probably what they eat and drink. I'm a well-trained listener, but this exercise is so revealing that it will give detailed information to anyone who's willing to listen carefully.

Do the exercise on audio 11 (male) or audio 12 (female), record it, and then play it back. As you do, use the following checklist to help yourself listen for the same indicators I do when I'm with a student. I want you to understand what's going on in my head so we can effectively share the same set of ears. Pay close attention, and take note of the answers to the following questions:

1. What happens in the range you normally speak in, those comfortable notes that feel as though they vibrate mostly in your chest? What is that comfortable voice like? Is it thick or kind of reedy or whispery? Does it have a nice resonance?

2. What happens as you approach the top of this range? Is there a buildup of pressure as you go higher? Do your throat muscles feel tight, as though you're doing the equivalent of lifting weights?
   Are you straining hard?
   Are you getting louder, and shouting as you move higher? (Notice that in the demonstration, I am just moving up and down the range, not changing volume at all.)

3. As you try to go higher, what happens?
   Does your voice seem to get thinner and less powerful?
   Does your voice crack, or yodel and flip into an airy nothingness?
   Does your sound change so dramatically that you sound like a completely different person?

Each of these questions will help you judge where your singing voice is today. If going higher was no problem for you, and you found that you could do it easily, with no (or small) breaks—great. If you sounded like Tarzan falling off a jungle vine—no problem. I'll show you how to climb back on and swing.

Don't let this test frustrate you. Use it as I do, to identify the weak spots. I promise not to expose anything that I can't easily fix with a little bit of practice and commitment.

Freeing Yourself from the Bad Habits

I hope you'll keep in mind that at every point you heard a sound you didn't like, or noticed a flaw, you were actually listening to the sound of a bad habit. Our work together will be a process of making you conscious of the bad habits and directing the body toward a more natural means of expression. Step-by-step we will exchange bad for good: pressure for ease, tension for relaxation, constriction for freedom, and pain for pleasure. Without the obstacles we've inadvertently set in the way of the voice's free flow, its real beauty can surface. The careful listening you've just done is a crucial foundation. Now follow along with me, and have a bit of faith. Your voice already sounds better.

· 3 ·
Breathing

THE MAGIC that I work with voices is built on a fundamental rhythm: the movements of the body as you inhale and exhale. Breathing smoothly and deeply works wonders for the body in general. It gives you more energy. It can center and calm your mind. And it will give your voice power and consistency. Once you learn to breathe as calmly and steadily as a child does, you are on your way to fabulous vocal reaches.

So how's your breathing? Let's find out right now.

Stand comfortably in front of a mirror and take a deep breath, inhaling through your nose. Fill up your lungs as completely as you can, then blow the air slowly out through your mouth. Take a mental snapshot of what you just saw and felt. What parts of your body were involved? What moved? How did it feel? The details are important here, so really focus on what you're doing. Breathe in through your nose, fill up your lungs, breathe out. We're all born knowing how to do this perfectly. But how easily we forget. To the smooth in-and-out movement of natural breathing, we add bells and whistles, superchargers, and huge dollops of effort.

When I stand in front of a group of new students and ask them to take a deep breath, giving them the same instructions I just gave you, amazing things happen. Chests puff up, and all over the room, shoulders pop up like bread from a toaster. Here and there, I'll see an occasional Buddha belly, from a person who's been told in the past that deep breathing involves filling up the lower abdomen. There's a strong sense of people actively pushing their bodies open to make space for more air, as though they're pulling on the sides of an empty balloon and holding them apart to make room for more breath.

The exhale is sometimes very forceful, another powerful push, as though they're trying to give birth to a beautiful sound by putting all their strength behind it. You can sometimes see the tension in their faces as they contract their stomach muscles to propel the air out of their lungs.

Does this picture look or feel familiar? Did you notice the toaster effect with your shoulders when you inhaled? Did you feel yourself actively pushing your ribs apart and trying to make your chest larger? How was the exhale? Did you tighten your stomach to get the last bit of air out and keep the stream strong? Did your stomach tense and remain locked while the air was trying to get out of your mouth?

The funny thing is, in breathing there's no extra credit for putting all your will, effort, and muscle into getting it right. In fact, all those elements get in the way. Forcing and pushing your breath is a bit like tap dancing on a five-mile hike. You expend a lot of energy, feel like you're giving it your all—and wind up way too exhausted to finish your speech or song with the same power you had when you started. Breathing with physical tension is exhausting, and it wreaks havoc on your stamina. But solid, effective diaphragmatic breathing is just the opposite. It isn't flashy. When you're doing it, air glides easily in and out. And you can do it forever.

In this chapter I'd like to show you how to strip off the layers of unconscious habits and misguided techniques that stand between you and perfect diaphragmatic breathing, that sheathed-in-mystery process that so many teachers have made complicated over the years. Breathing, as they say in California, is a Zen thing to experience: we have to *allow* it to happen instead of forcing it. We're meant to float through this kind of breathing instead of turning it into a grueling, athletic butterfly stroke. By paying attention to when it gets difficult, or when it seems to take special effort, you'll be able to relax and let the breathing be steady, smooth, and even, the perfect foundation for beautiful speaking and singing.

Natural Breathing

To understand how tension and effort get in the way of correct breathing, you need to know a little about what's happening inside your body. We're lucky enough not to have to think about how to make all the parts mesh when we inhale and exhale, but bringing some consciousness into this automatic process will help you step in and make the adjustments you need.

In a nutshell, this is what the essential breathing equipment looks like and how it works: Your lungs rest on your diaphragm, a large muscular sheet that separates the chest cavity from the abdomen. The diaphragm is attached to your spinal column, lower ribs, and breastbone. It naturally arches upward, but when you inhale, it contracts, moving down an inch or two. That little movement sounds insignificant, but it powers the breathing process. It not only gives the lungs more room to expand; it also changes the pressure within the lungs. Imagine that the lungs are a container with a false bottom. When the diaphragm drops, the "false bottom" falls out and air rushes in to fill the vacuum. When the diaphragm relaxes and begins to rise, the air in the lungs becomes more compressed in its smaller space, and it rushes out.

If the lungs are allowed to hang freely in the chest, and if the diaphragm is allowed to drop and rise, you'll be breathing like a baby, fully and naturally. That's the goal.

Now you try it. The instructions that follow are aimed at removing the obstructions that many of us allow to get in the way of deep and easy breathing. I'll stop to explain each basic step of the process, so you'll be aware of any "extras" you're unconsciously adding.

Step One: Good Posture

To begin, we'll need to create an unobstructed pathway for the inhaled air to travel to the lungs. First, stand up straight, with your feet shoulder width apart. Roll your head around to ease any tension in your neck, then hold your head level, with your chin parallel to the ground, not tipped up or down. Let your shoulder blades slide toward the center of your back so that they're back and down. If you do this, your chest will be open instead of collapsed, which is just what we want.

Slumping, or even rounding your shoulders forward slightly, partly collapses the upper rib cage and keeps the muscles between the ribs from being able to expand to accommodate the lungs as they fill with air. What we're looking for is the physical ease that comes from good alignment.

Now bend your knees slightly—just relax and unlock them—and tuck your pelvis under. This slight adjustment helps ensure that the diaphragm can function at maximum capacity. You could think of these movements as taking the kinks out of a garden hose so water can flow out easily. You're creating an open pathway for the movement of air.

Sure, it's possible to keep talking or singing if you slump, but it takes a lot more effort than you're probably aware of. If you'd like a vivid demonstration of what happens to the voice when the rib cage is obstructing air, try this:

Sit with your chest in proper alignment, with back straight and shoulders down. Begin to count aloud slowly to ten, and as you count, round your shoulders and move them toward your knees, as if you were doing a sit-up. Move slowly. You'll notice that as you get farther and farther down, your voice will begin to close, finally reduced to a squelched wisp of sound. Try to take a deep breath in this position and you'll feel the air physically blocked. Slight slumping and slouching won't constrict your voice this much—but they definitely put a pinch on the pipes.

Paying attention to alignment will help you eliminate much of the muscle tension that impedes good singing and speaking. I'm impressed by the ideas developed by movement specialists like those practicing the Alexander Technique, and I think they have definite applications for the work we're doing here. Alexander Technique experts believe that our bodies were designed to move and perform *easily*. Watch a healthy toddler in action and you will see an erect spine, free joints, and a large head balancing effortlessly on a small neck. Our natural posture is incredible. But without knowing it, we put unwanted pressure on the body, exerting more force than we need for even the simplest act—standing, sitting, or, I would add, singing. Paying attention to the alignment of the head and the spine can help correct the body's overall coordination and bring us back into balance. So can being aware of how much force we're putting into simple actions like lifting a book, opening a jar—or breathing. Balance, once we find it, is essentially *effortless*, and so is the flow of air into and out of our bodies. Discovering a way of standing that opens and lines you up may seem incidental to singing and speaking, but it frees space and energy for producing beautiful sounds.

Step Two: Inhale

Now I'd like you to put your hand on your stomach, with your middle finger on your belly button. All the action that follows should take place in the space between the base of your ribs and just below your belly button. Keeping your shoulders in that beautiful, open position, back and down, imagine that your stomach is a balloon, and as you inhale, let it fill with air. Concentrate on filling this "balloon" only. And when it's full, blow the air gently out through your mouth.

Try this for a few minutes, remembering that you just want to blow up the balloon without lifting your shoulders or puffing up your chest. How does this feel? Did you find that it was the opposite of what you usually do? Raising your chest and shoulders as you inhale is called accessory breathing, and it's the surest way to get the least amount of air into the body with the least amount of control. Often, people not only pull their shoulders and chest up as they inhale, but they also feel they should pull in their stomachs. That combination— I think of it as the Hercules breath, because when you do it, you take on the strained look of a guy in the gym lifting heavy weights— keeps all of the movement in the upper part of the body and results in very shallow breathing. Both of these styles of breathing, of course, can be so habitual that they feel completely natural.

If you're in the habit of dramatically involving your chest and shoulders in your breathing, you're only partially filling your lungs, and if you pull in your stomach as you do that, your diaphragm has no chance to drop. The quieter, much more subtle way of breathing we're using here may make you feel like nothing's happening, but rest assured—subtle is fine.

Diaphragmatic breathing is supposed to be completely relaxing to the body. But on occasion, in the early stages of learning, people can create all kinds of pressure and muscle tension. A few students, for example, say they feel a bit of tension in their stomach or lower back as they inhale. Some have even mentioned that the pain made diaphragmatic breathing an unpleasant experience. This kind of discomfort is not too common, but when it occurs, it's usually because the student is using the muscles of the stomach improperly.

As you expand the "balloon," you're not helping if you apply huge amounts of physical and mental force to push your stomach muscles out and distend your belly. All that pushing can cause you to tighten up, and with enough pushing, you'll feel like a bomb ready to explode. It may be that you're trying to fill your lungs too much, thinking that you have to cram every available space with air. It's a bit like trying to top off the tank at the gas station. It doesn't make sense, as the lungs will naturally let you know when they're filled to capacity. Going for unnatural expansion can put huge amounts of pressure on your back and even show up as pain there or in other parts of the body. Stop doing this, and see what happens as you consciously let your abdominal muscles relax while you fill your body with air.

Don't feel alarmed if you see only a small movement of your stomach when you quit pushing breath in and just let it flow. Many people experience only a small expansion in the front of their bodies as they inhale this way—but they feel their lower back area expand far more, because the diaphragm extends from the front of the body to the back, and its full motion affects the whole core of the body. You can detect the movement at the back of your body by putting your hands just above your waist on your back as you inhale.

When I worked with the actor and director Angelina Jolie, I couldn't see her stomach come that far forward when she breathed in, so I asked her to focus on filling up the lower part of her back area, as if air were going in there. That worked for her. Then, when she felt comfortable with that placement, we were able to shift more of the movement to the front of her body and she was able to let her stomach expand forward more.

In a very short time, your breathing should be free of chest and shoulder action, and you ought to be able to inhale without stomach tension. Don't worry if you get a little light-headed at first. People tell me that they sometimes feel a tiny bit dizzy as they begin to learn diaphragmatic breathing. That's because you're bringing more air into your system than you're used to, pushing more air out than before, and possibly hyperventilating. This will pass—and your body will appreciate all the life-giving oxygen you're feeding it.

Step Three: Focus on the Exhale

This is supposed to be the easy part, the release. As we exhale, the body is designed to allow the stomach to fall easily back to its normal position. It doesn't take muscle to exhale, just relaxation. But about 85 percent of the singers I work with, and many of the speakers, feel they have to try hard to push the air out. For them, exhaling is more like wringing the air out of their bodies, or straining to give birth, than stepping out of the way as the breath whooshes smoothly out of their mouths.

When we exhale, many of us use force. We tighten. We make it a hundred times harder than it's supposed to be, thinking, mistakenly, that to get the volume we want, and to hit the high notes, the best thing to do is to fire our voices out a cannon. We all know how forcefully we can make air leave our bodies because we've all coughed or sneezed. When our body tries to clear its air passages of obstructions, we automatically tighten the group of muscles located at the top part of the stomach area in the center of the chest where the ribs come together. Tensing this spot can create pressure strong enough to expel a foreign object from the body with more than ten times the force of a normal exhalation. It's very similar to what you might feel when you strain to force a bowel movement. It wreaks havoc on the body, and the reason we're discussing it here is this: Tensing these muscles blocks your access to the full use of your voice. When people have trouble with my technique, this tension is the cause about half the time.

Feel it yourself by placing your index and middle finger on the area I just described. In short, strong bursts, say "Go! Go! Go!" Do you feel the muscles under your fingers tighten and lock up when you shoot out that syllable? What you're doing, as you tighten, is cutting off the flow of air from your lungs.

Why do we do it? Lots of reasons. Many, many untrained singers tighten up the higher they try to go in the range because they equate high pitches with difficulty. As the singer moves up the scale, the brain and body go into what I call weight lifter mode. Believing that will, force, and effort will get them to the top, these singers push harder and harder as they go. And many people don't realize that's what they're doing.

In class one day, I asked my student Kevin to try some exercises. Kevin is a strong, muscular guy whose physique could come only from hours of pumping iron. I demonstrated some sounds, getting higher and higher, and as he followed me, I could see that he was creating huge amounts of tension in his body. When I put my hand on his stomach, I could feel the muscles locking up. It was impossible to miss the additional tension in his face and neck. But he *did* hit the high notes, and he was all smiles when he got there.

When I told him that I would show him a way to get to the same places without so much pressure and tension, he was confused. "What pressure?" he said. "There was no pressure." The other students burst out laughing, not quite believing that he could tense up so dramatically and not know it. I explained that when you get used to stomach spasms as you breathe, and experience other tensions in your neck and throat, *those feelings become the norm.* The strain is immediately apparent to others, but it may be invisible to you. Amazing, isn't it, how much we learn to ignore this kind of pain.

The fact that he could get the notes out made Kevin's brain think that he was fine. He hit the pitch he was aiming for, and despite what the effort was costing him, he thought he'd achieved his goal. Because he was strong and used to thinking "no pain, no gain," his tolerance for physical discomfort was a lot higher than many people's. So even though we all saw his eyes bulging and his stomach rippling, he didn't perceive a problem.

Like many of us, he was telling himself: "Singing is work! I'm really high, I'm really loud, I'm calling on my body to do incredible things—and of course there's going to be tension. That's what it takes."

There's just one problem with that line of thinking: It's baloney. There's no connection at all between the strain of power lifting and what's required for great speaking and singing. The more forceful the stream of air coming at the vocal cords, the harder it is for them to regulate the sounds they produce. Power, range, and consistency depend on smooth, even airflow, not bursts of supercharged breath.

Making the Exhale Easy

So how do we get from rigid to rag doll on the exhalation? A little awareness will go a long way. As you exhale, keep your hand resting on your stomach, and be conscious of when your muscles tighten. You can massage your muscles softly as you exhale to remind them to relax. And if need be, as you're learning, you can also help your stomach in by pushing gently with your hand, which creates less pressure than using your abdominal muscles. Remember, the goal is not to *pull* anything in. Just *let* your stomach fall to its neutral position.

There's no need to try to push every last bit of air out. There is always air in your lungs (unless one of them is punctured); when all the breathing muscles are relaxed between breaths, the lungs still contain about 40 percent of the volume of air they did when they were completely full. If you forcefully exhale as much as possible, you'll still have 20 percent of the air left. Take a breath and then blow out all the air in your lungs until you feel they're empty. When the stream of air stops, blow again. You'll notice that you still have more air. It's very difficult to get to empty, so it's not worth the massive effort so many of us make.

Deep Doesn't Mean Slow

Have you noticed that diaphragmatic breathing takes longer than "regular" breathing? That was a trick question. Actually, it doesn't. Sometimes my beginning students think that in order to get air deep into their lungs, they need to take long, drawn-out breaths. After all, they figure, the air has farther to go. But that idea is a fallacy. Once you stop raising your chest and shoulders, air will rush into the lungs in record time. Remember that when the diaphragm is free to move, its movement changes the air pressure in the lungs, and that shift sucks air into your body.

If you try to take in air very slowly, you're actually restricting the flow in and most likely inhaling through your mouth. You'll notice that your lips are partially closed and pursed, or your teeth are close together. You might even hear air get caught where your lips and teeth meet, creating the hiss of air being sucked through a tight opening. *This is not diaphragmatic breathing.* When you're doing it correctly, the air flows silently in through the nose and races into your lungs.

Getting It Right

For my client Tony Robbins, concentrated practice was the key to letting go of the need to push on the exhale. Tony has a powerful physical presence, something that's central to his ability to motivate people to be their best, and he tried to power and muscle his way through his first attempts to learn diaphragmatic breathing. Because he wanted to learn fast, we'd sometimes practice for twenty minutes at a time. He'd stand just the way I've told you to, and with his eyes closed and his hand on his stomach, he'd pretend to fill up the balloon in his abdomen. After five or ten minutes, it was no problem to get the air in smoothly. But he kept tightening his stomach to help the breath out of his body.

To counter that tendency, we did several breathing exercises that may help you.

The Slow Leak

Put your hand on your stomach and fill your stomach with air. Now close your teeth, placing your tongue against your bottom teeth, and release the smallest amount of air you can through your teeth. Make a *tse* sound as you release. Practice until you can make your breath last for thirty seconds or longer. (You can hear me demonstrate this exercise on audio 13 on the website.)

Remember that you are letting the air leak out of your lungs — you're not pushing or using any muscles. Most of all, you're not trying to get the last molecule of air out of your body. You're just watching as a small, steady amount of air leaves your mouth. As I'll show you later, your vocal cords often don't need any more air than this for beautiful speech and singing!

Blowing Out Candles

Next, try this: Take a proper inhale with your hand on your stomach. Imagine that you're facing a cake with a line of candles glowing on top. Imagine that the cake is level with your head, about three or four inches away from your mouth. Now softly blow out the candles one by one, opening your lips to blow, quickly closing them, and opening your lips again to blow out the next. As you do this the first time, notice what's happening to the stomach-area muscles. Do you feel them contracting each time you blow? Do you feel your stomach pushing out against your hand when you blow? Neither of those is the effect you want.

Try blowing out the line of candles again. This time, feel your stomach move in with little pressure when you blow, then stop. Feel it move in, then stop, with each candle you blow out. It shouldn't come out again until you take your next breath. (Feel free to inhale when you run out of breath.) Notice the difference between this "stop and start" and the more spasm-like jerks that you feel when you tighten your muscles.

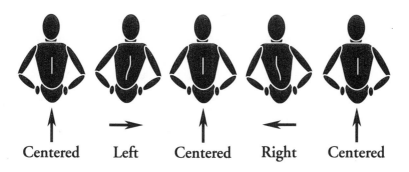

Centered   Left   Centered   Right   Centered

TORSO SWING

The Torso Swing

This exercise, though it's not for everyone, because it involves a movement the body's not used to making in its normal range of motion, is a great last resort for unlocking the stomach muscles. To do it, stand up and put your hands on your waist. Now, as the diagram above illustrates, move your rib cage from side to side without moving your hips. In other words, isolate your ribs and keep your body still from the waist down. Keep your shoulders level. I suggest that you try the "slow leak" exercise *while doing the torso swing*. You'll find that it's impossible to swing and clench your breathing muscles at the same time. And once you've experienced the feeling of exhaling without tension, you can find your way back to it without the movement. This will be a useful tool later if you find that your stomach tenses up when you do the general exercises.

One More Useful Breathing Trick

Lately, when working with students who are having trouble relaxing into diaphragmatic breathing, I've been pulling out what has proved to be a powerful prop: a large book. I find one that's several inches thick, and I put it on the floor near a wall, asking students to stand straight with their backs against the wall, with the balls of their feet and toes elevated by the book, heels on the floor. Standing in this position tucks your pelvis into correct alignment, which makes it much easier to breathe correctly. My student Aimee was thrilled with the results she got from using this simple technique. She'd been laboring through her diaphragmatic breathing and thought she'd never discover the ease that I'd been promising her. But she felt a shift right away when we tried the posture change, and after a week of practicing on her own, she came in breathing like a diva.

Now I point anyone with difficulties to this easy, accessible tool. Any thick book, or even a rolled-up towel, will do the trick.

Classic Breathing Exercises: The Good, the Bad, and the Ugly

Students sometimes come to me wondering about breathing exercises they've heard of or learned from other teachers. We tend to trust "the experts," and particularly if an exercise has been around a long time, we assume it must be effective. Sometimes we're lucky—and sometimes we've got a real lemon on our hands.

Take, for example, the belt.

I've heard of many instructors who teach diaphragmatic breathing this way: They tell the student to take a deep breath, filling up the whole lower abdomen, which we know doesn't really have much to do with breathing, and pushing the belly out. At the point of maximum expansion, the teacher takes a long belt and fastens it snugly around the extended stomach. Then the teacher tells the student to exhale, but to keep the belly expanded so that the belt doesn't drop.

This is somehow supposed to make the breath smoother and stronger, but forcing the belly out, and holding it there, only creates stress and tension, the very factors that get in the way of great breathing.

If this exercise is something you still do, STOP. And if you meet a teacher who advises you to do it, you know what to do. Find a new teacher. The sad truth is that teachers pass on what they have learned. Often no one challenges the master, and one generation after another builds its techniques without questioning or connecting with the underlying physiology. Voice teachers don't generally go to medical school, and doctors are often too busy to take singing lessons and correct teachers' misconceptions.

I don't want to weigh you down with complicated anatomy and technical information, but I do want you to understand the basic physical principles behind what we're doing. Believe me, when we work with the body instead of against it, the results are remarkable.

I'm certainly not out to discredit techniques just because they're old, sound weird, or were developed by someone else. Some funny-sounding exercises actually work, and they're worth holding on to. Case in point: the book on the belly.

Exercising by the Book

Lie on your back with your legs on the seat of a chair. Put a big book on your stomach, right above your belly button. Now inhale deeply into your stomach and exhale, taking care not to use your stomach or chest muscles to "assist" the exhalation. If you're breathing correctly, you'll see the book rise as you inhale and sink as you exhale.

Diaphragmatic breathing is easier in this position because when you lie with your legs up, your pelvis tips into good alignment, your back and shoulders are properly set, and you don't have to wonder if you're in the right position. Air has easy and full access to your lungs, your lungs are free to expand, and you can experience what good diaphragmatic breathing feels like. What's the book about? It's not to apply pressure or to facilitate the breathing—it's just a great visual aid. You don't have to wonder if your stomach is moving as it should. All you have to do is look down and see the book rising and falling. The movement's not huge, but it is easily visible.

The Bends

A final puzzling exercise that's quite common involves bending over from the waist as you sing an ascending scale. Students are told that if they do this, their sound will somehow improve, and because they feel the exercise does *something* to help them, sometimes they ask me about it.

Bending over as you sing does a couple of things. It does change the way you breathe out because when you bend until your torso is parallel to the ground, the movement helps push your stomach in to artificially send air out of the lungs. Actually, though, that's not the only reason the notes might have improved.

The real reason for the change is that as you bend, it's easy to become afraid that you'll lose your balance or fall. And when you're preoccupied with what your body's doing and how stable your position is, it's easy to forget that you're hitting high notes. Bending changes your focus—from "Oh my god, I'm singing higher notes" to "Uh-oh, I might fall." Lots of students freak out at the thought of trying to go high—until something distracts them.

Is it a real breathing exercise? Not really. But it does serve an interesting purpose for students whose minds get in the way of their singing. As we shape the breath into vocal sounds, I think you'll keep noticing the same thing: without the interference of tension and pressure (physical or mental), the body knows all about how best to release your true voice into the world. The trick is to get out of the way and let it.

The Tension Trap

The reason it's so important to drain the strain from breathing is that if you don't, you'll be forcing your vocal cords to contend with uneven blasts of air. Imagine trying to play a harmonica, never knowing if a lot of air or a little air was going to come from between your lips. Yes, you might make sounds, even interesting sounds, but it would be hard to know just what was going to happen when you opened your mouth.

When you create tension, you create a tourniquet effect on the air trying to leave the lungs. It's like putting a cork in a garden hose. Pressure builds, and the air eventually muscles its way through the restricted passage. The air that emerges under these conditions is very concentrated and pressurized, like the water you see spurting from a fire hydrant. And when it hits the vocal cords, it shocks them. The cords react by locking into a set position instead of being able to move. Believe me: for reasons I'll explain in the next chapter, you don't want this to happen. Gorgeous singing and speaking require you to be able to let sounds flow out without restriction. It's the tension blocks that cause problems.

A good way to think about solid breathing is what I think of as the "great waiter" model. If you've ever had dinner in a restaurant with four-star service, you've probably noticed that your water glass is never empty. You sip, you chat, you eat, and every time you reach for your water glass, it's full. The magic is that the refills are so unobtrusive they seem to be invisible. It takes practice to allow our breathing to be that easy and invisible as we make sounds, but once you do, you've got the best possible foundation for making any sound you choose.

How Long Will It Take?

For a highly motivated student like Tony Robbins, who was focusing on breathing for twenty minutes at a time, it didn't take long to experience the feeling of just letting the exhale happen. Within a few days, he had found his way from tension to tension-free in his exhalations, and that very small step immediately gave him access to a new freedom in his voice.

It may take you hours, or days, or even weeks to disengage the habits of muscles that are accustomed to locking up as you exhale. But keep working with the exercises and I guarantee that you'll see progress. I recommend that you stop two or three times a day and think about your breathing for five minutes.

Go for Optimum Results

Diaphragmatic breathing is part of the bedrock of the vocal technique that has made it possible for me to help every kind of person access the vast possibilities of the voice. It's the tested, proven way of giving the voice the natural fuel it needs for strength, stamina, and experimentation. But the unfortunate truth is that only a handful of singers and speakers have great diaphragmatic breathing. It *is* possible to make fabulous sounds and still be oblivious to this kind of breathing. I ask you to learn this technique for only one reason: I want you to have the greatest voice available to you. I want you to see, from the beginning, all of what your body is capable of doing, rather than learning to compensate for the things you can't do.

One notable singer who came late to the notion of diaphragmatic breathing was Luciano Pavarotti, one of the premier tenors of our time. Pavarotti, after singing for many years, was world-famous and starring in the most challenging roles ever written for the tenor voice. Yet he felt that something was missing from his technique. He'd sing like an angel one day, and the next he'd be able to perform but without the spark or the stamina. It bothered him that the quality of his voice would change so much from show to show, and he began to pay close attention to the singing of his favorite vocalists, who seemed able every day to sound as beautiful as the day before. His close observation led him to the conclusion that he had never really mastered the art of breathing. The singers he admired were breathing differently—more deeply and more fluidly.

Pavarotti emulated what he saw, and for the first time in his career, he began to use diaphragmatic breathing. When he did, he said, everything changed for him. He worried less that his voice would be strong one day and feeble the next. He felt he got a much greater level of consistency from his sound, and performing became much more pleasurable.

Taking the time to let the breathing techniques in this chapter become second nature won't automatically turn you into the next Pavarotti or Barbra Streisand—but it will relax you, focus you, and guarantee that you have all the necessary equipment for producing the full range of sounds available to you. Consistently. Easily. Powerfully.

· 4 ·

The Miracle of Middle Voice

Now that you've laid a solid foundation of easy, relaxed breathing, we can move into the heart and soul of our work together. I'm very excited about introducing you to the technique that sets my work apart from that of every other teacher. It's allowed me to create the miracles that have made my brand famous all over the world, and by the end of this chapter, you'll be on the path to mastering it.

As people sing from low to high, most of them concentrate on the extremes. How low can you go? How high can you fly? They work hard—sometimes for years—to expand their range, looking for ways to push the envelope. But very few of them have come to terms with the fact that a huge part of their voice is missing.

The exercises in this chapter, and the discoveries you'll make as you do them, will change your voice forever, and I guarantee that if you stay with me as we cover the material here and on the audio tracks on the website, you will feel and hear profound shifts in your voice that take you into undreamed-of territory. Where are we headed? Into the shrouded-in-mystery, overlooked, and unacknowledged key to vocal freedom: the middle voice.

The middle voice is the bridge between the familiar low voice most of us speak with (called chest voice) and the voice nestled way above our speaking voice (called head voice). This incredible, little-recognized part of the voice, which I specialize in helping people strengthen, is responsible for bringing a new kind of power and ease to both speaking and singing. Once you find it, you can sing without tiring your voice, relieve the pressure that builds in your throat and jaw, and, as you'll see, almost miraculously gain smooth access to the entire range of your voice.

For speakers, developing middle voice will give access to a new palette of resonances. What does that mean to you? Think about the range of colors you hear in the voice of a great actor, or a memorable speaker like Martin Luther King. That's the everything-but-monotonous world of possibilities middle voice opens up for you. And it's fabulous training for another reason: to find it, you *must* let go of pressure and strain in your voice. Using the middle-voice exercises is a litmus test for speakers. When you are able to find middle and play with it, you can be assured that you are breathing in a way that will keep your voice strong and powerful, and that you have learned to release the gripping muscles that keep your voice trapped, earthbound, or unreliable.

Middle voice will add gorgeous overtones to the way you speak. It will add a crisp, bright, and pretty sound to the lower register you've spent most of your speaking life in—and it will add high-end flair and color to a voice that's been low, husky, and dull.

Let me show you how the discovery of middle voice worked for two of my students, one a number of years ago and one more recently, because I'd like you to understand what's possible, and what you can expect, as you work with the exercises I'll teach you in this chapter. Yes, it will take effort. But the results will amaze you.

A Short Push to Freedom

A well-known manager in the music industry called me at the end of 1997 to ask me to work with a new group that was already on tour and starting to get significant airplay with its first single, called "Push." At that time I'd never heard the song, and I wasn't familiar with the group, Matchbox Twenty. The manager explained that the lead singer, Rob Thomas, was wonderfully talented but was becoming terribly hoarse from performing night after night.

Rob came in for his first meeting with me carrying a CD of his music as a gift and a guide to the kind of music he was making. He opened the cover, pulled out the photo, and signed it with the words, "Please make me sound as good as I do on this record." He explained that he was totally comfortable singing in the studio because when his voice got tired, he could say, "Later," and come back another day. But when he was onstage in front of a cheering audience, he didn't have that option. He wanted and needed help.

Rob has a bluesy, gravelly voice that's brimming with emotion and style. But because he was trapped in his speaking voice — chest voice — as the notes got higher in the range, he was straining terribly to reach them. I showed him the series of exercises you're about to learn, and as middle voice opened up for him, he realized that he no longer had to force the top notes. That revelation, he said, was like a gift from God. He and the band used practice tapes much like the warm-ups I'm about to walk you through, and with a program of fifteen minutes of practice a day, the whole band was able to perform, sometimes five shows a week, with no strain, no hoarseness, and no lost voices. In the months that followed, they went on to sell more than ten million copies of the CD.

Gwen Stefani had a similar middle voice revelation when I started working with her. I had been teaching her then-husband Gavin Rossdale, the front man for the group Bush, and Gavin bragged to her about the progress we had made with his voice. So as she was getting ready to head out on a yearlong tour, Gwen decided to come in for a lesson. When I vocalized her through some exercises to see what was going on, I realized that she had a powerful chest voice and head voice, but that she was still straining at the top of chest voice and not moving into middle. When I showed her how to do that, and she realized there was another voice she'd never heard about, she was shocked and excited. I gave her the exercises to make her middle voice grow, and sent her off on tour.

A year later, I saw her at a party and she came up to me saying, "Roger, you changed my life." I started smiling uncontrollably. "I practiced your warm-up exercises every night before I went onstage,

I used the middle voice, and I have never had greater performances," she told me. "My voice held up every night and sounded amazing."

That's what middle voice can do.

Meet the Zipper

To understand where the ease comes from when you find middle, you need to know a little about how your voice works. Remember, there are three different parts of the voice—chest, middle, and head—and each works in a slightly different way, as illustrated in the diagram below. When you're in chest voice, the vocal cords are supposed to be vibrating along their full length, like the long, thick strings of a piano. Chest voice—as you would guess—feels like it resonates in the top part of your chest. If you put your hand just below the seam where your neck meets the top of your chest and say, "I can speak in chest," you should feel a slight vibration in your hand.

As you move higher in the range, a kind of zipper effect begins to close off one end of the cords (this is called dampening). When this "zipper" moves up to the point where only 50 percent of the length of the cords is vibrating, you are in middle voice.

In middle voice, you should feel the vibration partially leave the chest area and move closer to the area just behind your nose and eyes. This area has been given many names over the years, but it's most commonly called the mask. The air and tone bouncing around the sinus area can feel as gentle as a minor flutter or buzz. Close your

| Chest | Middle | Head |

CHEST, MIDDLE, AND HEAD

lips and say *mmmmmmmm*. You should feel your lips vibrating as sound hits them from the inside of your mouth. This is very similar to the vibration you'll feel in middle, though in middle it's a bit closer to the nose.

As the zipper continues to close and only one-third of the vocal cords vibrates, you reach head voice. In head voice, you'll feel none of the resonance of chest voice, and you're far from the voice you use when you speak. Now you'll feel air and sound vibrating primarily behind your eyes and nose, in the highest reaches of your sinuses.

To achieve fluidity in your voice, the object is to allow the vocal cords to open and close smoothly through their whole range of motion without creating any strain or pressure. (What I've called the zipper is actually the result of phlegm building up at the end of the cords and creating the zippering effect.)

The main job of the vocal cords is to be a filter for the air. They simply decide how much air gets through. And to allow them to open and close smoothly in the filtering process, you need to send enough air to the cords to make them vibrate as rapidly as they need to, but not so much that it forces the zipper wide open with insufficient cord vibration.

In chest voice, the vocal cords are at their longest and thickest, so they can handle a tremendous amount of air. As the vocal cords zip together and get shorter in middle voice, they can't withstand the same volume of airflow, and in head voice, with the smallest area of cord vibration, they can handle even less. To make sounds through the entire range, I repeat: It's vital to send just the right amount of air to the cords as they change length.

There's an interesting irony here that emphasizes the same point I made about breathing: pushing hard, straining, and tightening up your body in an effort to make the zipper work is like using a jack-hammer when a gentle tug will do. All the straining we so commonly put into reaching for the heights, both musically and as we work to make points persuasively in speech, is completely counter-productive. The incredible stress that Rob Thomas was using to get to the high notes in his band's music kept the zipper from closing. The harder he pushed, the more the cords locked up and tried hopelessly to hold the air back. That made him more likely to get hoarse, not higher or stronger. The ease that freed him came from allowing his voice to slide into middle. The same thing happened for Gwen. Going into middle took all the pressure off the cords and kept her voice healthy for those long months of touring.

Where's Middle?

I teach middle to everyone because I consider myself to be the equivalent of a piano builder. My job is to ensure that the complete instrument—that is, your entire voice, top to bottom—is usable. In case you don't know how much ground your voice should be able to cover, let me get specific for a minute.

For the average man: Chest voice starts at low E or F, which is twelve or thirteen white keys below middle C on the piano (see diagram). It goes up for about two octaves (twenty-three or twenty-four notes), reaching middle voice at around the E or F above middle C. Middle voice runs from that E or F to about B-flat or B-natural. Above that, from C and beyond, you're in head voice.

The practical meaning of all this is that men can do almost all the singing and speaking they want to in chest and middle voice

MALE RANGE

(Pavarotti sang opera in the range covered by chest and middle). For you, head voice is probably going to be an interesting sidelight, but not much more. Mastering middle is essential.

For women: Chest voice starts at the F below middle C and continues up for just seventeen notes to the B-flat above middle C (see diagram). Middle voice covers the next six notes or so, and ends around E or F. And the rest is head voice. You'll hit middle sooner in the exercises than men will because physically you have less chest range—your vocal cords are thinner and shorter. (You do, of course, make up for it by having more head voice than a man.) If you're a singer, you'll want to practice moving smoothly from middle to head also.

Many people are shocked, after hearing me emphasize middle voice so heavily, that middle covers such a small span of notes. As we've seen, it's a total of about six half steps altogether. But middle is a pressure valve, a bridge and a proven pathway to strengthening the entire voice. Most people feel as though they're six feet tall in a room with a six-foot ceiling when they sing or speak higher in the range. At the top of chest, it feels as though there's nowhere to go but down. Middle raises the ceiling to ten feet, so you can jump up and down whenever you feel like it without crashing into a barrier.

You need *every* part of your voice. Together we'll shine, polish, repair, and replace any sections of the voice that don't serve you well.

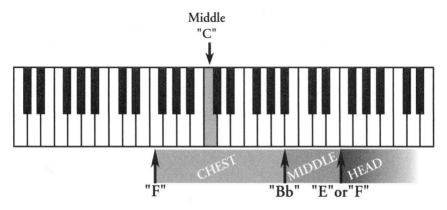

FEMALE RANGE

I never expect that every single note will be used every day, but I want to give you the confidence to reach for any one you want and know it's there for any purpose.

Let's Go for the Middle

Ready? First I'd like to be sure you understand what middle voice sounds like. Listen to audio 14 on the website and you'll hear a demonstration that begins with chest voice, then moves into the short passageway that is middle voice, and winds up in head. You'll notice that I point out just where middle begins and ends so there's no guesswork about it. Listen until you really hear it.

You'll notice that chest voice has a thick, open quality, while head voice is flutelike, with sweet, subtle high overtones. Middle combines the best elements of the two. The lower portion of middle is supposed to sound almost exactly like chest voice, and as we inch higher, it gradually picks up the sound colors of head voice. It's a lot like mixing paint. If you think of chest voice as being black and head voice being white, what we're doing with middle is blending the whole spectrum of grays that fall between the two. Skillful combining will create a seamless movement from low to high.

The One-Octave Exercise

Want to try it? To begin, I'd like you to spend a few minutes reconnecting with what you now know about breathing. Consciously practice letting smooth, deep breaths flow in and out. Then listen to audio 15 (male) or audio 16 (female) and follow along, maintaining your smooth breathing. What you'll hear—and then copy yourself—is your first vocal exercise, a series of sounds in a rhythmic pattern that begins a half step higher each time you do it. This exercise is called the one-octave series because—you guessed it—each exercise covers one octave of range. The specific syllables we'll use—goog, gug, moom, mum, no, nay, nah (which we'll repeat in many of the exercises)—are designed to direct progressively greater amounts of air toward the vocal cords. That means you'll start with small, easier-to-control amounts of air and move toward being able to shape larger amounts.

Basically, the syllables themselves, because they position your throat and tongue and help regulate the flow of air, set you up physically to find middle voice. What you need to do is keep going as the exercise gets higher—at the same volume from beginning to end. This is important: *Getting louder will not help you find middle.* It's almost sure to prevent it because it sends more air to the vocal cords than they can handle as they try to find the middle position.

If you feel a large buildup of tension and pressure when I say go to middle, stop and try it again, keeping your breathing even and your volume constant. Try this a few times. You're exploring—feeling your way toward middle.

What happened when you got to the top of chest and took your next steps up the scale? How smooth was the transition? Was there a big yodel-like break? At the top of chest, the voice may go into a very different place, which is thin and high. In fact, the low voice and the high one might sound as though they belong to two entirely different people. That's not the blending you want. It means you've skipped middle and rocketed into head voice.

Do the exercise again, this time trying to make the high sounds more like the lower ones. Don't expect the shift from low to high to be perfectly smooth in the first few attempts. This is a learning *process.* You may notice that there's a small break in your voice as you make the transition to middle, then a weak middle, produced without strain, that carries some of the resonance of the chest voice. What you're looking for is a voice that sounds almost as thick as chest voice but feels like it is vibrating both behind your nose and at the top of your chest.

I know this sounds complicated, but I want to remind you that the voice *wants* to find middle. It *wants* to shift gears easily, without grinding, stopping, or feeling that the body is squeezing so hard that only a squeak comes out. Play with this!

First Helper: The Cry

Sometimes you're just a step away from middle and one little push will get you there. So I'd like you to try the one-octave exercise again, singing only googs and gugs, this time using a special sound that I call the cry. You'll hear it on audio 17 (male) or audio 18 (female) on the website. The cry is an amusing sound that might make you feel like a cartoon character pretending to be sad. Imitate the sound as closely as you can, and enjoy yourself. This is supposed to be fun.

The cry works by concentrating the flow of air at the back of the throat and helps the air navigate successfully both below the soft palate and above it, into the nasal area. It works to give the breath a boost into the right position so you can feel and hear it.

If you're like many, many students, the cry may take you straight into middle.

But for those who get stuck, have questions, or want more illumination, let me show you how other students have dealt with the most common problems and concerns.

Slipping into Middle

Ryan is the choir director and head of the vocal department of a private school in Los Angeles. He has a substantial knowledge of music, but he had never fully grasped the concept of middle, and he was intrigued when we began to work together. Ryan's first attempts to find middle had him pushing and straining when he got to the top of chest voice. He was trying to muscle those rich sounds higher in the range while keeping them vibrating only in his chest. I made him aware of the straining, and as he allowed himself to relax, we tiptoed into a very thin, hard-to-hold-on-to middle voice that was light and airy. It was so fragile that only some sounds allowed him to cross into middle. He especially liked *mum* and had trouble with many of the other syllables.

You may notice this yourself. You may do well with one sound and not another—and at the beginning, this is fine. Our first goal is for you to have the sensation of getting into middle. Let me tell you a little about how each of the sounds works and what a preference for one sound or another might say about you.

Goog and gug. The g sound on both sides of the vowel momentarily stops the air from going through the cords (this is known as a glottal stop). At that moment, the cords have an extra split second to move to the right position before the air hits them. The vowels themselves allow slightly different amounts of air through: the *oo* is fairly closed, while the *uh* opens the throat up a bit more.

Moom and mum. These two syllables allow you to play with a wee bit more air. The *m* sound allows a small stream of air to keep coming through the cords, even when the lips are closed. Remember how I mentioned that middle voice vibrates in the mask area? The *m* sound helps redirect the air into that area by sending some of it above the soft palate (the back of the roof of the mouth).

No, nay, nah. When you use these syllables, you'll notice that the vowel sounds aren't closed off at the end by a consonant, so the airflow is a little stronger and less interrupted. The nay and nah sounds are a bit harsh. They're called pharyngeal (it means throaty), and they put the cords in a thicker, longer position for more volume and strength. When I give you a harsh sound to make, never worry that your voice will be trapped there. These are just tools to get you to the next place.

An important note about diction: Because these sounds are designed to place air in precise places, pronunciation counts. As you practice with them, be sure that your goog is a goog and not a good or a goo. It's easy to get careless as you're concentrating on where your voice is going and how it feels, so remind yourself to check in once in a while and go through an exercise focusing on quality control and keeping the syllables exact. It'll make a big difference. As you go higher, the corners of your mouth may start to widen. You need to be very careful to maintain the same mouth and lip position whether you're high or low. It's possible to drop your jaw to get more space, openness, and resonance for the higher notes without going wide with the corners of your mouth and losing the pureness of the syllable.

Accept, as Ryan did, that certain sounds will fit more easily, at the beginning, into your mouth and the back of your throat. And the rest will come with practice.

Preparing the Throat

When middle is tentative and elusive, as it was for Ryan, we often need to help the throat physically prepare to enter middle. Ryan found the "cry" sound, which you learned earlier, to be very effective, and that removed one obstacle from his path. He also had another easy-to-solve problem: his larynx was too high in his throat and was constricting the flow of air.

Go back to the personal vocal inventory you did in chapter 2 and see if you diagnosed yourself with a high larynx. If so, listen to audio 19 and you'll hear how it sounds to combine the low-larynx sound you learned earlier with any of the exercises. You can do this any-time you feel your larynx rising. A lot of you will have a high-larynx condition, and you'll want to work often with this technique.

If you find you continue to be troubled by this extremely common condition, do two things: keep working on the middle exercises in this chapter, and add the series of low-larynx exercises you'll find in chapter 7, which explains high-larynx problems and their solutions in detail. Like Ryan, I'm sure you'll see remarkable results.

Visualization: Watching Middle Happen

I'm a strong believer in the idea that the more you understand about what's happening in your body as you speak and sing, the bet-ter you'll sound. So I often ask students to visualize what's happen-ing inside as a way of making a stronger connection to the changes that take place as they move from chest into middle. In chest voice, the back part of your throat should be very open. You should feel very strong and powerful as a large amount of air comes through the vocal cords and the cords easily handle that.

As you get to the top of chest, though, you need to allow some of the air to move into the sinus area, behind the nose. I asked Ryan to use the following visualization to help him make this transition more smoothly:

Close your eyes and do the one-octave exercise. As you make the sounds in chest voice, imagine the air filling up the throat, coming into the mouth, and leaving through your lips. Give the air a color. Imagine blue or purple air moving up along this chest-voice pathway. As I say go into middle, visualize the color moving higher at the back of your throat and entering the area behind your nose. Feel the color vibrating there.

This sensory cue helped Ryan perceive the shifts his body was making as he entered middle, and helped him connect with and strengthen his sound.

Back to Breathing: Is It Popping?

Because Ryan had a tendency to tense up as he did the exercises, we checked in frequently to be sure that his voice had a consistently solid base of breath to build on. As you go through the one-octave set, especially if you're having trouble finding middle, be aware of what's happening with your stomach. Are you doing "popcorn breathing," pulling in your stomach with each goog or gug? If so, try the exercise again, this time consciously smoothing out the breath.

No matter what your throat and mouth are doing in an exercise that feels staccato, your breathing should remain constant: one inhale and one exhale instead of a series of rapid-fire puffs. The sounds themselves will break the airflow into manageable chunks — you can't, and won't, help by firing a series of short, percussive blasts at your vocal cords. As we've seen, that's a recipe for trouble. Your stomach needs to come back in smoothly and evenly regardless of the sounds made.

Too Much of a Good Thing

Ryan had one final problem, also fairly typical, that stood between him and middle: too much phlegm. Phlegm is mucus of the throat, and it's the substance that lubricates the vocal cords. Phlegm, as I tell all my students, is a good *and* a bad word. Without phlegm, even small amounts of talking or singing would irritate the cords. But too much poses an interesting problem: it keeps the cords from closing as they should.

You've seen how the cords need to zip closed to precise places to produce middle and head sounds. The edges of the cords need to meet exactly and close tightly. But when there's an abundance of phlegm in the throat, the substance holds the cords apart instead of sealing them. It's like trying to close a Ziploc bag around a pencil that's sticking out of the top. You can close both sides, but there's a gap at and around the pencil. This kind of separation in the vocal cords can create a slushy, airy, rumbly sound and makes it very difficult to hold the cords in the middle position.

Ryan learned how to control the amounts of phlegm his body was producing, using techniques I describe in detail in chapter 9, and he opened his voice to a realm of sound he'd never thought possible. If you find that you're clearing your throat a lot and hearing hoarse or slushy tones as you do the exercises, don't worry. Remember that we'll deal with this problem later in the book.

Working the Obstacle Course

It took Ryan a while to feel fully comfortable in middle and strengthen it to its full richness. As you've seen, he ran into a host of obstacles—just as you may. But he kept moving through them, as we will, together. If you identify with a problem that Ryan, or the other students you'll meet in this chapter, experienced, do what Ryan did: work on the targeted exercises to solve it. Then—and only then—move on to the next one. We're not talking about years of work. We're doing efficient, systematic problem solving. Your voice is likely to move through a lot of small interim improvements instead of presenting you with a five-minute miracle the first time you do the middle exercises. And that's fine. I want you to own the technique, not just borrow or fake it. That means savoring the small changes and listening as they accumulate into something amazing.

Going Higher

Women doing the one-octave exercise might notice that it carries them into head voice. The seam joining the upper part of middle voice to the head voice is similar in feeling to the first seam, where chest meets middle. You'll notice that, once more, pressure will begin to build; and once again, the way to make the smoothest transition is to relax, stop straining, maintain a constant volume, and allow your voice to go to a new place. This time it will feel as if air is concentrated high in your head, almost behind your eyebrows, and your voice will physically feel higher in your body.

A man needs head voice too, but by the time he gets to the top of middle voice, he's already at high C, and that will get him through 99 percent of what he needs to do. It's still important to me that both male and female singers reach vocal freedom by absolutely owning all three voices. I've given women more head voice in these exercises because they need it more. And at this stage of development, men won't use it nearly as much. Please keep in mind, if you are a male singer, that once you've mastered chest and middle, you'll want to go back and claim head voice as well.

Caution: No matter how much you'd love to hit the highest highs instantly, take your time. If you feel any strain at all, no matter where you are in the exercises, stop. If the voices on the audio track enter an area that's beyond you today, stop and listen, then rejoin the exercise when it returns to the part of the range you own today. The notes you claim slowly, and without pressure or pain, are the ones that belong to you. There's no rush.

A Note about Falsetto

Most people think that head voice and falsetto are the same thing, and the terms are used almost interchangeably. But these two places in the voice are entirely different. When you're singing in head voice, you're still allowing about a third of your vocal cords to vibrate. But falsetto is produced when so much air blows through the cords that they completely separate and only the outer periphery or edge of the vocal cords vibrates. Falsetto doesn't use any of the normal inner-edge vibration at all.

Where head voice has a bit of the same buzz, edge, and vibration as chest and middle, falsetto is an island apart, and because of the way it's produced, it will always have a detached sound. Many pop singers—think of the Bee Gees or Prince—have built their sound around falsetto, or used it to express a particular character in a song, but for our purposes, I'd prefer that you hold off using falsetto until you master the three genuine voices we've talked about. They'll give you more control, and more power, and they're much easier on the cords.

Expanding the Range

Now that the one-octave exercises have given you a handle on where chest, middle, and head voice go, how they sound and how they feel, I'd like to introduce you to the rest of the exercises in the basic vocal warm-up. The exercises we're using to find and refine chest and middle voice are the same ones I prescribe to all the singers and speakers I work with to strengthen their voices every day. Each one is challenging in a different way, and each adds one more element that will allow you to control that magic ratio of air to vocal cord length that will give you the master key to your voice.

My Favorite, Most-Used Exercise: The Octave-and-a-Half Set

Listen to audio 20 (male) or audio 21 (female) on the website and do your best to follow along. You might have to listen a couple of times to hear the pattern.

This exercise will send you into middle fast, and it's my hands-down favorite because it's so efficient: it covers more range and gives you more opportunities to move through chest and middle than any other exercise I know. Because you're covering more ground in this exercise, your voice learns more. And many people actually find it easier than the one-octave set because the top note is not repeated and it's a little easier to control the airflow.

The same things you observed with the one-octave set will probably hold true here: the cry sound will help you anytime you use goog and gug. And you can add the low-larynx exercise anytime, if that's been a concern.

You'll get a great sense of where the holes are in your voice, and what blocks might be on your personal obstacle course, and I encourage you to keep playing with all the variables—from breathing to pronunciation and even phlegm—until your middle voice begins to shine.

The Octave Jump

When you feel comfortable with the octave-and-a-half set, or you just need a change, listen to audio 22 (male) or audio 23 (female) on the website for a demonstration of the octave jump. In this exercise you'll hit a note, then hit the same note one octave above it (that might be a nice break after the rigors of the previous exercise). What makes this exercise interesting, and adds a new challenge, is that you'll *hold* the high note before you descend. Until now we've been stepping fairly quickly up and down the scale, touching but not stopping on any of the notes. That quickstepping lets you zip the cords open and closed without any buildup of pressure. But sustaining a note requires you to hold the cords at one length for a moment or so, and in that time, air can build up behind the closed area of the cords.

You can visualize what's happening if you wave your hand in front of your mouth as you're blowing out a stream of air. Your breath only hits your fingers when your hand is right in front of your mouth, and no significant pressure develops. The second you hold your hand in the path of the stream, though, you'll feel the air build behind the obstacle in its path. The effect, when this air buildup occurs as you're holding a note, is that there's a greater volume of air to control. It takes a bit more effort and strength—which you'll gain with practice.

We're using five syllables in this exercise, and two of them, goog and gug, are air-controlling sounds that make the sustaining easier. Experiment with these and see which one you like. Then work to build *all* of them into your repertoire.

Now That You've Got It, Use It

The series of exercises I've described will keep your voice going back and forth, up and down, until you start to feel and hear and get a sense of the real middle voice. At first it comes out of nowhere as a surprise. You'll be doing the exercise and suddenly you'll be singing very high, but still have the richness of your chest voice. The main difference, however, is that there is no pressure, no strain. You feel as comfortable as you do when you're talking—but if you were to look at a keyboard, you'd realize that you are much higher than your chest voice ever went before. You're creating a perfect blending of chest and head sounds that forms a unique sound all its own.

Whether you're a singer or a speaker, middle voice is the key to sounding the way you were meant to. Middle voice gives you the room to navigate freely all the way through your voice, giving you low, bassy resonant tones mixed with midfrequency warmth and high-end sparkle.

With this series of exercises, you've got not only a wonderful learning tool but the basic warm-up that I give to all my students. You may want to add additional exercises to help you with a particular problem, but this is the core, and I'd like you to spend fifteen minutes a day, every day you can, working with them. That's the best way I know to keep your voice, as an instrument, completely healthy. Vocal exercise is what the voice needs to maintain its freedom, and now that you've got the tools, you're halfway there.

Please spend as much time as you need to with this material. You may find that you're one of the many students who have an immediate epiphany the first time you do the exercises. Or you may fall into the group of students whose discoveries are earned by slow and careful experimentation. Your body, your habits, and your voice are unique—but the technique *will* lead you to a breakthrough.

I'd like you to practice what you've learned here for a week and see what you discover. In the next chapter you'll find hints on how to practice to the greatest effect. Use what applies to you, and if you have questions about middle and whether you're there, review the text and the exercises in this chapter. In chapter 6 you'll find a deeper exploration of the process of finding and working with middle voice. We're still on track and we have much to cover. Don't think you have to be perfect yet—there's more to learn. We're still taking small steps. Stay with me. You're doing great—and soon we will be running.

· 5 ·

How to Practice

Y<small>OU'LL BE</small> happy to know that if you keep working with the basic exercises you just learned, you'll be on the expressway to true vocal liberation, and there are few limits on how fast you can go. Let me also say that meandering is fine. Your pace is entirely up to you. But now that you've got your first vocal exercises under your belt, some of you may have concerns that didn't exist when you were just thinking about your voice. So let's take a few moments to talk about them.

How Fast Do You Really Want to Go?

This process is driven by you, and what you want will determine how you can best use this book. Keep in mind that the exercises are addictive, and once you begin to get the feeling of chest, middle, and head, it's such a satisfying discovery that you may want to practice far more than the daily fifteen minutes that I've recommended. That's fine. But remember that there are many ways to travel toward vocal bliss. Here are some that have worked for my students.

The overview approach. Did you manage to get all the way through the preceding chapters without actually trying the exercises? Of course I hope you'll do more, but I want you to know that just reading this book will help your voice. I often teach large groups — sometimes hundreds of people at a time. In the course of a lecture, I cover some of the basics you're learning here, and I've seen that students who only listen, without trying any exercises at all, are still able to improve their voices as much as 40–50 percent. That means you can expect changes even if all you do is read the book and listen to the audio tracks on the website, without ever opening your mouth. You'll benefit from learning how your voice works, how to care for your vocal cords, and how to avoid the activities that cause the greatest vocal damage. Then, if you're willing to make small changes in how you care for and use your instrument, you'll see gratifying results.

My recommended approach. I encourage you to be realistic about how big a commitment you can make to working with your voice. I feel it's better to start with small, manageable, and regular bites than to make promises to yourself that you ultimately won't keep. There's a kind of destructive guilt that goes along with making extravagant plans at the outset—"I'll start out with an hour of practice a day, and more on weekends"—and then feeling overwhelmed, falling further and further below the mark you set. It's easy to give up if you start out by putting yourself in what feels like a pressure cooker. I'd prefer that you start small and let pleasure and satisfaction be the motivation behind upping your practice time along the way.

Here's the foundation I'd like you to aim for if you're serious about improving your voice: a vocal warm-up of just ten to twelve minutes, as many days a week as you can. You can squeeze in this little practice session sometime in the morning before you head out to a day filled with speaking or singing. If morning slips away, or you've got an evening gig, warm up then.

I've made it easy for you to do that by creating a set of complete warm-up tracks for this edition of the book. For singers, audio 48 is the daily warm-up for women, and audio 49 is the warm-up for men. Those two have the most range. The two tracks for speakers are audio 50, for women, and audio 51, for men. It's fine for you to use *any* of the warm-ups that feel good to you. If you want to build your confidence by mastering the speakers' warm-ups before you try the singers', go for it. If you're a male singer who wants to stretch, try the female singers' track. Never strain. Just aim to enjoy yourself and see your voice get stronger.

The pull-out-all-the-stops approach. Every once in a while I meet a student who is so clearly committed that we design a high-powered program. Tony Robbins, the fire-walking motivational speaker, fell into that category.

Tony has a schedule that keeps him hopping from plane to helicopter to submarine, and at the end of our first session together, I wanted to be sure that we could come up with a practice schedule that wouldn't overwhelm him. I casually suggested that he practice a few times a week for fifteen to twenty minutes, and was about to change the subject when he stopped me. "Roger," he said, "tell me the straight stuff. Don't sugarcoat anything. If you think I need to practice every day for ten hours, tell me that." He said that he wasn't the kind of person who would do anything halfway, and that improving his voice was a top priority for him. He believed in total immersion and was ready to eat, breathe, and sleep voice if that was what it was going to take.

We agreed to a five-day-a-week program of exercises that he would practice for thirty minutes a day between his lessons with me. Though intensive, it would certainly yield dramatic results, first in his speaking and then in the singing he would like to pursue. This kind of regular and deep focus actively helps the body remember how to shape new sounds, and it speeds up the process of developing strength in all the parts of the body that influence the way you sound. The more you put into learning, the more quickly you'll achieve the results you want. I hope you'll think about working up to this kind of commitment—when you're ready. Experiment with different amounts of practicing and see what's most satisfying. Above all, remember that you want this to feel a lot more like play than like work. It's pleasure, not punishment!

For Those Who Want to Speak Better but Not Sing

It's hard to predict what you'll want to do with your voice once you've experienced middle voice. A good many people who come in intending simply to strengthen their speaking voice decide that they want to broaden their horizons and pursue secret dreams of singing. If you're keeping your focus tightly on speaking, the most intensive program I can suggest would involve practicing twenty minutes a day three to five days a week, as I initially recommended to Tony. You'd run through the speakers' warm-up tracks, which you'll find on audio 50 or 51, and then focus on putting sounds together using the additional material for speakers and presenters that you'll find in subsequent chapters. That regime is the fastest, most direct route to the most progress and mastery. But remember that you'll make light-speed advances if you simply use the warm-ups. Ten to twelve minutes two or three times a week should slide easily into even the busiest schedule.

Later in the book I'll introduce you to some specific speech-correction techniques that I would like you to practice in addition to the general warm-up. They're aimed at solving common problems such as sounds that are too nasal or gravelly, and you won't need to use them a lot. They'll make you aware of what you do, and they'll point the way out of your bad habits. But keep in mind that almost every problem affecting speakers will be addressed by the warm-up, which requires you to build a rock-solid foundation of vocal technique that will serve as a tune-up for your voice. As you'll see in the next chapter, the qualities you now have in your voice because of the initial work we've started with middle voice are already beginning to transform some of the problem sounds.

Adapting the Program to Your Life

Inevitably, when I've outlined the basic program, there's an enthusiastic nodding of heads, followed by the "Yes, but..." stage when questions, concerns, and objections come up. Let me address some of the most common ones:

OMIGOD! I'm gonna have to make noise. People will know I'm doing this. What can I do?

I'm fully aware that more than a few of you slipped quietly into the house with this book and were thinking of keeping it in your locked briefcase or tucked under something in a drawer or the back of the closet between readings. That's part of what I think of as the Ugly Duckling syndrome—the fantasy that one day, seemingly out of nowhere, you'll glide in with your fabulous new voice and all the critics and skeptics in your life will marvel that this proud, trumpeting swan has replaced the familiar old quacker. The transformation, the thinking goes, will be all the more remarkable because no one suspected it was happening. No one knew you cared how you sounded.

Miraculous change is a wonderful fantasy, but the fact is, achieving swandom takes practice—out loud. And really, have you ever thought less of a great performer, or of people who have made a big change in their lives, because you found out that they worked for their success? Most of us applaud effort, and chances are the people around you will hear the changes in your voice and offer you support, not pies in the face. But if embarrassment is threatening to muzzle your practicing before you've even begun, here are some remedies my students and I have come up with to ease the discomfort of practicing around other people:

♦ Practice while you're driving. This morning on the freeway, I glanced over and watched as the woman in the car next to me rushed to apply her makeup every time traffic slowed. I'm sure she would have preferred to be doing it between sips of cappuccino at home— but "stuck in traffic" was the only private time she had this morning, so it had to suffice. If you're a commuter who drives to work, you have a regular slot in your schedule for warming up your voice. You can use your phone to go to the website for the exercises, and wail away.

♦ Drive away from the house, park the car, and practice. Maybe you'd like to put your full concentration—sans lane changes—into doing the exercises, and you just need a place to rehearse. Some of my students get in the car, drive to a pleasant spot, park, and vocalize. If privacy is what you need to get started, by all means remember that many hours of great practicing have been done in portable, four-wheeled studios.

♦ Sing in the shower. The water's loud, the door is closed, and the acoustics are good.

◆ Be open to finding practice situations that work for you. Practice at the beach. Practice in the park. Practice in the backyard or in an empty conference room at work before or after hours. Practice while your housemates are out, or when their music is turned up. Practice while the trumpet player next door is practicing. Just be sure you can hear my voice, and yourself, when you keep your dates with me. If you practice with headphones or earphones, leave one ear uncovered so you can hear and judge the sounds you are making.

◆ Tell your friends and family what you're up to. I realize that this may seem like a last resort, but for many students it's been a great lesson. I know it was for me. When I moved into a new house several years ago, I was worried that my practicing would disturb the neighbors. I closed the windows and tried to contain the sounds, but I felt I had to say something to the people next door. I told them I was a voice teacher, apologized for bothering them, and promised to hold down the noise level. I was astonished when they said, "It sounds great — make it louder so we can enjoy you." Don't assume the worst. We live with the sounds of jets, crying babies, and construction. Vocal exercises, by comparison, can sound almost soothing.

◆ Remember that you're working on your voice, not taking tuba lessons or sandblasting. The volume level you'll be trying to attain as you practice is only slightly louder than that of normal, comfortable speaking. I'm not going to be asking you to project your voice to the far side of the block, and for our purposes, you won't be sitting in your apartment belting out "Over the Rainbow" either. Instead, you'll be making gentle, pleasing, and even soothing sounds that are easy to listen to.

◆ Beware of Apartment Singing syndrome. One thing to keep at the front of your mind is that you need to let the sounds out instead of doing the mental equivalent of singing or speaking with your hand over your mouth. That leads to what I call Apartment Singing syndrome, the soft, tentative, half-humming vocal style that I hear from so many of my beginning students.

"You nailed me," my student Terry told me when I stopped her midexercise to ask if she'd been worried about disturbing the neighbors as she practiced. "I close all the windows, turn on the air-conditioning, and sing really softly so no one can hear me." Unfortunately, both of us were still having trouble hearing her at her lesson—that muffled practice style was becoming a vocal habit.

As I pointed out to Terry, the work we'll be doing has everything to do with clearing and freeing the channel that the voice flows through, and concerns about making too much noise put a very large stopper in that channel. Terry decided to practice in her car until she felt more confident that her exercises sounded good enough to be heard by other people. It didn't take her long to realize that her practicing sounded musical, and after a couple of weeks she was able to do exercises in her room without self-consciousness.

Believe me, I've heard every conceivable excuse for not practicing, everything from "The dog ate my warm-ups" to "My husband makes fun of me." And there's a way around every obstacle. Throw the dog his own bone. Quit practicing in front of your partner for a while. Let yourself have some fun. You can do your vocal exercises anywhere, and in any free moments you have in your schedule.

Is there a best time to practice?

As I've been emphasizing, whenever you can practice works for me. But routine is good. The more you build your practice sessions into your regular schedule (for example, right after breakfast, right before bed, on the way to work), the more likely you are to remember to vocalize. By the way, it is possible to sing early in the morning, as long as you have the right technique. Practicing in the morning has advantages—it will warm up your voice for all the communications you'll have for the rest of the day and night. But I'll be happy with whenever you can do it. Giving yourself a chance to make practicing a habit will continually provide a reminder of what you're supposed to sound like and a chance to put your best voice into your awareness. I hope you'll do it.

It sounds weird, but I get the giggles when I do this.

Sometimes, when students begin to practice, they're shocked by how entertaining the exercises seem. There's almost always a moment or two of initial giddiness the first time you hear my slightly out-of-the-ordinary sounds. Don't fight that giggly feeling! These exercises are supposed to be light, fun, and a bit out of your normal spectrum. They come from out of left field, and because they're strange and new, they help move you to a place with no preconceived limitations. Enjoy them.

You're asking me to follow too many notes!

Some of you, because you're not used to matching your voice with a pitch instrument like the piano, may feel strange singing along. Actually, what you're doing with an exercise like the octave-and-a-half set is no more difficult than the melody of "Happy Birthday," but you'll be concentrating a little harder because you're trying to match the pitches you hear. That's a bit more demanding than singing along with the radio, when most of us don't pay attention to exactly what our voices are doing—but it's not complicated. After a while, your ears will get used to their new job of noticing when you're on and when you're off.

What do I do if I get confused?

Some students—in fact most students—get a sense of what I'm after right away. They listen to an exercise or a sound, try to copy it, and get the immediate satisfaction of being able to follow along easily. But it's not uncommon to get confused, and at some point it'll probably happen to you. It sometimes takes repeated listenings to understand the sounds you're trying to copy—and that's fine. Play an exercise as many times as you need to, until you feel you really hear it. This "ear training" is the key to being able to copy a sound. Listen until the qualities of the sound are clear to you, then jump in and imitate, following along with the voice on the exercise track.

Learning to listen is the most valuable thing you can do. It will get you unstuck when you're confused, and it will leapfrog you forward when you use it to fine-tune your voice work. Learning to listen will make you your own best teacher. Starting today, I want you to focus your awareness on the voices around you. Every time you think of it, tune in carefully and listen—to radio announcers, family and office mates, people in front of you at the supermarket checkout stand. What do you like about their voices? What would you have them change? Don't criticize, but pay attention. Being able to identify the qualities of other people's voices is an important first step toward being able to listen critically to your own voice. The more you listen, the more you can hear how you sound—and once you can do that, you can adjust the sounds you're making. Great speakers and singers can correct their voices midphrase, before their audience ever hears a "mistake," and you can develop that ability too.

Listen-copy-evaluate-adjust is the process you'll learn to use again and again as we move your voice toward its best and richest sound. And it all begins with listening.

What if I do it all wrong?

It will actually be hard for you to make a "wrong" sound because, as I've mentioned, the specific sounds I ask you to make put your mouth, tongue, and throat in particular positions and help you keep them there. The only "wrongs" are strain, pressure, and pain. If you feel them, stop. And don't worry. You'll learn what pressure sounds and feels like, what shouting and straining sound and feel like, and what it feels like to take the strain away.

My voice is just going to get better and better, right?

Well, I wish I could just say yes and move on, but actually, it will save you a lot of worry and concern if I let you know that there are a few curves on the road to vocal mastery. Typically, students' progress unfolds like this:

Stage one. In our first vocal exercises, you learned the basics of connecting with all the parts of your voice. In short order, you should be able to move up and down your range smoothly and without strain. Discovering that you can do this is the first breakthrough. You may go through a stretch of finding the new places in your voice—and then lose them again, but the exercises will keep leading you back.

Stage two. You'll probably stay at your new level of accomplishment for one to three weeks without sensing anything like the first breakthrough. You may feel that you're on a plateau, but remember that your speaking and singing have already improved markedly. Keep doing the exercises, and as you do, feel how natural it becomes to use your voice in this way.

Stage three, the setback. Almost inevitably, you'll go to do your exercises one day, after happily and comfortably doing them for days or weeks, and you'll feel as though your voice doesn't know what to do anymore. You may feel you're lost, or sliding backward. This is completely normal. Sometimes the learning process slows down when you come to new material, and you struggle to put it together with what you've already learned. Incorporating a new chunk of information or technique means turning on the part of your brain that is trying to fit together the pieces of what feels like a giant puzzle. It's clumsy, thinking hard about what you're doing instead of gliding. A setback may mean that you're taking in the knowledge you'll need for the next step forward. I'll be leading you into new vocal terrain and asking you to follow me by rote, but I'll also be explaining how you're making the sounds you do. Setbacks — and plateaus — are processing times, when you move from making sounds with no understanding of how you're doing it to owning the sounds and knowing them intimately.

A setback may also mean that your voice is just tired. You enthusiastically cheered on your team at a baseball game last night. You had a tearful fight with a loved one. You've got a cold. Any of these very human activities can cause your vocal cords to swell — and stop cooperating. This, too, is completely normal. The voice is the most unpredictable instrument on the planet. It's affected by your health, your thoughts, and the environment. Don't be alarmed if you feel that on some days your voice has been possessed by unruly spirits. You don't need an exorcism, you just need patience. Even if you think you sound ridiculous or strange, the exercises work to smooth the rough spots and put you back in control, so let them help you regain your sense of balance.

And remember that what follows is

Stage four, the next breakthrough. As you move out of that first slump, your voice will suddenly seem to have new life. You may wake up one morning feeling great and find that when you start vocalizing, something just clicks in your voice. The very things you struggled with the week before are now...no problem. Your body has become stronger, your brain has shifted gears from puzzlement to "I know how to do this," and you have a new vocabulary of vocal strengths to weave into new textures.

This pattern of breakthrough, plateau, struggle, and breakthrough is what you'll experience through the entire learning process. Your body and your mind need time to incorporate what you're trying to teach them, and if you can remember to practice patiently, knowing that every step is leading you toward the next breakthrough—whether today's work feels like a step forward or a step backward—you're on the path of mastery.

What about those setbacks?

I know it's one thing for me to say "Expect some setbacks" and quite another to be moving more slowly than you'd like to be. When you get stuck, reread the parts of the book that focus on the techniques that are giving you trouble. Listen to my audio examples. And try it again. But be gentle with yourself. If you find that you can't hear the exercise anymore, can't feel it, or it hurts—STOP. Give yourself a break, and come back to the exercise either several hours later or the next day. I'm not saying give up. I'm saying give it a rest.

If you find that you're so negative about your own sounds that you can't be a fair listener, you need to reschedule your lesson. Don't wait more than a few days to come back to the material, but be sure that you give yourself enough time to regain a sense of fun and perspective.

Please remember that you cannot fail, even if you think your voice is not changing. If you're consistently doing the exercises, then your instrument is growing, thickening, and strengthening, and you are gaining control of the sounds it produces.

Can I learn singing without reading music?

Yes. Some of the most successful popular singers and composers have never learned to read music. My guess is that fewer than 15 percent of all top singing stars today know how to read music, and the number is probably even lower than that. Aside from opera singers, who need to follow complex notation, many professional singers at the top rung don't read music. I teach people how to be musical and to have a musical ear, which is much more important, at the outset, than knowing what the notes look like on a page. You'll get plenty of practice discriminating among sounds and imitating them, and that's the skill you'll need most as a singer. Knowing that you're hearing a C or a D doesn't help if you can't imitate it. Don't get me wrong. I'd be overjoyed if you decided to learn more about music—like all the math you learned in school, it's a plus. For our purposes, though, it's not essential.

Do I have to have perfect pitch to sing?

People with perfect pitch can hear a tone and tell you exactly what note was played. It's a wonderful ability, but there's no correlation between having perfect pitch and being able to *sing* in perfect pitch. Just because you can tell when a note is on and when it's off doesn't mean you can automatically produce the note. And knowing that your voice is off doesn't necessarily help you correct it. If knowing your voice was off were all it took to get it back on track, we'd all have perfect voices. Willingness to listen and make adjustments is a thousand times more valuable to you than having perfect pitch.

All I really want to do is speak better. Can't I just skip this singing stuff?

I've found, over the years, that the part of a student's brain that asks that question is precisely the part that we need to quiet in order to make fundamental changes in his or her speaking voice. You can't think your way to a better voice—but you can sing your way there. I sometimes suggest making big shifts in a student's speaking voice, and it's natural for people to go into shock. They think, "That's not my voice. What are you trying to do to me!" But when I say, "Sing this sound," the mind of the average nonsinger has no frame of reference. All you're doing is copying me. And as you do it, I can move you onto a different plane, far from the limiting ideas you've had about what your voice can do.

I'll show you how to make specific singing sounds, then ask you to speak with the same kinds of sounds. I call the result speak-singing, and it's the most effective—and enjoyable—way to improve the speaking voice.

◆

I realize that some of the issues that I've described may not come up for you, or may arise late in our work together rather than early. Please consider this chapter a resource throughout the process, and refer back to it when you've got questions about how you're doing or how your path is unfolding. You'll do fine.

.6.

Staking Claim to Middle

Q UITE OFTEN when I work with a new student, the first lesson is a revelation. The first few exercises take the student right into middle, and the discovery is thrilling. My student Danielle, for example, initially experienced a lot of pressure at the top of chest voice, but when she learned what middle felt like, she was exuberant and left my office with her feet barely touching the ground.

When we met again two weeks later, she had a huge smile on her face. "I just had the best two weeks of my vocal life," she told me. "Once you pointed me in the right direction, I had a fabulous, positive learning experience on my own."

My experience as a teacher tells me that even when students are as confident as Danielle was, our second lesson together is crucial for their progress. That's because the second time students work with me, they've tried on their own to imitate what they heard in lesson one, and they've had time to get into trouble.

If you've been doing your homework and practicing for a week, you, too, have had time to experience the pleasures and pitfalls of looking for middle voice. In this chapter I'd like to take you through some typical lesson two experiences and let you see how they compare with your own search for the middle way.

SET YOUR VOICE FREE

Too Much Chest

Danielle was very clear on the concept of making middle voice thick and strong, but she was so focused on that powerful sound that as she tried to get into middle, she wound up mixing in too much of the chest sound. (Listen to audio 24 on the website to hear what middle voice sounds like when it's both too chesty and too heady.) Yes, she was in middle, but it was a middle overloaded with the lower resonances of chest. Trying to hold on to the thick chest sounds created way too much pressure as she moved toward higher notes.

When I explained that her middle was still too filled with chest qualities and that we needed to add a little more head to middle, she complied. But the second she did, she said, "Oh, I hate that! That can't possibly be right. That's not what I was doing—that's head voice. It's not middle anymore."

You Can't Judge by Feel Alone

Danielle was so skeptical that I played back a few moments of the recording we'd been making of the session. "If you're really jumping from chest to head, you'll hear a big break," I told her. "So listen carefully, and tell me when you hear the gap." Danielle was astonished to realize that the voice on the recording had gone beautifully from chest to middle without showing even the tiniest seam.

"Was that me?" she asked. "It felt like it was so much in my head that I thought it would sound completely like head voice."

The reason the physical feeling didn't match the voice, I explained, is that everything above chest voice feels as though it's resonating so much higher in the body than chest; middle voice and head seem to be resonating in almost the same place. Fortunately, you don't have to rely solely on what you're sensing to figure out whether you're in chest or head—you can use your ears. If you have any doubts about how you sound, make a recording to orient yourself. When you wonder if you're really going from chest to middle to head or if you might be skipping from chest to head, pull out your phone, play the audio from the website, and record a set of scales as you sing with me. Then go back and listen for audible breaks and gaps as you move from low to high. Remember that the point is not to judge. You're trying to determine where you are on the vocal map so you can find and stay on the path to middle.

Making Adjustments

Finding middle, I tell my students, is a little like being on the Yellow Brick Road. It curves to the left — too much chest. Then it curves to the right — too much head. But if you keep adjusting, looking for ways to relieve any pressure that builds as you ascend the scales, you'll eventually wind up at the Emerald City meeting the Wizard, which I define as having the perfect blend of chest and head to form absolute middle.

Danielle was concerned about using too much head voice, but I reassured her that it's perfectly acceptable for women to lean a bit toward head voice in the early stages of looking for middle, as long as there is not a huge break between chest and middle. Try it, listen, and adjust. And keep experimenting until you hit the smooth sound of middle.

Once we find middle and you spend a little time getting used to the way it sounds, we'll dress it up to sound gorgeous. Right now, just get used to making middle with any sound necessary. Many times in the audio exercises I ask you to make funny sounds to guide the voice into a specific place. Please use every extra trick — or trigger, as I prefer to call it — I give you. Use the cry sound. Use the funny voices. And when I say make it sound funny, I mean really funny. When I say make it sound absurd, try it! As the cords and the body accept all of the new placements, they won't need any extra help. But for now, go for it. The object here is to make the biggest and best changes in the shortest amount of time.

If you have a good ear and can match pitches on the piano (or the audio on the website), your ear will be your compass and let you know if you are veering to the left or right of middle. Even if you think you have a bad ear, and have trouble recognizing pitches, the best thing you can do is to keep listening to the exercises and singing along. You may be off 89 percent of the time, but every time you run through your scales again, you'll be on target a little longer. Step one of this process is to listen carefully. Step two is to sing along. And step three is to record your voice to give yourself a frame of reference. You need to know how you're doing—and with the objective ear of the tape recorder, you have the feedback that allows you to be your own best teacher.

"I Don't Like the Way It Sounds"

Sometimes the sound and feeling of middle are so different from what you've grown accustomed to that hitting a perfect middle isn't satisfying. It feels off somehow. My student Johnny, for example, found middle fairly easily, but he just didn't like it.

Johnny had been to a lot of teachers before he met me, and he'd spent a lot of time focusing on his head voice. He'd grown up singing along with great artists like the Beach Boys and Smokey Robinson, and because he was a good imitator, he could soar with them. Some of his teachers believed, as many do, that there was no such thing as middle. They concentrated exclusively on chest and head voice, treating them as separate units that would come together later, with a seam that is known in Italian as the *passaggio*, or passage area. But Johnny, in his years of study, never learned to smooth out the seam until he met me.

Learning about middle undeniably got rid of the gap between chest and head, but Johnny's first response to it was completely negative. It sounded strained and funny, he told me, and way too nasal. Middle shocked him with its brightness and its concentrated thickness. Compared with the light purity of head voice, this was a foreign animal, and as far as he was concerned, it was ugly. Not only that, he said, but he hated the way his voice was still breaking a bit.

Johnny was willing to bet money that he sounded terrible, but when I played back his voice for him, he was stunned. He couldn't hear a break when he moved in and out of middle, though he was certain that he'd felt it. We played the recording again, and this time he had to admit that he didn't sound nasal or strained at all. So what was the deal, he asked. He'd been so sure that he was way off the mark.

Once again, there was a disparity between how he felt and how he sounded. He assumed that because he *felt* a change in how he was producing his voice when he moved from chest to middle, we must have heard it. He was wrong. He figured that when he felt the resonance of his voice go into the nasal area, it must create a nasal sound. Wrong again. He insisted that it must be too harsh, because it felt so strong. Strike three.

Every vocal student learns that there's a huge difference between the way the voice feels and the way it sounds. That's why it's so important at the beginning to record your voice and listen to it. Listen a lot. Listen to other people too. When you can truly listen carefully, you can detect and correct problems before they become ingrained. As I've said before, the biggest gift I can give you, and that you can give yourself, is the ability to take in what you're hearing and to learn from it.

How the Pros Handle Middle

As you're working with middle yourself, you should be pulling out all of your favorite CDs, MP3s, and old records and tuning in to a new aspect of the sounds you love—the technique of the singers. To get you started, let's listen together to some of my favorites, old and new.

Whitney Houston. Whitney had an incredible instrument, with a rich, vibrant emotional quality that I love. But even her voice had a few problems. If you go back and listen to her hits, you'll notice that as she approaches the top part of her chest voice, she sometimes builds up too much pressure. She gets louder and louder as she goes, and her vocal cords are bombarded with air. You can hear the strain and sense the tension building as she ascends. As she leaves chest on her way to middle or head, I think you'll hear how the top of her voice just doesn't match the bottom. The high end seems much too airy and light. Listen to her hit "Saving All My Love for You." At the end of the song, she sings a final "for you," and you can hear a marked difference between the sound of "for" and the sound of "you." If she had total command of middle, they would sound like they were from the same family, rather than like estranged cousins.

This flaw in her technique took a heavy toll on her voice during the height of her career. She could never stay on tour long enough to get to all the fans who wanted to hear her live. She always had too many vocal problems. The cause: too much pressure at the top of chest voice.

If you want a modern-day example of someone who strains in a similar way, listen to Florence Welch of Florence + the Machine. There is simply too much pressure as she approaches the top part of her chest voice looking to get into middle. The result is similar to what Whitney struggled with. Florence wants to belt out all the higher chest-voice notes, but it has to be extremely hard for her to do without straining and losing her voice night after night.

Sting. Sing along with any of Sting's hits and you'll cover the whole range. He soars, even by tenor standards, and he keeps his voice strong without pressure as he moves from chest to middle to head. His transitions are smooth and seamless. He's an excellent singer to imitate.

A more modern example of that type of middle could be someone like Bruno Mars. He is certainly a tenor and can sing all the high notes. But he does so in a way that makes the middle part of the range still sound like he's low and speaking to you. When the notes are high and the tonal quality sounds low, like chest voice, that's a great indication that you are in middle voice.

Steve Perry. In his prime, Steve, the lead singer of the classic rock group Journey, had fabulous vocal technique. In fact, I believe he had one of the best middle voices in rock music. He's a perfect example of what we aim to do, moving from low to high with no breaks, equally strong at every part of his three-plus octaves of range. No matter how high he goes, he still sounds attached to chest voice. Steve's a great person to imitate if you're a tenor or wanna-be tenor. His middle is more than worth studying and emulating.

If you want to listen for middle voice, put on "Open Arms," one of Journey's most famous songs. Here's how one line breaks down: "So now I" (all chest) "come to you" (middle) "with open arms" (middle).

Aretha Franklin. She's a true diva, with a gorgeous voice that covers chest, middle, and head, completely connected at each seam. Listen, copy, and learn. When she goes swooping up to the high notes, she sounds like she never fully left chest voice. Her middle has a buzzy, nasal sound that is very easy to recognize and imitate. The top part of her range is not pretty and sweet. Instead, the middle she demonstrates sounds like it belongs to a person full of pain, longing, and struggle.

You can hear the same qualities in Jessie J. Her middle has a tonal ring very similar to Aretha's. The bite and presence of the middle are very clear as Jessie navigates from very low to high notes.

Ol' Blue Eyes. So let's talk about Frank Sinatra. Frank managed to be the most recognizable voice in singing history outside classical music — and he used *only* chest voice. The crooning style he and Dean Martin and Tony Bennett refined was all chest-voice derivative. It was all about mirroring a cool, cigarette-smoking, Scotch-drinking image, and chest voice worked for that image and era because it's so conversational. Singing in chest conveyed the idea that singing was easy, no sweat. Frank's voice was great not because of where he was going in range but because of his phrasing. He had the ability to group words together to make people believe and feel what he was feeling and thinking. We'll talk about phrasing in a later chapter. Meanwhile, aim at making your chest voice as strong as Sinatra's — then add a great middle and head and see what happens.

Elvis. Elvis Presley spent 85 percent or more of his singing time in chest voice, but I believe he was a closet tenor, and occasionally he would hint at a bit of middle voice. His access to higher realms gave him more pretty overtones than you hear in Sinatra's voice, and Elvis doesn't sound like he's running out of range when he hits his top notes. He could have had a great middle if he and I had met.

The point here is not to cast stones at famous artists. I'd just like to intrigue you with the idea of listening to the singers you enjoy with an ear to the techniques they're using to produce the sounds you love. You'll also begin to notice problems you've never noticed before. All voices are influenced by good and bad techniques, and no matter how incredible the instrument you were born with, it can still be easily damaged by strain and pressure. When you become aware of technique and how it affects the voices around you, you can refine your ear and listen more critically to your own voice—the one you can develop and change.

Still Can't Find Middle?

How's it going for you now? Many times, students come to me after they've been practicing at home and claim that they still can't find the middle voice. If you aren't clear about the difference between middle and chest, I'd like you to go back to the middle-voice demonstrations on the audio recordings (14 and 24). Can you hear the distinctive qualities of each part of the voice? Most people have no problem recognizing the differences between them, and that's a great start. Then it's time to look more closely at why you might not be able to reproduce the sounds you hear.

Let me reassure you that you'll know middle when you hit it. It's thick and edgy, and higher than chest voice. When you notice that you are high in the range, past where your break used to be, and that you are not straining to produce a large sound—you're there. And if you don't feel it, *you probably haven't hit middle yet.* Chances are you're still going from chest straight to head voice. And once you realize this, you need to go back to the exercises and try them again.

Without straining, don't let the voice get so soft on top. Run down this familiar checklist, and keep going back to these points in your practice sessions:

♦ Use your diaphragmatic breathing to help generate a stronger sound by *allowing* your abdomen to fall back in as you exhale, instead of constricting your stomach muscles to try to force the air out. Some years ago, when I taught classes at UCLA, I used to ask for a show of hands at the midway point of the term to find out who was still having trouble with middle. Most often, the reason the struggling students didn't find middle was that they locked up their stomachs and didn't give themselves an even flow of air to work with. It's easy to get the cords to zip into the middle position, but until you consciously stop pushing, and stop treating breathing and singing as though they're related to weight lifting, you can't produce the middle sounds. The blockage produced by locked stomach muscles allows so much air pressure to build that there's no chance that the cords can withstand it.

What does it feel like if you're locking your stomach? As you move up the range, you'll notice that you just don't have enough air to make sounds. You'll feel as though you're trying to blow through a pinhole rather than having your whole throat to work with. For a graphic demonstration, take a straw and pinch it together in the middle. Now blow hard into one end. The pressure you feel is the same as the buildup you feel internally as air tries to get from the lungs to the vocal cords.

Most people start doing vocal exercises and immediately put breathing on the back burner. It's not dramatic. It seems inconsequential. It's invisible. But anytime you run into a wall with your vocal technique, the first place to go is back to your breathing exercises. Without the right amount of air, the cords are powerless to help you make beautiful sounds.

Check the position of your head. When I look at a piano keyboard, I see it as a horizontal object. It's no more difficult for me to place my left hand all the way down on the bottom than it is for me to noodle around the middle keys or place my right hand near the top. All the notes are in the same horizontal plane. Your voice has a similar configuration, but a lot of inexperienced speakers and singers imagine that the notes they want to use, the sounds they want to make, are arrayed top to bottom like a piano turned on end.

To play a keyboard in that position, a person would have to lie down on the floor to reach the low notes and jump into the air to touch the high keys. And vocalists often believe that that's what's required to make sound. They lower their chins to their chests, thinking that's where the low pitches are. Then they raise their heads to the sky, stretching their necks like giraffes eating leaves from a tall tree, as though this position will somehow help them hit the high notes. It just doesn't work like that. And the pain in the neck that results is just one more source of strain that keeps them from gaining access to the middle. Use a small hand mirror as you do the exercises to check your chin. Keep it level, and let your breath and the sounds themselves do the work of taking your voice where it needs to go. I repeat: If you feel like Annie straining to sing "Tomorrow! Tomorrow! I love ya...," you may not have a voice tomorrow. Getting rid of every source of strain is the way to achieve tremendous gain.

♦ What are your shoulders doing? Has accessory breathing crept back in? To give yourself a memorable demonstration of how much effort it takes to involve your shoulders in your breathing, try lifting your shoulders to your ears and holding them there as you continue through an exercise. Exhausting, isn't it. Let them drop to the proper position, and keep them there.

♦ Use helpful tricks like the cry sound, and over exaggerate them.

♦ Use flip-flopping to build on the sounds that are most comfortable for you. What's flip-flopping? It's a technique of substituting sounds that are easy for you in the vocal exercises for sounds that are difficult. There are a couple of ways to do this, and I suggest that you try them and see which way works for you, listening to the demonstrations on audio 25 on the website.

1. Substitute the sound you like for the syllable I'm singing on the audio example when you get to the high notes. In the one-octave set, we do a pattern of sounds that ends with a high note repeated four times. In a gug exercise, my student Ryan would sing gugs until he reached the repeated high notes. He'd sing the high notes as mums, which were easier for him.

2. Do a set of a syllable you like, then follow it with a set of one of the sounds that's more difficult for you. Ryan would first do a set of exercises in which he substituted mums on all the high notes. Then he'd do a set of all gugs and a set of all mums. It's easy to get a little confused with all this switching, and that's part of what makes it effective. You trick your mind into thinking that your voice should be in middle, even when you're mak-

ing a sound that's hard for you, because it gets harder to associate a particular sound with "high" or "difficult." Your brain just wants to send you back to the low-stress feeling of releasing into middle — no matter what syllable you're using.

♦ Are you yelling as you get higher? Turn down the volume! Your vocal cords find it annoying to try to cope with your sound-level changes when you pour extra effort into high notes by getting louder. As you ascend the scales, aim for an even volume, and record yourself or ask a friend to listen to you if you're not sure how you're doing.

♦ And finally, *stop going from chest to head!* It's that difficult and that simple. Work harder.

When I tell you to work harder, by now you know that I don't mean strain. I simply mean use all the energy necessary to achieve your goal. Some people are under the impression that in order to speak and sing without pressure, you need to keep your body completely relaxed. That is not 100 percent true. The body still needs to work hard to go from chest to middle to head, and it can work most efficiently and strongly if it's not impaired by muscle tension and strain. You may think great speaking and singing happen to a body in slumber mode, but that's not the case. Focus and intent and energy will make your voice sparkle, and without them, it will stay flat and lifeless.

So use your mind to help you. Stop telling yourself that you can't find middle, and allow yourself to play, experiment, make funny sounds — even look a little foolish. Make a point of using the preceding checklist and the information in chapter 4 to be sure that you're putting together all the elements that make for great sound. If you remember learning how to drive a stick shift, you know how much you had to think about all the components of shifting, using the clutch, and stopping before the actions became automatic. Learning to use your voice in a new way requires the same kind of concentration and coordination. And the more energy you put into the adventure of finding middle, the greater your rewards will be.

If You Want to Go Higher

I want to be sure that you master chest and middle voice before we spend more time with head voice. That's why you won't find a lot of head voice in many of the exercises. As far as I'm concerned, there's so much potential for strain and pressure in trying to take the voice to its greatest heights that for 95 percent of us, it's not worth the effort. When students are in front of me, I can monitor any unwanted pressure and help to alleviate it. So when I can't be standing with you in person, I want to offer you only the safest exercises and ranges to play with. The exercises you've learned do cover almost three octaves. Done just as I've demonstrated them, they will give you a more connected, usable range than you ever dreamed of.

But for the small percentage of you who can and want to go higher in head voice, let's discuss how to do it with the audios I've recorded for you. When the scale gets to its highest point, simply put the audio on pause and continue using the same syllables as you extend the exercise past the point where I left off, taking it up a half step at a time. Go as high as you can, keeping the same pattern and rhythm you used to begin with. As you reach your limit, start down the range again, until you reach the point where you paused the audio. Turn it back on and resume singing with me. Feel free to do this with any of the exercises. BUT DON'T STRAIN!

You may notice that if you spend a lot of time vocalizing on the high end of the scale, using a lot of middle and head voice, when you go back down to the bottom of chest voice, you may temporarily feel as though the bottom notes have evaporated. It may seem as though you've lost a little of the bottom range. This effect might be startling, but it's quite normal. The vocal cords get used to being in a shorter position if you spend a great amount of time only on the high end of the scale. The effect is temporary. Your full low range will be back in a few minutes.

Please keep in mind that a lot of women have a false conception about head voice. You may have encountered teachers in the past who stressed it so much that you feel guilty when you're not making that sound. Be sure you absorb all that chest and middle can offer before you become preoccupied with developing a very high head voice. Understand this: I have worked with many opera singers over the years, and I studied and performed operatic pieces for much of my first twenty years of singing. I teach opera singers the same way that I teach everyone else: everyone, even high operatic sopranos, starts with chest and middle before moving to head. Those lower parts of the range create the perfect foundation for a head voice that is full and strong, with powerful resonances. You must climb this ladder one step at a time, without skipping rungs and without neglecting any portion of your voice.

When the Going Gets Rough, Remember: It's Worth It

We all want instant results, and my technique is faster than any I've encountered. But as I've pointed out, true mastery takes time. Keep your eyes on the prize, cherish your successes, and remember: when the going gets tough, the tough go to PRACTICE.

My client Sara had recently joined her church choir, not as a star, but as a happy member of the alto section. She'd grown up listening to gospel music, and she loved the powerful swoops and flights that fill it with such incredible joy. But she'd always thought that the ability to create those sounds belonged to superstar recording artists, not regular people. She was startled when she realized that the same richness was coming from soloists who were standing just five feet in front of her in church. It wasn't just that these mere mortals could hit the high notes. It was that the quality and resonance of every note they sang was so even. The highs sounded just as thick as the lows. Every note, no matter where it was on the scale, rang like a crystal bell.

The question in her mind when she came to see me was: How do they do it? Could she develop that quality too? The beautiful and simple goal of our work together was to find out.

Sara had a lovely voice. In fact, she had *two* lovely voices. There was the gorgeous soprano she'd developed when her parents sent her to the local mom and pop vocal studio in her neighborhood, where they emphasized head voice. She'd been proud of being able to hit the heights, but as she got older, she realized that this kind of singing had its limits. If she used her trained head voice when she was hanging out with her friends and singing along to the radio, she sounded like a strange opera singer from some other century. It was pretty... embarrassing. So she did what most people do: she abandoned the high notes and began belting out everything in chest. It didn't excite anyone, but she was happy being an alto. At least she sounded like she was from the same planet as the people around her.

By the time she came to me, her chest and head voices were two islands with a vast sea between them.

In our first session together, I showed Sara the exercises you've been working with, and in half an hour, she started to feel and hear and get a sense of the real middle voice. Sara struggled a little in the following weeks. She found middle, she had trouble connecting, middle got stronger again, and little by little it became a part of her voice that she could count on.

After Sara had worked with me for a time, she invited me to a concert at her church. As I watched, she stepped out from the chorus and sang a soaring, heart-filled solo. Maybe it was the day or the place, but at that moment both she and I felt ever so slightly closer to God.

It was the kind of hard-won miracle I see in my work every day. Patience, persistence, and practice will take you there too.

· 7 ·

Making Your Speaking
Voice Sing

How's your speaking voice? Are you noticing a difference in
it yet? If you've been doing the exercises consistently, paying attention to the smoothness of your breathing and the position of
your larynx, you're probably noticing some positive changes in the
way you speak. You've left a lot of pressure behind, and your voice
should be stronger, less strained, easier to listen to. If that's the case,
congratulations! You've allowed the exercises to do exactly what
they're designed to do—fix your voice naturally, without any other
special adjustments on your part.

The exercises are full of sounds that force the air and cords to
work with each other in an optimal way through the whole range of
your voice. Each time you do them, you remind the body how comfortable it feels to produce sound so efficiently and naturally. In fact,
if you've spent several weeks faithfully practicing, you've already
fixed 50 to 75 percent of the problems in your speaking voice. You've
reshaped it, strengthened it, and drained stress and pressures from
the body.

But you may not feel that way. You may be enjoying the singing
you're doing and happily venturing into middle voice, yet when you
step away from your practice sessions, perhaps you find that you slip
into the same problematic speaking voice you'd hoped to improve.
Or you may be frustrated because you're having a lot of trouble getting into middle voice. If you're like some of my more pessimistic

students, you may have decided that your singing is still downright pathetic—and worse, maybe you're not aware of your speaking voice changing at all.

Why is this happening? The simple answer is that you're still thinking of singing and speaking as two different, unrelated activities, and you still haven't mastered the concept of speaking the way you sing.

In this chapter I'd like to help you bridge the gap between the way you sing your exercises and the way you speak. I'll show you how to carry the sound qualities you're discovering in the exercises into the strong, resonant speaking voice you've dreamed of.

I'll be asking you to concentrate very specifically on a lot of small components, and it may seem overwhelming to have to think about what your vocal cords are doing as you make particular sounds, or what's happening as you try to adjust your breathing, volume, and what seem like an endless number of pieces of a giant sound puzzle. Please stay with me. When we're a little further along, all these little pieces will fit into a whole that requires no conscious thought. Your voice and body will relax into place, and everything will automatically come out right.

Remember, too, that you don't have to have a flawless voice to have a voice that works well for you. A number of years ago I was helping a noted actor work on his singing voice. One day I noticed that when he spoke, he was restricting the air too much at the ends of his sentences and the resulting sound was a little gravelly, so I mentioned this and told him I thought we could make a few simple changes. He stopped me and pointed out that he had been the voice of God in a couple of the most famous biblical movies in history. I quickly agreed that if his voice was good enough for God, it was probably good enough for a successful actor as well—though we'd probably want to do a little work to ensure that God didn't get hoarse.

The point is not perfection. Our goal is to find a speaking voice that expresses who you are and delivers your message effectively. Don't feel compelled to fix everything. Just work on the sounds that get in your way, and keep what works.

It takes guts to stick with singing exercises, especially if being a singer isn't your ultimate goal, and I applaud you for the work you've done so far. Now I'd like to challenge you to step up and claim the changes you've made in your voice, then let them come through in the way you speak. It's easier than you think.

Making Chest Voice a Treasure Chest

First I'd like to reassure you: the quality of your singing, especially as you enter the higher end of the exercises, isn't a proper gauge of how wonderful your speaking voice can sound. Finding middle will enable you to add gorgeous resonances to the words you speak, so I want you to keep aiming for it and playing with it when you practice.

But if you've made numerous tries to find middle but still haven't gotten comfortable there, don't give up — and don't think your speaking voice isn't improving just because you feel unsteady as you move higher in the exercises. Most of the sounds we use for speech reside, as I've mentioned, in chest. The fundamental question for speakers is: How is your *chest* voice doing? Does it feel thicker and stronger now? Are you doing diaphragmatic breathing and experiencing what it feels like to let your vocal cords vibrate powerfully with a smooth flow of air? Do you find that your larynx is staying more stationary, instead of rising to block your throat?

Let's put middle voice aside for the moment and focus on using the improved chest voice you've gained with the exercises to help improve your everyday speech. I want you to get the gravelly, brassy, nasal, breathy, and otherwise irritating qualities out of your voice, once and for all. Not only do they detract from the message you want to deliver to your listeners, they're also extremely harmful to your voice. For the health of your vocal cords — and this is vital for singers, by the way — you *must* take the stress- and strain-induced sounds out of the way you speak.

As we take these steps, what we're really doing is allowing your voice to be as interesting as you are. Significant, powerful, and lasting change is well within your reach right now, as we use the basics you've been practicing to make your voice sparkle.

Updating the Diagnosis: How Do You Sound Now?

Let's start by listening to your voice once more. Because you may not be aware of the way it has shifted over the period you've been practicing the basic exercises, I'd like you to go back to chapter 2 and quickly run through the diagnostic tests again. Record them, then compare them with the set of tests you did when we began working together. Are you noticing changes? What's improved? Do any specific problems pop out? Below you'll find combinations of exercises that you will use to adjust any qualities that still bother you. In the process of using the exercises consciously to change your speaking voice, you'll be teaching yourself how to make a direct link between what you do when you sing and what happens when you speak. I promise you that you'll be very pleased with what you hear. Speaking the way you sing is the key to vocal magic.

Still Too Much Air?

If the voice you heard on your progress recording was still too soft and wispy, I'd like you to concentrate on a few select sounds in the vocal exercises. Most helpful to you will be gug and goog. The gs at either end of those syllables are highly effective at restricting the flow of air to the cords, and both of the syllables allow your vocal cords to move into position and vibrate without being bombarded by too much air. Try these sounds now: return to audio 15 (male) or audio 16 (female) on the website and sing the first two exercises using goog, then gug. I'm betting that your singing has more thickness and power than what you heard yourself speaking on the initial recording—a better blend of cord and air.

When you do the exercise, be sure to sing it in a bigger-than-normal volume, the volume you'd use if you were trying to address someone one hundred feet away, instead of two feet away. Concentrate on how both goog and gug make your voice jump out.

Now go back and speak something—whatever's on your mind (or just read the preceding paragraph if you like)—into your recorder. Look for a way to speak from the same place you just used to produce the googs and gugs. Try for the same volume, the same intensity and thickness. It's helpful to flip-flop between words and sounds, and to make the speech a little singsongy at first, so that you might find yourself sing-speaking a phrase like "Gug, gug, this is how I say gug." (You can hear a demonstration of this kind of flip-flopping on audio 26 on the website.) Keep trying until you feel that the exercise syllables and the words have exactly the same qualities. Your speech will be louder. Thicker. A lot less airy!

You'll also get a lot of benefit from using the throaty sounds in the exercises—nay and nah. These two sounds are exceptionally good at making the vocal cords vibrate in a long, thick position. Go back and do the nay and nah sections of the general exercises. Let the exercise sounds reposition the way the air and cords are meeting, then slide immediately into speaking. Carry the sound of the short *a* into a spoken sentence, much as you did with the gug and goog sounds above. Sing a few nahs, then try a sentence like "I *caaaaan* nah nah nah do *thaaaat.*" Hold out the *a* sound, which will intensify the thickness. "I *caaaan haaave* thaaat."

Most people sing the nay and nah exercises at a thick, strong volume because it's so easy and pleasurable to do that. But when they speak, it's common for them to pull their voices way in and turn down the volume. As well as making it seem that you're afraid of being offensive or bothering someone, speaking at low volume has a direct effect on the speaking voice: it provides insufficient air to the cords for proper sound.

Make your speaking voice louder. I ask my students to do this dozens of times a day, and 90 percent of the time, even the most outgoing among them complain: "But I'm shouting now!" Please remember that speaking is supposed to use and energize the whole body. I've noticed that many people, especially those with very airy voices, are using about a cubic inch of their bodies, and a cubic centimeter of their energy when they talk. Great speaking is about grabbing hold of the words and sounds you want and directing them forcefully, but without pressure, out of the body. In chapter 11, I'll show you some tricks for fine-tuning volume and ensuring that your sound is always rich and inviting. But for now just enjoy what it feels like to take up more space by getting louder.

Am I saying there's no place for a soft voice? Of course not. If you're in a romantic situation, for example, naturally you want to sound as approachable, alluring, and passionate as you feel—and shouting in your beloved's ear is not going to do the trick. What lets the person you love, or your partner in an intense but hushed conversation, know you're completely present, that you're interested, and that you mean what you say? Your listener will hear it when every bit of your body is connected to the voice—and every word you speak is connected to true cord vibration. Listen to audio 27 on the website for a demonstration of the difference between airy whispering and a soft voice that is *connected*.

Practice infusing your speech with the vocal intensity that arises so naturally when you use gug, goog, nay, and nah. You'll feel the airiness in your speaking voice being steadily replaced with a new, and appealing, presence. *Your* presence.

Smoothing Out the Gravel

There's no mystery about what it takes to keep your sentences from ending on a rough, gravelly note. The cause and cure, as we've seen, is air. When you run out of air and keep on talking, your voice simply runs out of gas. Many of you have probably found that your voices become much smoother and much less likely to run aground on gravelly sounds when you're working with diaphragmatic breathing. But it can be so easy to lose the connection between breathing and speaking that I'd like to reinforce some basics.

You know that as you breathe, if you put your hand over your stomach just above your belly button, your hand should move in smoothly as you exhale. If you keep your hand there when you're talking to someone, the same smooth movement should be happening the entire time you speak. If your stomach is always making that inward motion when words are leaving your mouth, it's very hard for airflow to be restricted. So let's get back into breathing mode and see if you can experience what it feels and sounds like to eliminate the gravel from your voice.

Turn your full attention to your breath. Standing with your toes propped up on a book for optimum alignment of your body, breathe fully and deeply, keeping your chest and shoulders from rising. Feel the full extension of your lower stomach area and concentrate on freeing your breath so that you feel no pressure on either the inhale or the exhale. When your breathing feels smooth and effortless, pick up something and read aloud, or simply start talking about what you plan to do today. As you do this, keep your full, deep breathing pattern in place. Keep your hand on your stomach around the belly button and stay conscious of the way you're bringing your stomach in as the words flow out. Anytime you're speaking, your stomach should be moving in. When you pause during a sentence for a comma or a period, it will stop its inward motion for a moment, and when you resume, it continues its path back in until it's time to take another breath. As long as this inward motion is happening, you will not hear the gravelly sound in your voice. Give yourself the experience of speaking with lots of air, using the hand on the stomach as a guide.

I'd also like you to pay close attention to your volume level. You can throw your voice immediately into a gravelly mode by pulling back the volume (without whispering). Doing that leaves the cords vibrating but without sufficient air, and causes them to hit each other roughly. What's the proper volume for speaking? I encourage you to set your habitual volume at what I call the "listen to me" level—also known as the "It's very important that you hear me" level and the "I'm not willing to be overlooked for another promotion" level. I don't mean yelling. I'm talking about a volume that attaches importance to every word you say. After all, if it's not important, why should you bother to speak it? And why should I listen?

It's interesting to me that the same level of energy that makes a voice command attention and gives it the most interesting and appealing qualities is the level that's required for superior sound production. It's as though our voices are designed to be compelling, and listened to—if only we let them. Try speaking more loudly for even a day and see what happens to the way people respond to you. People who are used to turning down the radio and leaning in to hear you may need a little time to adjust to the new, sculpted voice you've built, but I know they'll be energized by your new vocal energy.

Many of us are in the habit of letting our volume drop at the end of every sentence, and it's no coincidence that this loud-to-soft pattern is so common. We're getting soft not because we want to but because we're running out of air. But with just a little practice and attention, you can easily build the strength and skill to set the volume and energy level of your sentences where you want it — and keep it there.

The exercise that's most effective for correcting this problem is the octave jump. If you go back and listen to audio 22 (male) or audio 23 (female) on the website, you'll hear how all through the exercise, I keep the same level of intensity. I'm *not* just hitting the high note and letting it peter out. The volume and strength of the sound are constant, and that's precisely the quality you want to take with you when you leave the exercises and begin to speak.

Make the transition from the octave jump to speaking like this: Do the first section of the octave jump exercise (just the chest voice parts) using the gug sound. Practice until you feel you can hold the high notes with real power. Then substitute words. Sing: I-CAN-if-I-want. I-CAN-do-it-right. I-WANT-ev-'ry-thing. Now I'd like you to try speaking those words in the same way you sang them. Keep your voice strong and present through every word, and feel the power of your breath bringing each one to life. Listen to the demonstration on audio 28 to hear how this can sound.

Connecting your diaphragmatic breathing to speaking should feel smooth, as though you're blowing out one big candle instead of puffing at ten small ones. Think of your sentences as a string of beads with breath flowing through them, *connected* — and each one significant. Speak each sentence as though there's not a throwaway word in the bunch, and not a single syllable that you can afford to lose by allowing it to become soft or gravelly.

Turning a Brassy Voice to Silver

If you listen to your progress recording and still detect a touch of the irritating brassiness you heard me demonstrate on audio 7, it's time to review what we've learned so far about the larynx. Brassiness is first and foremost a larynx problem. When your larynx rises as you speak, cutting off the flow of air, your voice loses all its warmth and richness, gaining, instead, a harsh, buzzy quality. You may not hear in your voice the extreme sounds I demonstrated—few of us do— but you may notice grating traces of brassiness. Listen carefully, and if you detect them, take heart—this condition is easily fixed.

Please go back to audio example 19 and practice the Yogi Bear voice that moves your larynx down. Start by adding the smallest of amounts of the demonstrated sound, and see if your larynx stops rising. If that does it...great! If not, keep adding more of this sound until the larynx stops rising. It sounds funny, but it's highly effective. As you use the sound, you're giving your larynx a few moments to find its most comfortable position. And after even a short period of talking like this, the larynx is ready to stay in its proper place. Make sure that you're not creating too much pressure in the area right under your chin as you practice. Sometimes when I ask people to do the low-larynx exercises they tighten the muscles under the chin way too much, using them to pull the Adam's apple down. Instead, I would like you to think more about lowering your Adam's apple by lowering your tongue in your mouth. Not by pulling the tongue backward, but by placing the tongue lower in the mouth. Play with it.

As you practice your vocal exercises, keep your finger on your Adam's apple, and when you feel your larynx rising, use the low-larynx sound to bring it down again. This low-larynx training should open up the back of your throat and take most of the brassiness away.

I'd also like you to use a small hand mirror to check the position of your mouth as you speak. Recite the alphabet and watch what the corners of your mouth are doing. When you reach letters like *e* and *g*, do you feel your mouth becoming wide, the corners flaring apart? Some people say *e* with a very wide smile, their eyes nearly closed and their cheeks high. I appreciate the energy and enthusiasm of that mouth position, but it doesn't serve you well at all for speaking.

When you let the corners of your mouth go wide, you restrict the amount of resonating space inside your cheeks, which changes the way your voice sounds. Ideally, air is supposed to bounce around inside your mouth and cheeks, picking up resonances that make it sound rich and full. It's a bit like what happens inside a big bass drum after you strike the top: the sound bounces around the interior space and is shaped by it. When you widen the corners of your mouth, it's as though you've taken the sides of the drum away. The sound is flat, brassy, and tinny.

To correct the too-wide habit, try this: Put an index finger on either side of your mouth. Push your lips in just a bit, so they're just slightly pursed. Now, start the alphabet again, or tell me about what you're doing for dinner tonight, and as you speak, don't let your lips go any wider than their starting position. Keep the corners of your mouth *in*.

I know you may believe that you have to stretch your lips wide to say *e*, but that's not true. To prove that to yourself, say *oo*, and hold your lips in that position. Now say *e*. You *can* make the *e* sound with *oo* lips. And you *can* get out of the habit of making your lips so wide as you speak. The payoff for practicing with this is substantial: you'll love the rich tones it adds to your voice, and you'll notice how dramatically the brassiness fades.

Rx for a Too-Nasal Voice

When your voice sounds too nasal, the reason, as you might recall, lies in the amount of air flowing to the nose. Too much air and you will certainly sound nasal. Too little and you sound like Sylvester Stallone playing Rocky. Remember, as you listen to your progress recording and compare it with my demonstrations on audios 2 and 4 on the website, that you're listening for *traces* of the sounds I'm demonstrating to the extreme. If you know you're nasal but you can't figure out which camp you fall into, experiment with both of the solutions below. Which accentuates the problem? Which seems to correct it? This is your chance to really learn about the factors that add particular flavors and colors to your voice.

The extreme example of the nasal sound is a direct result of a high larynx. When your larynx rises, the back part of the throat closes and directs too much air toward the nasal cavity. The pinched, unflattering tones that result disappear instantly when you lower the larynx using the low-larynx sound I discussed in detail in the previous section. Interestingly, though, it's likely that you'll be a little shocked by the new sounds you hear when the nasality is gone.

Quite often when I work with students, we target the nasal sound, fix it with a touch of low larynx, and then the student stops and says, "That sounds ridiculous!" The voice the student now hears seems to have way too much bass. What I hear, and what we've really created, is a healthy, harmonious blend of air moving above and below the soft palate. But it feels strange, as though it couldn't be an improvement, and the cure seems much too fast. There's got to be more to it than that.

Actually, there's not. Your nasality is really fixed—that quickly. Be sure to record your voice speaking with this new larynx placement before you judge it too harshly. Compare it with the too-nasal voice on your progress recording and I think you'll find that your voice sounds great.

What about the Rocky "stuffy nose" nasal sound? To get rid of it, you'll need to allow more air to resonate above the soft palate, and that really means you'll need to concentrate on the physical feeling of middle voice. Middle voice requires you to allow correct amounts of air above and below the soft palate, and *every time you hit middle, you are moving away from the blocked, stuffy-nose sound.* In the early stages of going to middle, a lot of students mistakenly think that they're making their voices more nasal, but that's not true. It's just that they're feeling more air vibrating around their noses—which is just what we need to fix the stuffy-nose nasal-sound problem. I can show you a test to see if you are actually letting too much air come through your nose. Pinch your nostrils closed and say the word "Helloooooooooo." If you sound normal, you are in great shape, without extra nasality. However, if you sound blocked and funny, you are too nasal and will want to use the techniques above to fix that.

As you go through the general warm-up, concentrate on the one-octave and the octave-and-a-half exercises, which take you quickly and repeatedly toward middle. You'll notice that the throaty nay and nah sounds, which help direct air above the soft palate, are especially effective. Pay attention to when you go to middle, and notice how the sound vibrates a bit behind your eyes and nose. That's the feeling you're looking for, and this is all the awareness you need to open up a stuffy, nasal voice. Use the flip-flopping technique I described earlier: Sing through an exercise until you feel the high sinus vibrations of middle voice, then stop and speak a few lines, trying to add a bit of that new sound quality to your speaking voice.

If You're Still Too Husky

It's unlikely that many of you will be having problems with the husky, Louis Armstrong voice at this point, since we've had so much practice regulating the flow of air to the vocal cords. That husky quality, which results from blasts of air causing the outer edges of the vocal cords to vibrate, probably began to disappear as soon as you tried your first exercises using goog and gug. The glottal stops produced by the gs are the perfect antidote to the rushing sound of air that hasn't been slowed enough to be shaped by consonants.

If you're still hearing traces of huskiness, go right back to goog and gug and let them continue to help moderate the flow of air to the cords. One more time, try to carry the richer, more controlled sound you hear in the exercises into your speaking voice by doing a few googs and gugs, then speaking with the same intensity. As your body and brain jump from exercise to speech, you'll find that you begin to expect your speaking to sound like your singing—exactly the habit we're working to develop.

You May Get Tired—But It Won't Last Long

Making changes in the way you breathe and speak can feel strenuous at first. My student Evette told me that when she tried diaphragmatic breathing, she hated the "side effects"—it made her light-headed, and she felt as though she might pass out. She was also concerned because after even a small amount of practicing, her voice would give out, and she'd have to rest until she felt her vocal strength returning.

As Evette spoke, I noticed that her soft voice seemed tight and constricted, with a slightly nasal quality. Were these problems—the lack of strength, the light-headedness, and the soft, tight, nasal voice—related? Absolutely. And by looking at how Evette worked with her voice, you'll begin to see how you can treat the voice as a whole instead of separating it into tiny parts with different instructions for each. Improving your voice goes beyond fixing specific flaws. It's really a matter of strengthening the basic technique that supports and improves your entire voice.

Watching Evette do the basic warm-up, I noticed that she was still raising her chest and shoulders. To remedy that, I asked her to place her open palm on her upper chest area, several inches below her neck. As she inhaled, I told her to keep her hand still and not let it rise. (Doing this, instead of thinking specifically about keeping your chest and shoulders down, is a helpful trick when you're learning diaphragmatic breathing.) As Evette accomplished this, the air very easily went lower in her body, and her breathing was much better.

But she still felt light-headed. I explained that the hyperventilation she was experiencing is normal as the body tries to get used to the increased air that proper diaphragmatic breathing provides. But if you don't take deep breaths consistently, your system can't regulate itself. To get past the dizzy feeling, you need to stick with the correct breathing until the body adapts. This should take no longer than a couple of days if you stop going back and forth between deep and shallow breathing. What's really necessary here is consistency—twenty-four hours a day of proper breathing, regardless of your activity or mind-set.

Once Evette had proper amounts of air coming into her body, we needed to work on how much came out when she spoke. Remember that if you place your fingers directly in front of your mouth as you speak or sing, you should feel a solid stream of air. Evette did not; in fact, she could feel almost no air hitting her fingers at all. We remedied that by using the steps below, which I described earlier:

♦ I told her to increase her volume by 500 percent to get a better balance of air and cord thickness, and we knew we'd hit it when she could feel a sizable amount of air against her fingers and hear a fuller, richer sound.

♦ Next we used the low-larynx sound to correct the nasal tones in her voice. I spoke several words using the low-larynx sound and asked her to repeat them back to me with the same tonal quality. Her larynx responded instantly, because like many people, she didn't have a serious high-larynx problem. Instead, she'd gotten so used to "speaking small" over the years that her throat tended to close up.

As soon as we opened up the back part of her throat with more air, more cord, and a lower larynx, a strong, normal-size voice popped out. But using that bigger voice was exhausting for her. After a few minutes of speaking that way, she felt as though she were losing her voice and getting hoarse. That was the combined effect of a couple of factors:

♦ The larger amounts of air were a bit drying to her vocal cords, which needed more lubrication. I asked Evette to start carrying a water bottle with her and to drink from it constantly.

♦ The thicker cord vibration was more physically taxing, and it also required a greater amount of mental concentration. Extra mental focus often tires the body because in trying so hard to make a particular sound, you can exhaust yourself emotionally, using huge amounts of energy. The solution is patience. Keep making the new sounds, but rest when you need to.

Evette's homework was similar to the prescription I give many students: Concentrate on diaphragmatic breathing, using all the tricks and suggestions you've seen in this chapter and in chapter 3. Then, remember to maintain the same volume levels for singing and speaking. That doesn't mean start singing more softly. It means speak as loudly as you sing when you practice. And finally, don't give up. It took Evette three or four weeks to integrate these new habits into her life, but she persisted, and now she's got the improved strength and stamina she deserves. You will too.

Taming the Tongue

The final element I'd like you to think about at this point is your tongue. I often find that my students do well with the exercises but inadvertently find themselves tripped up by the position of their tongue, something they've never given much thought to. The position of the tongue is crucial for great sound, but it's also central to swallowing—and the swallowing functions can sometimes influence speech in negative ways.

Go ahead and swallow now without drinking. Notice where your tongue goes. You should feel it push up against the back part of your closed teeth. Its job in this position is to seal off the mouth when you swallow. As the front part of your tongue pushes forward to seal off the teeth, the back part of your tongue rises and closes the back part of the throat. Swallow again and look for that placement. This is very important, because if the tongue does this rising and closing motion while you are trying to make a sound, it will drastically constrict the back part of your throat and restrict the amount of free air that can exit.

As you speak, your tongue is supposed to stay pretty much resting at the bottom part of your mouth, with the tip practically touching the back side of your bottom teeth. It can move slightly away from the teeth, but only *slightly*. Practice saying the vowels with the tip of your tongue almost touching the back of your bottom teeth. I'll bet many of you will notice that on certain letters your tongue wants to move back, and that's a problem. When your tongue retreats, the back part almost always begins to rise and close off the air. Work with the vowels and try to get used to keeping the front part of your tongue closer to your teeth.

A Recipe for Success

With the work we've done here, you have the tools to use your vocal exercises, and your work with the larynx, breath, and tongue,

SET YOUR VOICE FREE

to make dramatic improvements in the sound of your speaking voice. Keep recording yourself to monitor your progress, because your ear may take a while to catch up with and embrace the positive changes you've made.

Enjoy the new richness and energy in your voice, and be open to the new kinds of expression it leads you to. Knowing you sound better, you may want to speak up more, or even step into the spotlight. The investment you make in your voice is certain to reward you by energizing your whole life.

Coming chapters will give you the information you need to care for and fine-tune your instrument. Once that's done, we'll work on adding even more interest, variety, warmth, and color to your strong, healthy voice. I want you to leave monotone behind, and I'll show you how to use your voice dynamically to capture and keep your listeners enthralled. Everything builds on the basics you've learned here. They're the springboard to vocal mastery.

. 8 .

Songs without Fear

I F YOU sat in on lessons with me for a week—or even a day— you'd see the immediate changes that create breakthroughs in people's singing voices. It's as though people were driving around in Ferraris that behave like Volkswagens because of a tiny malfunction they never knew was there. Your "malfunction" might be a high lar- ynx, or a weak middle voice. Maybe it's as simple as a clenched stom- ach that builds pressure as you try to breathe. The interesting thing is that these factors don't completely keep us from singing. When we run into roadblocks, we just build alternate paths. You might tell yourself that you can sing in only one key—and so what? You sound great there. Or you figure that everyone knows it's hard work to hit the high notes that your band wants you to add to its songs, so it's no big deal that singing wipes you out. You're getting gigs; what's the problem? In other words, what's wrong with a Volkswagen, anyhow, as long as it runs?

Believe me, being a great vocalist is not just about driving from point A to point B; you want to be the Ferrari. And if you listen care- fully to the way you sing songs, you can learn to do what I do: find that hidden glitch and fix it. I'd like to help you identify the physical reasons that are making you limit your choice of songs and the way you deliver them. The clues are all there in the places you hate the most—the songs that are "way out of my key," the notes that make your face turn purple, the phrases that tie your tongue. If you learn how to work through the spots where you would ordinarily stop, you can immediately begin to use them as stepping-stones to amped-up vocal power. So let's start singing and see what happens.

Singing Along

A lot of teachers will tell you that you need to practice vocal exercises for months, even years, before you're ready to try a song. One school of thought says: Teach them breathing until they're bored, then let them do exercises forever, and when the exercises are perfect, bring on the songs. There are even technique teachers on the planet who never let their students graduate from exercises at all. These approaches might be great ways for singing coaches to wring the maximum amount of income from dedicated students, but the problem is that vocal exercises on their own aren't what you set out to master. You know, and I know, that while you're learning the vocal technique exercises, you're going to sing songs, even if I tell you not to.

Since I'm a vocal producer as well as a technique teacher, I can't see the point of technique that doesn't flow directly into making music. My feeling is, once you have a sense of where middle is, and you have some control over chest and head, it's fine to begin to put your new skills to work in songs. I'd just like you to do it in a smart way that will multiply the progress you're making using exercises alone.

What You Hear versus What I Hear

There's nothing I love more than an ambitious student who's eager to jump into the tough stuff right away. I've met thousands of you, and typically, I find out who you are when, in your second lesson, you bring me a Sia or Justin Timberlake song and tell me, "I'm ready to do this." Instead of being scared off by the vocal acrobatics and pure daredevil highs and lows of the music, you're inspired to go for it. And I say: Fine. I take the sheet music, start to play, and then I just listen. Almost inevitably, the singing I hear is way off the mark.

At the points where Sia is soaring, the student has settled into a comfortable monotone that doesn't come close to the peaks, and when I point this out, the student says: "But I don't have this problem when I'm singing this at home."

When you're singing for the joy of it, just you and your music player, it's easy to fall into the illusion that you're singing the same pitches as the recording artist. Part of your brain hears the artist and part hears you, and when one is on and one is off, it's natural to give yourself the credit. "I was right there with the singer," you think. "That was great."

Imitation is a great way to learn a song, and you've taken a big step in the right direction by taking the time to listen or play the music repeatedly. You can't even think about being technically proficient until you know the words and melody completely. Once you've reached that stage, though, it's good to start listening to yourself. And if you learn to listen a little more critically, you'll hear what I do—the places where the voice is straining, or where there's a break between one note and the next. You *could* cringe and criticize yourself every time you identify a rough spot. But instead, I'd like you to keep your ears open and make notes of exactly where you're getting into trouble. In effect, you'll be plotting out your own hazard course. Ask yourself:

- Where does the song get difficult?
- What particular words in the song trip me up?
- What passages seem to build up too much pressure in my chest voice?
- Where am I breaking between one note and another?

You might notice that one part seems high for you, so you're straining. Is that a place to leave chest voice? Move into middle? Move from middle to head? How can you reduce the pressure?

Keep in mind that there's no magic way to leapfrog from where you are now to instant divahood just by choosing more difficult music and knowing where it's hard. I don't mind your struggling through songs if you're not technically perfect, but I want you to struggle through the same areas that we're working on in the exercises. That means I want you to start with songs that go a little way into middle instead of immediately jumping into songs that go way up into high middle and head. Choose songs that let you sing with chest and a bit of connected middle, and then, as you get stronger, work upward.

I'm not sentencing you to remain stuck in a limited range. In fact, in my studio I don't even allow students to sing simple songs that cover no ground at all. I want you to own the entire range, but as you set out, I'd like you to avoid songs that go from the lowest note in chest to the highest note in head voice. I know this sounds obvious, but it's easy to fall in love with songs that are technically demanding and try them without really thinking about what they're asking of your voice.

Finding Music That Works for You

If you look at the sheet music of the song you're interested in, you can easily see how much of it falls into chest, middle, or head. Women should watch for the notes that fall between B-flat and E or F and know that in that range they should move into middle. If you're able to get into middle but it's still weak, look for songs that peak around B-natural to C-sharp. That's a part of middle that can still be very chesty. Check out the singer Tori Kelly, who sings a lot in this territory, and you'll see that you can do real songs, with beautiful possibilities, within this range. (Look at the diagram to see what these notes look like on sheet music if you're not sure.)

If you're a man, you'll see middle on the sheet music in the notes that run between E or F and B-flat or B-natural. Your first songs

STAFF NOTATION — FEMALE

should have their highest notes around G and A. In this range you'll have a chance to taste middle without having to strain incredibly. (The diagram shows you how these notes look on the page.)

Keep in mind that 85 percent or more of popular songs for men and women have *no* head voice in them at all. That means that any song you love probably requires only chest and middle—unless it's superhigh gospel, or performed by Mariah Carey or Jennifer Hudson, who love middle and head voice. As you sing along with your favorite recording artists, try to be acutely aware of where your voice wants to leave chest and go into middle. Because you've worked with the exercises, you've learned how to allow air to get above the soft palate and into the nasal area, so when you feel this as you sing, you won't be in the dark. You can allow middle to happen. Don't be surprised if middle just pops out. The exercises have cleared the way.

If what you hear as you move beyond chest voice is soft and airy, or if you notice that your voice bounces from chest to a higher voice that is drastically different, you'll know you've missed middle. Having that awareness is vital! And once you've got it, you can back up the audio and look for middle in that spot. Try it again. Keep concentrating on finding a place to go with your voice that doesn't strain.

STAFF NOTATION — MALE

For convenience in popular sheet music, men actually follow the same treble clef notation as the women, but singing an octave lower.

You know what to do when you run into trouble with the exercises. Use the same techniques as you sing along with recordings. Check your breathing and be sure it's smooth and "unaccessorized" — no chest and shoulders involved. Stop straining at the top of chest voice. Put your finger on your larynx and be sure it's in the correct position. Use all these techniques — they are there for you when you sing.

The Songwriters' Obstacle Course

You might notice, as you launch into songs, that problems you think you've mastered in the exercises suddenly reappear. Breaks, squeaks, and strains can surprise you at places in the range you've started handling smoothly when you do your warm-ups. That's because you've left the ultracontrolled environment I created in the exercises, which was designed to allow you to make sounds easily.

Your ease and comfort are about the last thing on a songwriter's mind when a new piece is flowing out. I assure you that the composer is not thinking, "What words, what consonants, and what pattern of notes in what range will make this song easy to sing?" Few composers are great technical singers, and a lot of them don't sing too well at all. More important, they don't want to limit the magic of the song, or their own creativity, by confining themselves to sounds and notes that are easily accessible. They don't *care* how hard the music is as long as it sounds good and creates the perfect emotion.

Not surprisingly, the words and melodies in songs don't tend to focus the amount of air that goes to the cords the way the exercises did. Singing gug, gug, gugs gives you controlled amounts of air to work with, but replace them with words and a tune like "And now, the end is near" (from "My Way") and your cords may feel like they're in a wind tunnel. You're making quick switches, and suddenly your body has a ton of information to handle.

The exercises train your cords to move into place without your thinking about where they go, but it's difficult to slide into singing without some thought. You're not just working with nay and goog, you've got dozens of combinations of vowels and consonants that open and close the back of your throat, challenging you to try to control the air. Frequently, there's a fight between you and the music, and you'll have to work consciously to make a smooth transition between the sounds you've learned in the exercises and the sounds the song requires.

Taming the Musical Beast

Start by scanning the music and getting an idea of how much is in chest voice and how much is above chest. Spot your "middle" notes — E for a man (that's the fourth space on the treble clef), B-flat for a woman (a flatted note at the third line of the treble clef). Then start to sing, using your diaphragmatic breathing.

As you reach middle, pay close attention to the position of your mouth. In singing, even more than in speaking, the corners of your mouth should never widen into a smile, especially as you go higher. When you sing "no" at a comfortable place in your range, your lips purse slightly, but you may notice that when you try to sing it higher in the range, the pouty lip position disappears, and the *o* sounds more like an *ah*. It's a natural tendency to slide into a smiley face when you go higher than chest voice, but if you let it happen, you'll hear strange things happening to your lyrics. "Go" becomes "gah," and the sound of *ah* becomes *aaa*, as in *splat*. In fact, you'll find your lyrics splatting all around you. Not too attractive.

Worse than that, you can trap yourself in chest voice, with no possibility of getting to middle. When you let your mouth widen, the air that was going to bounce around in the cheeks and travel above the soft palate to the nasal cavity has no room to move, and it goes straight out the corners of your lips.

Some of you have probably encountered the crazy solutions that many teachers use to deal with this problem. Thinking that the vowels will change as you go higher, they ask you to sing new sounds — made-up words that will, they hope, sound like the right ones when they're sung. That's silly, confusing, and unnecessary. All you really need to do is to make a conscious effort to control the position of the corners of your mouth. No matter what you're singing, your lips should remain relatively narrow instead of changing drastically.

This technique is called focusing the vowels, and it sounds simple, but I can't tell you how many singers it's helped. Try it, using a small hand mirror to keep an eye on your mouth, and you'll sound richer, more resonant. If you ever have a question about how a word should sound on a high note, stop, speak the word, and look at the position of your mouth. That's the position you should try to duplicate when you sing. Just as I've told you to speak the way you sing, I want you to sing the way you speak—with the same clarity. Don't do goofy things with your mouth just because you're singing. It confuses your brain—and your audience.

That said, there *is* one specific change I'd like you to make in the position of your mouth as you go higher: I want you to drop your jaw without tilting your head down. As you ascend the scale, the back part of your throat tends to close a bit, making the sounds coming out of your mouth seem smaller. Dropping your jaw compensates for that change by creating a large resonating cavity in your mouth that amplifies the higher notes. Be careful not to throw your jaw down in a spasmodic movement. Let it slide up and down in a gentle fluid motion that creates no pressure in the muscles of the jaw.

At first you might feel that I'm asking you to do two opposing things at one time. After all, I want you to drop your jaw—and not distort the words you're singing. First of all, don't drop your jaw three inches, just let it fall slightly, without tension. Practice these mouth positions—corners of the mouth in, jaw down as you go higher—and you'll find that your words are clear and beautiful without distortion or strain.

When the Words Get in the Way

If you're having trouble getting from chest to middle at some point in a song because the words are acting like obstacles, switch from words to exercise sounds. Instead of singing "Some-where over the rainbow," you might sing "Some-mum over the rainbow." Putting a sound like mum at a trouble spot can help you recapture control over how the cords and air are mixing. You can even sing a whole song in an exercise sound, to get a good sense of where middle needs to come in, then begin to switch to words, going back to the exercise sound only when you need it.

The old habit of thinking "Wow, I can't hit that high note — time to back off" is something you can change if you stop thinking you have to use chest voice for the whole song. You know how to allow middle to happen in the exercises, and the same guidelines apply here. As you approach the high notes and seem to hit the wall, concentrate on the basics:

- Are you getting louder as you go higher? Keep your volume constant.

- Are you allowing big bursts of air to come through in some parts of the song and feeling a more restricted flow in other parts? Try to keep the airflow at one level throughout by using a hand on the stomach to be sure you're exhaling smoothly and evenly.

- Are you assuming that you'll get more power and energy in your voice if you just push harder and tense the muscles in your stomach? A lot of my students see a high note coming and want to use muscle to get up the mountain. It sounds effective, but let me repeat, it just doesn't work.

I got a great demonstration of where true physical power and energy come from when I worked with Bruce Jenner many years ago. This was long before he became famous on the reality show *Keeping Up with the Kardashians* or made the transition to becoming Caitlyn. I knew him as the man who won the 1976 Olympic decathlon, meaning he could throw farther, jump higher, and run faster than any man alive. My job was to teach him how to sing for a project he was doing. During that time, Bruce continued to maintain his well-toned Olympic body, but he would go to the gym and look scrawny next to the power lifters all around him. He liked to bet them that, as small as he was by comparison, he could lift more weight than they could. The funny thing was, he always won. Why? It was a matter of technique. The big guys would inevitably hold their breath and push.

Bruce, on the other hand, would focus energy on the muscles he needed and lift on a smooth, deep diaphragmatic exhalation. There was no tension at all in his stomach as he hoisted hundreds of pounds. Maximum physical—and vocal—power is a matter of using your breath correctly.

Remember to record your voice from time to time. Recently, one of my students was singing the Katy Perry song " Roar," and though I assured her she sounded great, she was certain that she'd jumped straight from chest voice to head. She felt a definite difference in her body when she left chest and was sure her listeners could hear it. *All* instruments make shifts in sound as they move from range to range. A piano, for instance, is fat and bassy on the bottom but tinkles into treble on the top. The key to making both sounds fit comfortably together is in the transitions, and it's the seamless connections that I'd like you to concentrate on. The seam areas will undoubtedly feel strange at first. But as we've seen along the way, you can't judge your sound from the inside alone. Record and listen to yourself before rushing to the conclusion that everyone heard the big change you felt as you moved out of chest voice. You might be pleasantly surprised to hear that it sounds a lot better than you thought.

What Key Are You In?

You might be wondering, about this time, if you could make things a little easier on yourself by choosing songs that are in "your key," the magical musical neighborhood that will show off the real strengths in your voice and maybe even let you avoid the struggle with middle or head voice.

I'd like to make things as simple as possible for you, but I'm afraid assigning you to your key isn't going to do the trick. The key signature of a song tells us how many sharps and flats are in a piece, but it says nothing at all about how high or low the notes go in the range. For example, the key of C has no sharps or flats, and while staying in that key, I could play the notes that correspond to every white key of the piano. That means that if I scooted all the way to the left side of the piano bench and played the lowest white notes, I'd be in the key of C—and there's no way I, or any human, could make my voice that deep. On the other hand, the notes that correspond to the white keys on the far right side of the piano are also in C, and none of us is going to be singing those either. So to say "I love to sing in the key of C" makes no sense.

It does make sense, however, to figure out what key you like best for a *particular song*. That's a question an accompanist might ask you, and there are a couple of ways to decide how to answer.

The first is to listen to where the artist who first performed it sang it. This can put you in the ballpark if you're the same gender as the original singer, but it can cause a bit of confusion if you're, say, a man who's drawn to music that was made popular by a woman. My student Evan loved Taylor Swift, and he'd endlessly play her records and sing along as he danced around in his apartment, waiting to be either discovered or evicted. Although Taylor's voice isn't super-high, when Evan tried to copy it, he wound up spending all his time in middle and head voice. As I've mentioned, both men and women should keep the low notes of every song in chest voice, and for Evan to let his voice develop, he needed to transpose Taylor's songs into a key that would allow him to dip into chest voice and expand his repertoire of vocal sounds. You can sing along with, and be inspired by, performers whose voices are very different from your own, but it's important to avoid getting stuck in limiting imitations and to look for ways to bring the unique qualities of your own voice into the mix.

Most people do end up choosing keys based on what they see as their own vocal limitations. If all you have is chest voice, it's natural to feel inclined to stay low in your safe, comfortable range. And if you're a woman who has studied opera for years and are trapped in head voice, it's typical to pick keys that keep you stuck in the stratosphere. This method, though, is like going to an ice cream shop that offers fifty flavors and choosing vanilla—not because you love vanilla, but because you're too timid to try the others.

I recommend taking a chance on the new possibilities of your voice. You've got an instrument that has chest, middle, and head voices, and with that kind of versatility, you can place your song anywhere in the range that makes the music and your voice sparkle. Does the song sound great high? Put it there. Does it sound sultry and sexy down low? Put it there. Each song has a signature and an emotional resonance that begs for certain vocal sounds. A driving, fast-paced rock tune screams out for a certain amount of chest voice. A slow love ballad may require the conversational sound of chest voice on the bottom and the lilting excitement of middle, even head voice, on the high notes. With a few tries, it should be easy to uncover the perfect key. Look for the combination that excites you, even if it's difficult. Make the choice to take a chance on sounding great — even if it takes you time and practice to get there.

Joining the Rhythm Nation

Singing in perfect rhythm is not always so easy to do. Yes, I've taught dancers like Julianne Hough, who could sing wonderfully in time when I coached her for the starring role in the movie *Rock of Ages*. I've also seen many students who concentrate so hard on singing the words correctly and hitting the right notes that they wind up separating themselves from the flow of the music — the rhythm. My student David was a classical pianist and conductor, yet when he sang for me, I noticed that at times he was too fast or too slow, and often he was out of sync with the music. We stopped our session and did a simple diagnostic exercise that I'd like you to try.

Follow along with audio 29 on the website and join me as I accentuate different beats at different times. We'll use a basic rhythmic pattern called 4/4 time. First, clap with me on the first beat of every 1-2-3-4, 1-2-3-4 cycle. Then clap on the first and third beats. You can count aloud if that makes it easier for you. Finally, we'll clap only on the third beat.

It sounds easy, but David had a considerable amount of trouble accentuating different beats — and he was a professional musician. When he listens to other people making sounds, vocal or instrumental, his internal sense of rhythm operates quite proficiently. But when he tries to sing, his rhythmic sense goes out the window. Why? I believe it's a matter of concentrating on the details — those tricky lyrics, those daunting high passages—and never quite connecting with the big picture.

It's common for students to say, "I don't have rhythm," but that's an argument I just don't buy. Listen to your breathing. That's rhythm. Look at how smoothly and regularly you walk. Or pay attention to the sound of your heart—which is so regular that when it adds or skips a beat, you know something is wrong. If you've got a body, you've got rhythm.

You can translate that natural gift into a consciousness that will help your singing by attuning your ears to the pulse of your favorite songs. First, focus on finding the straight-ahead beat—the toe-tapping rhythm that the drummer is providing as a backbone of the song. (If you get confused, listen for the snare drum, which usually signals the main beat.) Second, use audio 29 on the website to get accustomed to clapping out the main rhythm of songs as you sing. The more you do this, the more you'll be able to keep a simple rhythm going in your mind even as you're singing notes and counter-rhythms that move and weave all over the song. David was a little embarrassed about going back to the rhythm basics he thought he'd learned in grade school, but he practiced them anyway. And he quickly stopped losing the main beat of his songs. I know this will work for you, too, if you'll take this musical essential as seriously as you do the other components we've worked on. You'll step out of the notes and into the music.

Handling the Old Bugaboos

Whether you know it or not, you now have all the tools you need to guide yourself back and forth between your warm-up exercises and songs, and I hope you're feeling the close relationship between them. The feeling and placement of "mum" can become "love" easily in a song if you let it, and you can flip-flop your way into handling even the most complicated lyrics with ease. If the pieces are clicking into place for you now, and your technique has switched to autopilot, you're probably having a lot of fun and enjoying what may seem like a brand-new voice.

If you're still having trouble getting a particular part of the technique, though, I know you may still be frustrated. So I'd like to tell you about a couple of students who patiently and persistently solved what looked like insurmountable problems. Remember the path I described to you earlier, the road that leads to vocal mastery. It's lined with great successes but also with plateaus and with places where adding some new element—like dropping your jaw or facing the challenge of singing words instead of just sounds—seems to throw you backward. Work gently and take small steps. The next breakthrough will amaze you.

Singing the High-Larynx Blues

My student Chuck was a keyboard player for a popular band. Aside from playing, he also handled a lot of the background singing, which required some amazingly high notes. Chuck and the band were very successful, but for him, performing was a nightmare. Whenever he approached the top of his chest voice, he would create huge amounts of pressure. His face would turn red, and he would look a little like he was being choked. He would even cock his head over to one side, and his tongue would stick out—while he was onstage. I know this doesn't sound like a pretty picture, and it wasn't. Chuck loved what he did, but he hated the physical experience of singing.

His problem was an extremely high larynx, which forcefully rose when he hit high notes, closing off his throat like a cannonball stuck in a cannon. We spent several months on low-larynx exercises alone. Months of singing like Yogi Bear, months of keeping a finger on the Adam's apple to keep track of when it rose and when it went down. In the beginning we seemed to stand still. The muscles controlling the larynx were so used to pushing his throat closed that they hardly seemed to respond, no matter what we did. But we kept working, despite our worries and doubts. One-eighth inch by one-eighth inch, Chuck's larynx began to move down and find a new, slightly lower resting place in his throat. And eventually, after all those weeks of dedicated work, his body accepted that he could allow sound to come out while his larynx remained in its proper place. It was miraculous to sit in the audience and watch him perform without pressure or strain. There were no facial spasms, just the occasional smile — his and mine.

Had Chuck been faint of heart, or believed that his miracle had to be instantaneous, he never would have reached his goals. Remember that some changes will happen fast, and some will happen slowly for you. But whatever you need to fix, I promise you, the body will eventually make the necessary changes. We simply need to keep moving in the right direction and refuse to give up.

I offer you the same advice I'd give the star of *The Exorcist*: "Remember, Linda, even though you might not feel in charge right now, it's still your body — and if you just stay with it, you'll soon be in control."

The Mirage of Middle — and How to Make It Real

I know we've talked a lot about middle and how to find it, and that you've been practicing for some time to strengthen that part of your voice. If you're still wobbly when it comes to leaving chest voice, read on to see how I worked with my student Carol. The techniques we used may be just what you need to get beyond what's blocking you.

Carol had a terrific chest voice, and she'd been singing with it for thirty years, never venturing beyond the notes she knew she could always count on. As we worked with the diagnostic exercises, I noticed that as soon as she got to the top of chest voice, she strained, pushed, and inevitably hit a concrete wall. We tried to break through with the whole range of exercise sounds, but no matter what sound I gave her, we couldn't seem to find middle. For her, the next voice after chest voice was a weak, airy, falsetto-like sound. I know that some of you can definitely relate to this dilemma.

The first thing we needed to do was to establish the correct place for the seam between chest voice and head voice. Because her chest voice was overused and overworked, she needed to make a conscious effort to draw a border where chest voice would end and middle could begin. I drew the line at B-flat. Even though we couldn't get access to middle, we left chest at that point and went anywhere we could get without pressure, then came right back to chest on the way down each scale.

Let's say we were doing the one-octave exercise using goog. As we sang the first three notes we were in chest. Then we left chest for any of the high notes above B-flat. We came right back to chest on the way down. It went like this:

CHEST . . . CHEST . . . CHEST . . . SOMETHING . . . SOMETHING . . . SOMETHING . . . SOMETHING . . . CHEST . . . CHEST . . . CHEST.

I told Carol to be sure she didn't ride her high voice back down the scale. It's easy to leave chest on the way up and get caught in that new place as you descend.

By making sure that Carol was at least going back and forth at the right place, we were paving a place where middle could exist when she found it. We were finally telling her voice and mind that we were no longer going to accept the belted-out, pressured sound that resulted when she brought chest voice too high. And by not allowing the old habits to surface, we were telling her body to find a new way to sing higher than chest.

For a full half hour, we kept searching unsuccessfully for the middle, while I assured her that it would come. It was a long thirty minutes for her. Though she might have believed me, she couldn't help feeling impatient when the middle voice wouldn't thicken up. Every time she looked for middle she would either get caught in a strained chest or go too far toward head.

Then I gave her the octave jump exercise on mum. I told her to sustain the top note and increase the volume as she held it. As she hit the high note in a headlike tone, I told her simply to add more of the chest-voice feeling to that. Though she didn't fully understand, she tried. We also did this with the nay and nah sounds, which really helped to get more of the vocal cords vibrating. Within a few minutes, she was suddenly in the middle. She could feel that it wasn't chest, because it had no pressure, and it wasn't head because it was too strong for that. She understood and agreed that it must be middle.

Because Carol sang all the time, she was locked into the specific sounds she called upon so regularly. But when she realized that there was more to her voice than she'd ever used, she began to accept that her voice could, indeed, have the magic of middle. Though we were still only getting a small amount of volume in that part of her voice, at least she could feel the right spot, and that feeling would be the compass that pointed her back to middle when she felt lost.

If you're stuck in chest and feeling that there's no way out, I hope you'll try allowing yourself to make any nonstrained sound when you cross the border where chest should end. Like Carol, you'll quickly teach your body that the middle voice truly does exist, in all its glory.

Claim a Great Sound

From here, the sky's the limit. Stay with the exercises, develop your strength, and when you run into trouble, don't stop. Just stop worrying. Persist, as Chuck did. Be willing to take a risk and try something frighteningly new, as Carol did. I've offered you a whole range of techniques and tips to help your body become accustomed to its power and its possibilities, and I hope you'll use them in any combination that helps you today.

Later in this book we'll put the icing on the cake and decorate it, adding style and advanced presentation skills to your singing. For now, though, enjoy making the cake itself. Let your voice flow into new places, and savor its richness. You've earned it.

· 9 ·

The Care and Feeding of Great Voices

THE MORE time you spend doing vocal exercises and concentrating on your speaking and singing throughout the day, the more you'll probably come in contact with odd bits of advice about the voice. I've noticed that not only do my students become more sensitive to information in magazines and the media but people who know they're working on their voices inevitably want to pass along things they've heard. These bits of guidance, from friends, celebrities, "experts," and the manufacturers of helpful products for your throat, cover the whole gamut. I know, because I've probably heard them all.

Many of my students ask me about old standbys, like drinking hot tea with lemon and honey for a sore throat. I see people sucking on special lozenges before big speeches or presentations. I take calls from parents whose children love to sing but who have been told that voice lessons are bad for kids.

Who and what do you believe? What really works and what does more harm than good? It would take an encyclopedia to sort out the facts from the folklore, but in this chapter I'd like to address the most common questions that come up about the care and feeding of the voice—both yours and your children's. I've drawn my conclusions about what's effective from my own experience and the impact I've seen on the voices and vocal health of thousands of students. You'll find a whole range of techniques here for improving your voice from the inside out. Try even a few and you'll feel and hear amazing changes.

What's the best thing I can do for my voice right now?

The most important piece of advice I can give you if you want to get the maximum performance from your voice consists of three words: drink more water. If you're serious about sounding better, have a glass of water as soon as you finish this paragraph. In fact, sip water whenever you think of it, and prompt yourself to think of it by keeping a water bottle with you all day.

Water is vital for your voice because it helps your body provide the lubrication that protects the vocal cords. The cords vibrate the whole time you're speaking or singing, and they even vibrate when you're asleep and dreaming of talking. All that movement could easily be irritating, but when you take in enough water, the body can produce the ideal protective substance: thin, watery phlegm. Like oil in an engine, it keeps friction from damaging the moving parts.

Just imagine what would happen if you rubbed your hands together for the entire time you spent using your voice today. First, your bare skin would turn red and swell. Then, if you continued for a long period of time, your palms and fingers would protect themselves by developing extra layers of skin at the points of contact. If you've ever taken guitar lessons, you've seen how irritation creates calluses.

Your vocal cords, when they're not properly lubricated with phlegm, do essentially the same thing, first swelling and reddening, then forming their own variety of calluses: nodes or nodules. Nodes and nodules have a drastic effect on the voice because they keep the cords from fully closing, and sometimes, even after they've been removed surgically, they can still cause problems. There's much evidence to suggest that the first one you get predisposes you to more, so this is a cycle you definitely don't want to set in motion.

Don't get paranoid about nodes, by the way. As long as you follow the program I describe in this chapter and remove the strain and pressure from your voice, you're at extremely low risk. I've worked with many of the top laryngologists in the country, who send their patients to me before they consider surgery. With the right techniques, I've been quite successful at eliminating the problem.

OK, I've got the message. How much water do I need to drink?

For the average person, eight glasses a day is adequate. The kidneys tightly regulate the water content of our bodies, and under normal circumstances they do an incredible job on eight glasses. If you want to be sure you're drinking enough, just watch the color of your urine. When your system is adequately hydrated, it will be clear, and if you're running low on water, it will be more yellow. Keep in mind, if you use this test, that vitamins and medicines can significantly alter urine color and distort this technique's accuracy.

Humans are more than 70 percent water, and we need to keep replenishing the source. Most of us don't realize that our bodies are losing water all the time. Even at rest we lose half a liter of water a day, and that amount increases with any activity—including singing. Water vapor leaves your body with every breath, so to stay properly hydrated, you'll have to either stop breathing or drink enough water.

I know you're concerned that you'll spend half the day in the bathroom if you consume eight glasses of water every day. Still, I think you'll find that a couple of extra trips to the loo are a low price to pay when you see how much more efficiently your vocal cords operate.

When you start drinking enough water, your days of having a dry throat before you go onstage, or step in front of your board meeting or jury, will be over. Now, you may have tried to soothe a scratchy voice in the past with a glass of water before going on and noticed that your drink had very little effect on the way your voice felt or sounded. That's because you can't just pour water down your throat as though you're watering a plant and expect it to go straight to the vocal cords. Remember that there are two passages in the throat, one for food and liquid and the other for air. When you drink, water doesn't go anywhere near the cords—they're in the other passage. So the water you drink right now, hoping to help your throat right before your speech or song starts, can't do the job. But the water you drank last night or an hour ago can. Water gets absorbed by the intestinal tract, and it's then transported through the bloodstream, which acts as an elaborate sprinkler system, bringing moisture to all the tissues of the body.

Won't drinking too much water wash the vitamins and minerals out of my system?

Yes, but it's almost impossible to do. If you drink six to eight *gallons* of water a day, your blood chemistry may go out of whack, a condition called hyponatremia. But don't spend a lot of time worrying about this. It's tough enough for most people to drink eight glasses of water a day, much less eight gallons. Your body is designed to absorb the nutrition it needs. A general rule to remember is: If you need it, your body will keep it.

You keep saying water. Won't any fluid help my cords?

What I advise my clients to drink is pure, unadulterated water. Cool H_2O, straight, no bubbles, no chasers. At least half a gallon of it a day. Coffee, tea, and soda are liquid, but they're not the same. The problem is that the "added extras" in these other substances can create a different kind of phlegm problem: too much of the wrong kind.

A little phlegm is good, but when your body begins to supply more than you need, the result isn't pretty. Your cords can wind up covered with thick, sticky mucus (remember: phlegm is just mucus of the throat). It's a bit like having peanut butter on the rim of the jar when you're trying to close the lid. Your cords can't meet completely, and as a result, it's harder to produce sound.

The following list will help you make an informed choice about what you want to drink by clueing you in on the effects of the problematic ingredients in many beverages.

Caffeine. If you're a coffee, tea, or soda fan (the labels of your sodas will tell you if they're caffeinated—it's not always obvious), you may already have noticed that you need to clear your throat a lot. That's because caffeine acts as a diuretic and flushes water from your system. Loss of moisture makes the mucus in your throat more concentrated—thus the throat clearing.

What's happening is that when your body gets dehydrated, it pulls water from tissues that are less vital to survival and sends it to the ones that keep you alive. The mucous membranes, salivary glands, and other nonvital tissue give up water to maintain normal hydration for organs like the heart, liver, brain, and kidneys. That's why your mouth gets dry and your phlegm gets thick.

In addition, because caffeine speeds up your whole metabolism, it stimulates the mucus-producing cells and they work harder and faster, creating higher-than-optimal levels of thick phlegm. A faster metabolism also uses more water, which leads you right back to dehydration.

If you're a serious coffee drinker, I won't stand between you and your morning cup of joe. One cup won't really hurt. But I strongly advise you to stop there and to switch to decaf (or water!) later in the day.

Sugar. Some doctors believe that excess amounts of sugar may add to the production of thick mucus. But unless you're diabetic, your body should be able to regulate itself, as long as you're drinking adequate amounts of water. That said, I'd still like to caution you about your sugar intake. Many people, including me, believe that excess sugar consumption is bad for the voice. Many of my students have noticed that they have more thick phlegm when they're eating a lot of sugar. Do your own test and see if cutting back on sugar helps—then adjust your diet accordingly.

Acid. Carbonated sodas are acidic. If you live in a cold climate, pour a can of cola onto the ice on your windshield and watch it act as an instant defroster. Or just watch the ice cubes disappearing into your glass of soda.

What happens to this kind of acid inside your body? Actually, many scientists say, not much. The acid level in your stomach is so high that the soda has no tangible negative effect. But I've personally observed that drinking sodas leads to substantial increases in mucus production for many of my clients. And even natural acids, like those in citrus fruits, have a similar negative effect. Citrus, in the mouth, makes you salivate, and even though that doesn't necessarily make the phlegm thicker, extra saliva, even the watery kind, can be bothersome.

Many people think that citrus cuts phlegm, but strange as it sounds, I've noticed that the opposite is true. I remember working with Def Leppard during a tour and seeing that one stagehand was assigned to make a mixture of warm water, sugar, and fresh-squeezed lemons before the band arrived. For good measure, the drink also contained eucalyptus and an over-the-counter product that was supposed to coat the throat. I asked for a taste, and it was good, good, good. Joe Elliot, the lead singer, drank it constantly through the rehearsal.

At the end of the day, I took Joe aside and told him I had good news for him — he was going to have a lot less of a problem with thick phlegm . . . but he was going to have to trade in that lemonade for water. Joe's basic response was: "Lemonade! How can you take away something as innocent as lemonade?" But three days after the drink disappeared, so did most of his phlegm trouble.

Alcohol. Most of you know that alcohol dehydrates the body, bad news when you're trying to keep your cords hydrated. But a lot of singers and speakers swear by a drink or two before going on. The truth is, with your first one or two drinks, alcohol lowers your anxiety and is actually somewhat stimulating. Most people have trouble focusing when they're anxious, and that's why they often feel that a drink not only calms them down but makes them more alert. If they continue to drink, however, they feel the sedative effects of the alcohol, which makes the normal performance of every muscle in the body slower and less accurate, clearly affecting both speaking and singing. These effects may show themselves after even one drink if you're like me and have a low tolerance for alcohol.

The choice is yours. As long as you have four to six hours for your body to break down the alcohol before you need to perform, and you're not pregnant or an alcoholic, two glasses of wine a day, or a couple of beers, is probably fine. (Keep in mind that the less you weigh, the less tolerance to alcohol you have.) I don't recommend hard liquor simply because its high alcohol content makes it more difficult to deal with. While an American beer may be between 3 and 5 percent alcohol, 100 proof whiskey has a 50 percent alcohol content.

These are my guidelines: If you have a big presentation or performance scheduled at 8:00 P.M., don't drink with dinner. If you need to count on your voice at ten the next morning, it's fine to drink with your evening meal, but be sure not to continue at breakfast. Also remember that it's best not to drink without eating. Alcohol alone can lower your blood sugar, and you need normal blood-sugar levels to maintain the energy required to think and make great sounds.

If you're going to drink, think moderation, hydration, mastication (chewing, that is, eating), and duration (that is, give your body time to recover).

I hear I should avoid dairy products? Any truth in that?

When I have a student who's always clearing his or her throat and who has obvious problems with too much phlegm, sometimes all I need to do to clear up the problem completely is eliminate dairy products. My student Carly Rae Jepsen, the artist who recorded the song "Call Me Maybe," is one of many who owe their rattle-free voices to cutting back on milk, cheese, and yogurt. For a substantial number of my students, eating dairy products is a troublemaker, and because this is such a common problem, I think it's worth experimenting to see if avoiding dairy products will help you.

Medically, it's unclear how or why dairy products increase the production of mucus in your air passages and intestinal tract. One theory is that in order to digest dairy products, the body secretes specific pancreatic juices and, at the same time, releases more mucus into the air passages. Without getting any more technical, let me simply add my voice to the millions who see dairy products as problematic for vocalists and wholeheartedly advise restraint in this area.

If I'm working with a professional musician on the road who tells me, "I can't survive without my cheese pizza," I'm sympathetic. After all, we're talking about a major food group for the rock 'n' roll industry. So I try to suggest a compromise. I think it's OK to stop off at a pizza place, if that's what you like to do, but get the pasta with tomato sauce (tomatoes are excellent phlegm fighters) instead of the giant wheel topped with mozzarella.

If calcium is a concern, look for alternate sources. Broccoli is a great one. Your voice will thank you, and the rest of your body will too.

Hot drinks are so soothing! They're good for the voice, right?

Many people believe that a nice hot cup of tea is comforting to the voice. But even after you remove the caffeine, the lemon, the honey, and the sugar, you still have a problem: the heat. The temperature of any fluid affects the size of the tissue it comes in contact with. Heat causes blood vessels to dilate (open up), allowing the liquid portion of the blood to leak into tissue spaces, which causes swelling. (Cold, on the other hand, causes blood vessels to constrict, lowering the amount of fluid in the tissue and causing it to dry.) Even though the liquid you drink goes nowhere near the vocal cords, they're affected because all the blood vessels in that area—head, neck, and throat—respond to the heat of your tea.

If you want to be in great voice, drink cool water, or warm decaffeinated tea, but try to avoid both piping-hot and iced drinks.

Someone told me that red meat was bad for my voice. Is that true?

When you eat red meat, or any heavy meal, your body diverts blood to your stomach and intestines to aid in digestion. This takes blood away from the muscles you use to speak or sing. Digestion is energy intensive, and while it's in progress, there's less energy available to the throat and related muscles.

On days when you really need your voice, have something light to eat. That way your body can focus on producing sound, not be diverted by breaking down food.

Are you kidding? I can't do all this. I didn't sign up for a diet makeover!

Every body is different. You may be one of the lucky few who can eat a whole cheese pizza, wash it down with a couple of glasses of lemonade, and see no effects at all on your voice. But if too much phlegm is coming between you and a voice you can trust, I hope you'll do an experiment: Add more water to your diet. If you can't drink a half gallon, drink three more glasses of water today than you did yesterday. Try cutting back on caffeine. See what happens when you reduce citrus or sodas. Give yourself a vacation from milk and cheese. You needn't do everything at once—play with the variables and see what works best for you. Only you can determine the benefit you're gaining from these changes.

And if you can't make a long-term change, think about making short-term shifts when you need to count on your voice for an important job or performance. If you want to sound great on Wednesday, enjoy your dairy foods the weekend before, but cut way back from Sunday night through Wednesday. As you cut back on dairy, increase the amount of water you're drinking. By the time you step into the spotlight, you'll be able to concentrate on presenting your material rather than worrying that you're clearing your throat too much.

Ultimately, I can't tell you what to eat and drink, but I will tell you this: Hundreds of my students have taken these suggestions to heart, and they've got the clear voices to show for it.

What should I do if I wake up hoarse?

First, swallow. Does your throat hurt when you do? If so, you may have an infection that needs treatment. I don't advise doing any exercises when it hurts you to swallow. Instead, rest your voice. Limit the amount you speak to what's absolutely necessary, remember your diaphragmatic breathing, and see your doctor.

For all other levels of hoarseness—the days you wake up sounding extremely scratchy or gravelly and the sound persists for more than an hour but your throat doesn't hurt when you swallow: You might be dealing with edema—swelling of the vocal cords as a result of minor vocal abuse. Maybe you used your voice improperly at a ball game or in an argument. Whatever the cause, the problem can be fixed by doing the general exercises.

As I've mentioned, the best thing you can do to reduce swelling of the cords is the low-larynx sound, so add it to the exercises. Start with the one-octave exercise, using the normal sound of your voice, then do the exercise again, adding the Yogi Bear sound. It may seem odd, especially if you're used to going silent anytime you feel hoarse, but this is therapy time. Do the exercises in this way for about ten minutes, then start removing the low-larynx sound. I'll bet that you'll feel much better. If not, keep doing the low-larynx sound all the way through the general warm-up routine. If your voice is stronger, keep your voice in good shape for the rest of the day by doing a quick review of the problem-solving techniques you used to correct your particular vocal problems. Don't let yourself fall into old habits that add gravelly, brassy, or airy qualities to your voice and strain it in the process. Don't forget to speak up!

If you reach the end of the general warm-up and still feel hoarse, you've done everything you can by yourself and there must be a medical reason your cords are still swollen. Be gentle with your voice the rest of the day. Don't talk unless you need to, don't yell, and don't forget your technique: be sure not to use airy tones or whisper, and check in to be sure you're breathing diaphragmatically. Then, the next day start right back in using low-larynx sounds on the general warm-ups.

I've performed vocal-exercise first aid for many singers and speakers with important meetings or performances that just couldn't be canceled, and I can assure you that if you use the technique I described above, "miracles" are the rule, not the exception.

I met John Gray, the best-selling author of *Men Are from Mars, Women Are from Venus* under the tensest circumstances imaginable.

He was about to start filming a three-day seminar that would be turned into a series of videotapes for a new television infomercial. Hundreds of thousands of dollars had already been spent on sets, cameras, and crews, and the cameras were ready to roll. There was just one problem: John's voice was almost completely gone.

By the time my plane landed and I got to the hotel where he was staying, it was thirty minutes till showtime. I listened to him speak and could tell that his cords were inflamed and swollen, so we started in immediately on the low-larynx exercises. Within about ten minutes he had 40 percent more voice than we started with. I asked him to speak a few more lines and noticed that his voice was airy, definitely a problem that would dry out his already troubled cords. We solved this problem quickly the way I've shown you, primarily by using thick-cord sounds like nay and nah, and using googs and gugs to regulate the air. We also increased his volume. And finally, I showed him the basics of diaphragmatic breathing.

In about twenty minutes he had recovered 90 percent of his voice, and he sailed through the next few days.

You've got a powerful, and healing, set of tools in the techniques you've learned so far. Don't hesitate to use them. It's cheaper, easier, and more effective than popping a lozenge or buying a throat spray when you're hoarse.

So what about those lozenges and throat sprays? My friends swear by them.

I don't think you should rely on them. What your vocal cords need is moisture, and they're not getting enough of it from these products. When you suck on a lozenge, most of the benefit comes from swallowing. As I've mentioned, the movement of swallowing actually helps to lubricate the cords slightly. Water, free from the tap, is a better solution. I also find that people run into trouble especially with products that numb the throat because they don't address the cause of the problem; in fact, they mask it.

When you see throat sprays made especially for singers, keep in mind that they're mostly just water, with additives like eucalyptus.

I've nothing against eucalyptus, but the real effect of the spray comes from the water you inhale. It certainly wouldn't do you any good to drink a concoction like this.

I also see people chewing gum, thinking that it helps keep the throat moist. This, too, is a misconception. There's no moisture in the gum itself—you supply the moisture, and your mouth tries to help by producing more saliva. That can throw you out of balance, and create problems rather than solve them.

Save your money. I recommend vocal exercises and plain water. If I do find a lozenge that works, I'll put my name on it.

I've heard that spending time in wet saunas is really great for the voice—is that true?

Wet sauna. Sounds good, doesn't it? All that steam must be doing something fabulous for your vocal cords. Well, I wish it were true, but remember what happens when you sit in a sauna or a whirlpool: you sweat, becoming dehydrated. Making your body lose water only takes moisture from the cords, and that's hard on them and your voice.

Next you're going to say humidifiers are bad....

Humidifiers, I'm glad to tell you, are wonderful. Sitting in front of a cool mister and breathing is great for your voice. I like cool misters more than the hot, though if you already have a hot one, that's fine. When you inhale, water droplets actually do come in contact with the vocal cords and topically moisten the tissues. It feels wonderful— and it is. Some high-tech Japanese companies make small handheld humidifiers with attachments that fit over your nose and mouth like an oxygen mask. If you see one, get it.

Most of the time, by the way, I suggest using a humidifier only when you are feeling vocally under the weather. The rest of the time, the body should do quite well keeping the cords hydrated, especially now that you are drinking more water. Please remember to clean the unit often, when you've been using it, to keep bacteria and fungus from building up.

Someone told me that swimming wrecks your voice—could that be right?

Swimming is great exercise, but chlorine can irritate the linings of the nose, mouth, and throat. I know you're not drinking the pool water, but you can't help but ingest a little when you move your head in and out as you breathe. Watch for irritation, and drink a lot of water if you're a swimmer.

You haven't mentioned smoking....

Let me start by telling you how smoking affects the vocal cords (we'll skip all of its other well-documented negative effects). Remember that there are two openings in the throat, one for water and so forth and one for air, and because of that, the vocal cords don't get moistened directly when you drink water. But when you inhale anything—cigarettes, cigars, pot—the smoke goes straight to the cords. Take a drag and a hot, chemical-filled cloud begins to dry up the natural moisture there, reversing most of the good work you've already done.

No amount of smoking is healthy for the cords. I tell people that if they want to study with me, they have to stop smoking. I do have some students who are legitimately dealing with their serious addictions by cutting back. But in my heart of hearts, I believe that singing and smoking are opposite functions, and if you want to sing well, or to speak well, you must make the change and quit. Lots of smokers point to Frank Sinatra as an example of a person who could light up the stage while he kept lighting up, but I can guarantee that if Frank had quit, he would have had a hundred times more voice at the end of his life than he wound up with. You say he was good? I say he could have been a lot better—and that's the level that interests and satisfies me.

The key point is that any smoked inhalant, whether cigarettes, cigars, or pot, directly irritates the vocal cords with heat and chemicals. It also damages the lungs and eventually decreases the amount of air available for singing or speech.

I want to make one note concerning cocaine. It is a powerful vasoconstrictor and can limit the supply of blood to the tissues to the point that they actually die. Imagine what coke is doing to your throat if it can burn a hole in your nose. You can sing when you're high, but the long-term effects of pot and coke will send your voice straight into an early retirement, if the life problems don't.

My voice is no good in the morning. Is that common?

A lot of singers and speakers are adamant about not wanting to make appearances in public or the office in the early morning because they think their voices don't "wake up" until much later. Actually, their voices would be fine at any hour if they used my consistent and effective way of warming them up. A number of my students are dancers, and some of them don't get out of bed without stretching. If you rely on your voice to sound great, you need to build a little vocal stretching into your day.

The real reason our voices often sound lower in the morning is that fluids collect in the tissues of the throat from lack of use, mucus builds up, and the throat is dry from mouth breathing during the night. When the cords are dry, they don't move as well, and in order to make higher pitches, the cords need to move together and dampen. Until they can, you sound low.

Can I warm up by singing songs?

It's a bit of an old wives' tale that you can warm up your voice by simply singing songs. Actually, if you knew a song that went from chest voice to middle to head without building pressure, that would start the ball rolling in the right direction. But most songs aren't structured that way, and without the help of technique, people can't get through them without straining. The general exercises, though, offer a fail-safe warm-up that puts your voice in great shape, so you don't have to worry about it for the rest of the day. You don't have to do the whole warm-up. Just five or ten minutes, starting with gug, will get the engine running.

I know you've got things to do, kids to dress, breakfast to wolf down. But you may want to set aside time before work so you're in top form for your first phone call. This kind of thing can be fun if you just change your mind-set about it. You'll enjoy yourself more if you say, "I love doing this—can't wait to practice. It makes me feel good," instead of "That's a chore. I don't want to do it." It sounds funny, but you might get the boost you need by describing your brief warm-up time in a new way: "Today I'm empowering my voice." "I'm doing my vocal strengthening." "I'm a vocal goddess." If it brings a smile to your face, it'll probably make warming up easier.

I work weird hours—does that harm my voice?

Some of the artists I work with have wild schedules. I got a glimpse of this when I traveled with Eminem. On that tour I was coaching the warm-up acts, Papa Roach and Xzibit, as well, and I basically kept the same hours as the performers. The schedule was grueling: They might finish a show at eleven or twelve, but then it was time for meeting and greeting—talking to the press, executives, backstage folks, as well as fans who wanted autographs. It was typically 3:00 A.M. before we got on the bus, and after the excitement of performing, no one wanted to sleep. We'd get into the next town at six or seven, and that's when we'd go to sleep, getting up again around noon.

This kind of routine is very hard on the voice. In fact, any schedule that keeps you talking more than twelve hours a day takes its toll. If your voice were perfect, you could speak effortlessly nonstop, but for most of us humans, any amount of vocal work—speaking or singing—beyond twelve hours pushes us into vocal twilight time, when our voices are susceptible to the greatest damage. Your whole body is tired, and you're probably more dehydrated. If your schedule is crazy, try to give your voice a break after that twelve-hour mark. My best recommendation, though, is to get enough sleep. It doesn't matter all that much when you get your seven or eight hours in, but you need it. Vocal wear and tear is cumulative, and rest is a great way to recover. A biological clock sets physical and mental changes in motion as the sun sets and the moon appears, slowing your body down to prepare for sleep. The best way to keep this natural process from affecting you adversely is to get adequate rest and take excellent care of your body.

Do I have to be as big as a house to sing opera?

We've seen so many zaftig divas that it's common to think a bigger stomach means a bigger voice. That's a huge fallacy. Increased body fat has no positive effects on the way you sound. It makes the body work harder, and it doesn't do anything to change important factors like the capacity of your lungs. No, you don't need greater body mass to achieve fabulous vocal resonance. You need great technique, and dedication to developing it.

I'm sure my child's got vocal talent. What do I do now?

Over the years, I've worked with students of just about every age. Every child can sing, and those who love to will receive extra benefit from exposure to music and good technique. If a small child wants to take lessons, and has a sufficient attention span to focus on a teacher for twenty or thirty minutes, you might want to give lessons a shot. I'd suggest letting your child listen to the audio exercises on the website with you and join you in imitating sounds. (I'll talk more about this later in this chapter.) You'll get a chance to impart solid technique in a way that suits your son or daughter—a little at a time. Just hearing the sounds will help. There's no need for perfection. You'll know you're getting it right if both of you are laughing and enjoying yourselves.

Many child psychologists have argued that it's potentially damaging to tell a child that there's a right and a wrong way to sing, and some experts believe that parents ought to reserve their comments, except for a hug at the end and an encouraging "Louder, honey," along the way. I understand the point of that advice—lasting harm can come from critiquing a child with statements like "You're straining. That's bad. You're bad," or "Too bad you're tone deaf," or "Let's not think about singing anymore. How would you like to try the tuba?" But I believe that there are warm, loving, positive ways to expose a child to the basics of music and solid vocal technique. To stick with the "louder, honey" school of vocal coaching for a diva in diapers limits a child's perspective and possibilities.

I've worked with my daughter, Madison, since before she was born, and I'd like to share a few of the lessons we've learned. I hope they'll inspire you to share your own love of music and singing with your child. Broad exposure to music, to your own good technique, and to lessons that come in the form of play can make a lasting difference to a young person who's just discovering his or her instrument.

Starting Young

Doctors have told us for years that children in the womb hear sounds from the external environment, and legions of expectant mothers and fathers have talked and sung to their unborn babies. I was curious about the effect of such conversations and lullabies, so for several months before Madison was born, I'd put my head next to my wife's abdomen at the same time every day and sing the baby the same three songs. I hoped that those songs would somehow be meaningful to her, and a week after she was born I put that early exposure to the test. I heard her crying, and to comfort her, I decided to sing the three songs I'd been piping in. Her reaction was dramatic. She didn't sing along, of course, but she stopped crying immediately, looked directly at me, and seemed extremely happy. It looked like recognition to me. I had sung other songs to her since she arrived and had never gotten that response.

Perhaps I was a little zealous about teaching her music. From the day she got home from the hospital, I'd set her next to the piano and sing a few minutes' worth of scales. As I played and sang, I would sing out the letter names of the notes I was hitting. We also took care to fill her environment with music, playing children's songs and classical music in the house and even in the car.

By the time she was one and a half, she was singing continually. And by the time she was two, she was singing along to the Disney classics. She'd wander into a room as Belle from *Beauty and the Beast*, transform into the Little Mermaid, swim around a bit, and exit as Snow White. I had ended my little experiment in exposing her to music long before, but she had, on her own, become the diva of the house. People would hear her voice, on pitch and connected from chest to head, with vibrato, and stare in disbelief.

Yes, thankfully she's got great genes, and that's a wonderful head start. But I know that it takes nurture, as well as nature, to make a singer. Without the music that was put so easily within her grasp, her talents might have remained dormant, along with the obvious pleasure she gets from singing.

I took a much more relaxed approach to exposing my second child, Colin, to music. I didn't sing songs to him while he was still in the womb. I waited until he started asking me for bass lessons and piano lessons and guitar lessons and wanted to join a band. He's thirteen years old now, and driven by his own desire, he has the same love of music as his sister. Expose your little ones to music you love and that they enjoy. And don't be afraid to play. I taught Madison vibrato while we were watching the Cowardly Lion sing "If I Were King of the Forest" during *The Wizard of Oz*. When the song ended, I exaggerated the funny-sounding vibrato we'd just heard and asked if she could do it. Together for a moment or two, we both made the sound. I even shook my head so that she could put some kind of physicality together with the sound. Within a couple of days, she was singing vibrato perfectly, and not shaking anything. Did I really teach her how to do it? No. Did I open the right door? Yes.

Another way to open doors for a small vocalist is to let him or her study an instrument. Call me old-fashioned, but I believe the piano is the best choice for developing musical knowledge. Studying piano combines music theory, ear training, sight reading, hand-eye coordination, and rhythm practice. It's a pretty unbeatable package. Yes, I know I've said that you don't need to play an instrument or even read music to be a successful singer. But in this virtual reality, where we can plot out ways to give children the best grounding possible, I'd have to say that music lessons are an advantage. If your child is just not interested in piano, any instrument will do. Understanding how music works will make it easier for your child star to navigate the world of notes, structure, and imagination that's encoded on a sheet of music.

Let your children sing with you, and if they want to imitate the sounds they hear on the audio recordings, let them try. Just remember that play and joy are the keys to a child's discovery of music and voice. When Madison and I sang along with the Cowardly Lion, we were just having fun. It was a game, not a singing lesson. She didn't feel any pressure from me to achieve certain sounds. We just enjoyed ourselves — and learned something in the process.

Kids and the Exercises

Everyone can eventually have chest, middle, and head voice, but in children perhaps five and under, both boys and girls, it sounds as if only two voices are present. The vocal cords are still changing, and they're simply not long enough to produce three distinct colorations. Instead, there's a definite lower voice that I still call chest, and a higher area that is not completely head but not thick enough to be a real middle. As the child gets a bit older but has not yet reached puberty, he or she will begin to show signs of having all three voices. To work with my exercises with your children, both boys and girls, use the female exercises, which are set in the right range for maximum benefit. Don't expect to hear middle if your child is under five, just let your very young singers move back and forth from the low voice to the higher one. The aim, here, is to break down the walls that could otherwise keep them locked in either chest or head voice. As they smoothly work through the crossover points, and get a little older, their voices will be making way for the middle that will miraculously appear as they grow. Until then, the single most valuable thing you can do is to make sure that they don't get caught in chest voice, or strain. And, of course, make it fun.

Only You Can Decide What Level You Want to Reach

Some of the suggestions I've made in this chapter no doubt seemed extreme. A half gallon of water a day? Cutting out dairy foods? Singing to babies in the womb? Yet these are the tested techniques that have resulted in excellence, for the professionals I teach, for my own family, and for the students who are just starting out. I hope you'll take this information and run with it. Experiment. Eliminate the physical obstacles that are standing between you and a fabulous voice. You'll transport yourself—and maybe your lucky child—to the next level.

· 10 ·

Essential Extras for Singers

A VAST WORLD can open up for you when you have full command of chest, middle, and head voice. Like a violinist who's mastered the scales and technical aspects of the instrument, you're ready to step into the realm of musicality—making a deep, full connection between the music you're singing, your audience, and you. At this point your own individual voice, which reflects your personality and your sensibilities as well as the basic equipment you've been blessed with, takes center stage.

In this chapter I'd like to add one additional vocal coloration—vibrato—to your repertoire, then focus on the process of laying claim to a singing style that's all your own. There are whole volumes to be written on developing style as a performer, but I want you to have at least a taste of how I teach my students to transform themselves from Lady Gaga or Chris Martin wanna-bes into strikingly original singers who sound inspiringly like…themselves.

That may sound funny to you, but I'm absolutely serious. My goal, in this book, has been to make possible the kind of genuine expression that comes from connecting great technique to your own quirks and feelings, strengths, and soulfulness. You can't hope to find satisfaction or success as a pale imitation of someone else's unique vocal package. I want you to sound like you. It's the most profound gift you have to offer as a singer—when you learn to unwrap it.

Finally, I'd like to give you some fundamentals of handling yourself onstage. There aren't a lot of rules, and when you're familiar with the basics, you'll be ready to tailor your own presentation to your material and message.

Secrets of Great Vibrato

Once you've mastered the art of hitting notes and holding them, it's natural to want to color them with feeling. One of the most commonly used shadings is vibrato, a wavelike oscillation of the pitch that you'll often hear when your favorite singers sustain notes. For many a new singer, vibrato is a mystery. People feel as though you're either born with it or you'll never have it, and they don't quite know how to get from the straight, solid sound of notes that are purely held to the more intriguing sound of vibrato's rich waves. They can sometimes produce the sound with elaborate manipulations, but it feels forced.

Actually, all vibrato involves manipulation, and the secrets of great vibrato lie in knowing how it works, what makes it sound the most pleasing, and how to make it feel more natural and effortless. It's easy to veer off into strange, and downright funny, sounds when you're venturing into this technique on your own, but with the simple tricks I'll show you, you'll be able to discover the essence of vibrato without the amusing add-ons. Let me show you how it sounds on audio 30 on the website, then I'll run through a few facts.

How it works. When you speak or sing, your vocal cords normally move at a rate that ranges from a hundred to a thousand vibrations per second. The tension on the cords determines the pitch, and when that tension is perfect—neither stressfully tight nor too loose—a slow secondary vibration begins to develop. This secondary movement causes the sound to move in a wave at the speed of five to six vibrations per second. That's what we hear as vibrato. You can see the very same kind of vibration if you try this experiment: Pick up a sheet of paper and put one corner in your mouth. Now blow, directing even amounts of air down both the front and the back sides of the paper. If you watch the far corner of the sheet, you'll see that it's moving up and down, and if you could measure the movement, you'd find that it's traveling at the rate of five to six vibrations per second. These very regular up-and-down movements—of the paper and the cords—are created by something physicists call the Bernoulli effect.

Without getting too technical, the Bernoulli effect reflects the way the flow of air or a fluid across a surface changes the pressure above and below the surface. Changes in pressure cause the waves. You might be interested to know that it's the Bernoulli effect that allows you to roll your rs when you speak a language like Italian or Spanish. The effects of airflow across your tongue enable it, too, to move a lot faster than you can move it in normal speech.

What makes vibrato sound good—and bad. The fascinating thing about vibrato is that it is great for the cords, since it is a product of a perfect amount of tension, and it only sounds right when you're producing it at the right speed—five or six vibrations per second. Some artists, like Madonna or Stevie Nicks, have a vibrato that's on the faster side, and both have been hugely successful. But I want you to start learning vibrato at a more natural speed. When you master that, you can go faster, if that's the sound you want. It's tricky, though. Vibrato that's too fast all the time can make a singer sound nervous, or even a little sheeplike. Too slow is just painful. It worked well for Bert Lahr when he played the Cowardly Lion, but mostly we tend to associate it with old people singing off-key in the choir. If you don't pay attention to your vibrato, it does have the tendency to slow down as you age, and if you use it at half speed you'll sound old, wobbly, and vocally abused. I've had students in their eighties and nineties who sounded as if they were still in their twenties, so I don't expect voices to implode with age—as long as you use good technique. As you work with vibrato, be sure to keep it up to speed, and don't let it tag you with a label or an image you don't want.

Where it fits. Many students think that vibrato belongs in opera or musical theater—period—and they've decided that if you're not Sarah Brightman, or Idina Menzel, you don't need it. But I believe that vibrato will tastefully fit with every style of music, from rock to country to gospel and yodel. It doesn't belong everywhere, and it's a condiment, not the main course—but it's a flavor you need. Don't skip it. When you learn to control the sound of vibrato, you are getting a great lesson in how to control the way air leaves the body. When you experience correct vibrato, you're feeling the correct balance of air and cords in a stable, healthy instrument.

Don't Shake It — You'll Break It

If you've found your way to vibrato on your own, I'd like to be sure you're doing it correctly, not producing an approximation that's going to harm you. A rule of thumb is that you don't have to shake any part of your body to make vibrato, and if you are, something's not quite right.

Have you ever seen singers shaking their lower jaws up and down in pursuit of vibrato? Whitney Houston was quite famous for this, and a number of other prominent singers use this technique to get the sound, but it's not great for the body. It creates a huge amount of tension in the throat, and the constant movement of the jaw makes the powerful jaw muscles tense. Some of them are connected to the larynx, and when they overwork, they can raise the larynx and partially close the back of the throat. Use this technique for long, and you might wind up with not only a sore jaw but an impaired ability to produce the sounds you want. Worse, the vibrato you make this way doesn't create even waves of sound, and it can end up sounding harsh and shaky.

Don't beat yourself up if you've been doing this. You just imitated the wrong people. When you watch videos of a superstar like Whitney Houston and notice that she was shaking her jaw to the tune of millions of records sold, you figure she must have been doing something right. And indeed she was — she's just not a great role model for the way you should make vibrato.

Are you shaking your stomach in and out to make this sound? Some people shake low, below the belly button, and others aim higher, from the belly button to the bottom of the ribs. Either way, if you're doing this, you're creating a sizable amount of tension around your stomach, and you're not getting the kind of vibrato you really want. There's no hope of moving your stomach in and out fast enough to create the six oscillations per second you need for perfect vibrato, so using your stomach as an aid generally produces a slow, labored vibration that adds unwelcome years to the sound of your voice.

Doing It Right

If you just hold a note and think vibrato, believe me—nothing much will happen. It takes a special kind of effort to release the bursts of air that produce the wave effect. So chances are you'll have to make some big changes in the way you feel and think before you find the right sound. Try the following exercises, which will escort you right to the edge of a vibrant vibrato, and as you play with them, go all the way. Exaggerate everything! In the beginning, you'll feel a little silly, but let yourself try the over-the-top approach. If you're feeling self-conscious, now might be the perfect time to find a remote part of the island on which to practice.

Helper Number One: The Handshake Point

Though I've said that I'm against shaking anything to make vibrato, when you're starting out, I bend the rule a little to help you experience how it's supposed to feel in your body. Ready? Stand up and extend your dominant hand as though you were going to shake hands with someone. Instead of keeping your fingers in a handshake position, close your hand, keeping just your index finger pointing out. Now pretend that you are shaking hands with a huge polar bear who is a thousand times stronger than you are. Move your hand hard and fast. As you make this motion, sing *eeeee* and try to match the sound of your voice with the motion of your hand. It should come out in little bursts: *ee-ee-ee-ee-ee*. Let your voice take on a rhythmic pulsing.

Concentrate on the back part of the roof of your mouth as you're making the sound, especially the place where the top of your mouth comes together with the back of your tongue. This is where you should be feeling bursts of air. Repeat the exercise and see if you can feel the air pulsating there. Forget about sounding funny. Just concentrate on making your voice move up and down like your hand.

After you get used to this, try stopping your hand motion and see if you can still make the vibrato sound. Keep trying. And when you're using your hand, remember to keep its movement quite fast. You'll need that speed later, as this manipulation evolves to an effortless vibrato.

Helper Number Two: The Belly Dance

Make a fist and place it at the top of your stomach, where your ribs come together. Cover that fist with your other hand. Now say *eeeeeeeeee*, and as you do, push your hands in and out in a rapid pulsing motion to send quick bursts of air to the back of your throat. Once again, you should hear the smooth *eeee* sound break into a vibrato-like *ee-ee-ee-ee*. Keep your hands moving in and out rapidly, repeat the sound, and pay attention to where the air is pulsing in your throat: at the juncture where the roof of your mouth meets the back of your tongue.

All I'm trying to do is to help you get acquainted with how big vibrato feels in your throat—it's not a small thing. It takes a lot of air bursts to create the effect. Remember that as we manipulate the air and sound, it's tough, at first, to get the proper speed of six oscillations per second, and it may feel as though you're making phony sounds in completely unnatural ways. But once the body begins to understand how vibrato feels, a miracle happens. The voice begins to feel as though it's making vibrato on its own.

The main reason vibrato ever feels natural is related to speed. Early on, your vibrato is likely to be too fast or too slow, but as you get used to playing with it, the air and cords find the perfect relationship, and the cords find the perfect tension. At that point, vibrato just happens—and you'll feel as though you were born with it.

Making It Yours

Once you've mastered vibrato, play with it. Six oscillations per second is generally ideal, but if you're a high-strung person, your vibrato may mirror that energy and be a bit faster than the norm. Conversely, if you're calm and laid-back, your vibrato may be better a

SET YOUR VOICE FREE

touch slower. Try to get control of this sound, and learn to be in charge of every beat. When you want it fast, speed it up. When slow is the right effect, you know what to do.

Many people think that vibrato shouldn't come in until the end of a sustained note, and quite often my students start a note straight out and add vibrato halfway in. You can hear the slightly odd effect on audio 31 on the website. Who's responsible for this strange technique? Frank Sinatra, who would sing "I did it my way," adding just a touch of vibrato to the end of "way." You can do this later if you want to, but first learn to make the sound from the beginning of your chosen word all the way to the end, even and strong.

One last habit to avoid is closing your teeth to make vibrato. You can hear what this sounds like on audio 32. I find this sound very unattractive, and I think it's a good idea to keep your mouth open when you're trying to reach your audience. It will help your overall sound if you remember not to close your mouth until you've finished singing a whole word or phrase.

The Elements of Style: Putting Your Stamp on the Music

Within a couple of seconds of hearing Shakira, Ed Sheeran, Taylor Swift, or Drake, you know exactly who you're listening to. They've got style—their voices have a personal character that sets them apart. Style is perhaps the single most important factor in determining whether a professional singer succeeds or fails, and it's the element that often feels the most elusive, even to the most proficient performers. It's easy to say "Be original," but many singers have set out on the road to uniqueness only to get caught in a limiting copycat sound. That doesn't mean they did anything wrong—only that they stopped too soon.

Imitation is actually the key to developing your own style. The best way to shape a personal sound, strange as it may be, is to be able to sound exactly like someone else. There's really no such thing as something that's never been heard before. The masters in every realm of the music world all began by imitating their idols, and so should you. If you follow the program I've developed for my students over the years, I promise that you'll come out on the other side with a sound all your own.

Stage one. Start with your favorite singer, a vocalist you love for the range and positive qualities of his or her voice. Study this voice intensely. In fact, immerse yourself in it as though you were trying to learn another language. Listen to it until you're familiar with every nuance, every habit, every flourish and breath. Then sing along, imitating as closely as you can. Your goal is to *be* your dream singer. Use a recorder to help you impartially evaluate how close you're coming to the mark—it will give you an entirely new perspective and allow you to hear with the ears of an outsider who's listening in. This process may take you weeks, but stay with it until you've got that voice down cold.

This is what I call stage one imitation, and it's something every aspiring singer does intuitively. Like a lot of female students in the summer of 2014, my student Emily was taken with Taylor Swift and her hit "Shake It Off," which seemed to be playing every time you turned on the radio. Emily was crazy for the sound and studied all of Taylor's albums. Soon she was a walking, talking Taylor wanna-be, and no matter what she sang, it came out in a semi-Swift rendition. While she was in this phase, I encouraged her to sing all her material as Taylor would. And when she'd gotten as far as she could, I asked her to pick another artist and do the same thing.

Stage two. Mastering the sounds of a *series* of artists is the key to successfully developing your own style. You may be a passionate fan of Rihanna or The Weeknd, but when you've got either mastered, drop them and move on. That's stage two imitation: broadening your repertoire. Your voice may be very different from the one you're trying to capture, but as you memorize the notes and words, you are subconsciously storing the specific sounds of that singer's voice. And as you move from artist to artist, giving each one your full energy and attention, what you're really doing is building a library of vocal sounds that are varied and distinct.

At stage two, I want you to cover some stylistic ground. Copy an

R&B artist. Copy Carrie Underwood or Keith Urban. Copy Elvis or Aretha Franklin. Choose your favorites, but hit a range of genres. And with each one, do the same thing. Listen, soak up the sounds, and imitate until you can mimic them. No matter how much time and energy you spend impersonating each of the artists you choose, you'll never sound exactly like any one of them. Because you have a different instrument, the closest you'll ever come is to pick up the flavor, the nuances, the overall resonance and character of your models. But those are great raw materials. Be diligent about collecting them.

Stage three. You've stocked your library with impersonations of many of your favorite singers, and you can, at will, sing like Jessie J, move right into Beyoncé, then Miley Cyrus and Carrie Underwood. When you sing, however, people are most certainly aware that you are trying to imitate a particular person. They hear you move from one recognizable singer's sound to another. No, they're not thinking of you as an original stylist at this point, because you're coming across as more of a vocal impersonator. And that's OK for right now.

In stage three imitation, all we want to do is become proficient at moving from one artist's sound to another. Practice doing this by taking a song you love and splitting it up, so you sing the first verse as one singer, the chorus as another singer, and each subsequent verse as yet another singer until you reach the end. Yes, it's odd, but it's a pivotal skill you're developing. And it is the doorway to stage four, where real originality takes place.

Stage four. Let's say you've made it through the first three stages of imitation. You easily impersonate the artists you like. You sing uptempo R&B like Jessie J, country like Miranda Lambert, ballads like Lana Del Rey, and so on. But it seems pointless. You still seem to have no style or originality, and you can't see how this hodgepodge you now possess makes any difference.

That's where my student Annika found herself one frustrating summer. Annika had worked her way through all the homework I've given you, and she had become incredibly proficient at copying other singers. But every time she recorded her voice in the studio, she hated what she heard. One session she sounded like a bad imitation of Madonna, and the next she was a cartoon version of Iggy Azalea. She just couldn't find the voice that was all hers, and her producer didn't know what to suggest—all he could tell her was that the magic was missing.

So one day she just gave up. "Forget it," she told herself. "I simply accept that I have no style at all. There is nothing in my voice that sets me apart as one of a kind. I accept that. In the studio today, I'm just going to sing it straight ahead. I'm not going to put anything into it. They'll all laugh, and I'll just take the ridicule."

And that's what she did. She sang her song as her genuine self—just plain, no embellishments—stopped, and waited for the chuckling to begin. She was astonished when the people listening to her went crazy. Everyone said she had just given her best performance ever, and they asked why she had never sung that way before. Somehow, when she least expected it to happen, she found the style she had been looking for.

Stage four of the imitation process is where everything you've done comes together. Like Annika, if you do the hard work of imitating your heroes, your brain and your talent will process all the information you've provided them and create a new whole that's much greater than the sum of the individual parts. The real Annika was a blend of everything she had learned about vocal technique, everything she had absorbed by copying, and everything she was. And she sounded great.

Annika's story is far from unusual. Over the past twenty-five years I've heard it thousands of times. Each time, the singer has worked hard at copying voices, then seemed to get stuck in a frustrating place where nothing sounded original. Then, after much struggle and effort, the person has given up the hope of finding even a molecule of originality in his or her voice and dropped any attempt to dress it up. Each time, style has appeared suddenly, surprisingly—wonderfully.

Can you skip the work and the struggle and cut straight to style? Nope. It just doesn't happen that way. You need to lay the best foundation you can. We never know when or where all the work we've done will fall into place, but I assure you it does, and the results are magical. I highly recommend the path of imitation if you're searching for your true style. If you're exceptionally good at imitating, your journey will be shorter and less frustrating. And if not, don't worry. Keep practicing, keep listening, and keep imitating anyway. Nothing you take in will be wasted.

Phrasing: *Singing It Like You Mean It*

As you work to make the music your own, I'd like you to think about the way people really use words to communicate with each other. We pause, we stress certain words for emphasis, and we smooth the edges off words so that a question like "Would you like to go to the movies" actually comes out of our mouths sounding like "Would ya like t' go t' the movies." All these factors make us sound like people, instead of robots, and they make us sound believable.

But when we sing, a lot of the believability that naturally comes with speech is lost. A certain stiltedness creeps in, and to make things worse, the audience is skeptical. The moment they hear singing, their brains on some level think, "This isn't real—it's just a song," and they get ready to tune out the message. The challenge for a singer is to bridge the gap between the believable realm of speaking and the more artificial world of the song.

As I've mentioned, the master of this art was Frank Sinatra. When you listen to Frank sing, he makes you think he's telling you stories about his life, and that all of them are true. With every note, you feel the emotion. When he hurts, you hurt. When he's happy, you can't help but smile. He can reach right into your heart and communicate with you on any level he chooses. That's the goal, whether you're a rocker or a folk singer–songwriter. The key is to sing as though you were speaking.

Many developing singers move through songs in baby steps, note to note and word to word, and the result is, at best, mechanical. I'd like you to think in phrases and shape the song into the same patterns you use in normal, everyday speech.

Let me give you a simple exercise to help with this: Look at a piece of sheet music you're familiar with. Go ahead and speak the first lines of the song. You don't have to be Shakespeare; simply speak the words in a relaxed, conversational way. If you can, make a recording of yourself—you'll be able to use it for reference later.

Now go back and try to sing the words in the same way you spoke them. Go up and down with the melody, but try to make a connection between singing and speaking. If you need to, play back the recording of yourself reading the song and make pencil markings on your sheet music to remind you of how you said every word. When did you get louder or softer for emphasis? Which consonants did you punch up? Which were gentle? When did you stretch out a word and when did you clip it off? Try to put all these sounds into the song.

It's not always easy to do. The melody of the song seems to push you into a particular pattern that feels hard to break out of. But remember that all great singers use a song the way an adventurer uses a map. Most of the time they stay on the main road, but they leave themselves open to the smaller paths that could lead to someplace wonderful. You can do that too. Usually a great song suggests a particular phrasing, and the words are crafted so that they roll easily off the tongue. But there's always room for interpretation—you're not locked into anything. Experiment a bit and invite inspiration.

If you work with songs this way, recording yourself as you read the lyrics and making notations to remind you how you want to sing them back, you'll open the door to phrasing that's all your own and to sounds that communicate as intimately and naturally as speech.

Riffs: Bringing Out the Ornaments

As you move out from the note-at-a-time, word-by-word school of singing, you may find yourself wanting to add extra touches to the music itself. Some singers like to use the written note as a starting point and create little clusters of complementary notes around it. This grouping of notes is called a run or a riff. All you have to do is listen to ten seconds of Stevie Wonder or Aretha Franklin or Mariah Carey or Jessie J to know what I'm talking about—they embellish and embroider almost everything they sing.

SET YOUR VOICE FREE

When beginning singers come face-to-face with these acrobatic movements, they often shudder in terror. The masters move through riffs like race cars, and when you try to imitate them at full speed, the early results are bound to be messy and inaccurate. Too much speed too soon only leads you to the crash-and-burn school of voice. If you want to try riffing, start out with someone like Drake or Demi Lovato. I've noticed that they make riffs a bit more slowly than other performers, and that slightly reduced speed will help you out early on.

To start, listen repeatedly to the riff or run you're trying to learn. Then try to plunk out the notes with one finger on the keyboard. Go slowly, taking the time to figure out every single note in the pattern. Over and over, more and more slowly. When you feel that you have the pattern down on the keyboard, sing along with what you play, one note at a time. Don't be in a rush—keep the pace slow enough to be accurate. When you've learned the notes, stop playing the piano and begin to sing the riff over and over, making it a tiny bit faster each time. If you start to get sloppy, slow it back down.

If you can't play the notes on the piano, you can still use the same idea to learn. First listen, then imitate at a drastically reduced speed. Think of it as the slo-mo style of riffs and runs. Stay at that speed for a long while (maybe even as long as a few days), then start to increase the tempo.

Luther Vandross once said that some singers do riffs as if they're being paid by the note and need to cram in everything and the kitchen sink. It can reach the point of absurdity. I remember the first few times I heard the duet Mariah Carey did with Boyz II Men on "One Sweet Day." It was like listening to dueling riffs, and I don't think it was possible to discern the actual melody line.

But if you keep it sane, maintaining a basic number of simple riffs is important for the advanced singing student. Riffing is so much a part of gospel and R&B music that you have to do it if you want to legitimately sing that style. The skill is less important if you're in opera, musical theater, or country, or even if you're singing classic rock 'n' roll, but whatever you sing, give it a try—with a light touch, so you don't get frustrated. And when inspiration tells you that what your song needs is a riff, you'll have the skill at your disposal. The greatest little piece of advice I can give you on this subject is to slow down. Rushing won't get you there.

The Hunt for Great Material

No matter how much skill and style you have, you need great material if you want to showcase your talent. What does that mean? Let me state the obvious: It's a lot easier to sound original when you have original music. If you work on previously recorded songs, you're walled in by what the original artist did, and unless you're an accomplished arranger or have a great musical imagination, it's likely that your cover will sound like a partial imitation of the original. But the whole picture changes when an artist decides to work with music that's new. Ears perk up, especially in the music industry, which bases itself on the new songs played on the radio and streamed. That's why, if you want to succeed in the business, it's almost essential either to write or to cowrite your material or to find terrific new songs.

Acquiring potential hit songs is the most important "business" part of the music biz, and it's where the money is—the songwriter generally makes more profit on a record than the singer. So it's worth it to dip your toe into writing and see what happens.

I know that you're probably thinking, "Great. I'm just trying to learn how to sing right now, and the idea of becoming a hit songwriter is a bit more than I can bite off at this stage." That's fine. I want you to concentrate on your voice right now. But in chapter 13, I'll go into detail about how you can create your own material—or collaborate with others to do it.

As you're learning, remember that you can always seek original songs, too. Get out there and find a young writer who loves your voice and wants to be the gas for your engine. You'll be working with virgin songs that are just waiting for the imprint of your original style.

If you can't work with original songs, I want to suggest a tactic that's the flip side of imitation: reinvent a song. There are a couple of ways to do this. First, you can learn a song you've never heard before from the sheet music alone. Don't listen to another singer perform it, just plunk out the notes on a keyboard, or ask a friend who plays to help you. I know that learning a song takes a lot more time this way, but the rewards can be phenomenal.

You can also learn a song the usual way—by singing along with an artist—and then turn it inside out. Make a slow song fast or take a fast one down in speed. Change the melody or some of the words. The goal here is to shake things up. Once you've made major changes, you cut your ties to the standard rendition and put yourself in a place where you might feel more creatively open.

Give yourself as many opportunities as you can to imagine new sounds and to find them if you can. The song you develop with a buddy, or your country blues–cabaret rendition of a funk classic, might spark a vision of the way you want to sound and push you into a truly original space. Inspired? I've got more in chapter 11 on finding the sounds that will make you stand out.

Where Originality Counts—and Doesn't

Keep in mind that originality is embraced and expected in some realms of the music world and it's just not appreciated in others. If you're in opera or musical theater, the goal is not to sing differently from the norm but to copy it. In fact, voices with distinct character are most often weeded out rather than pushed up the ladder. In this kind of technique singing, everyone makes vibrato, each note is held to the maximum, and the focus is on the voice as structural instrument, not as a staging ground for vocal experiments.

Pop music opens up the territory and welcomes original sounds, but there, too, what's expected depends on what you're singing. Ballads—slow-tempo songs—are generally classically based: they're musically related to the straight-ahead tunes you hear in musical theater. That leads listeners to expect a certain easy, smooth, and peaceful sound. They want to get the words on first listening and to be soothed, not jarred by experimentation. Up-tempo songs, whatever the genre, give you more room to move away from sounds that are technically pristine and into those based on energetic emotion.

I hope you'll all want to develop a style of your own, but please tailor your expectations about originality and style to your chosen genre. It'll make things easier.

Of Course, It's Not Entirely about Singing

People ask me all the time what it takes to be a successful singer, by which they mean "a singer who's making loads of money." Though my specialty is vocal technique, and I stress the idea that great technique can lead you to a standout voice with an original sound, I have to admit that in reality the voice is simply one component of success.

At the beginning of my career a record company executive called me and asked me to work with a new artist he was developing. He told me that the guy was incredible and destined to be a huge star.

"Can he sing well?" I asked.

"Nope."

"Does he write the music or the lyrics?"

No.

"Does he play any instruments?"

Not one.

"What's his name?"

"Billy Idol," came the reply.

The record company was not that interested in Idol's natural musical talents. They realized that he had the right look, the right vibe for the time. And they were betting heavily that the young record-buying public would pick up on his animal magnetism and charisma. It was a bet that paid off handsomely. Billy Idol went on to sell millions of records worldwide.

Am I saying that music doesn't count? Of course not. Am I saying that style and charisma win out over talent? No. I just want to point out that there's a world beyond music that factors into stardom. Stagecraft and performance are arts all their own. If you're just starting out, I'd like to give you the briefest of introductions to those arts.

As you turn your attention to putting your talents out in the world, just remember that, Billy Idol aside, you're best poised to succeed in the music business if you've got the goods vocally. I've seen many singers build great, long-lasting careers on the confidence that comes from hard work and talent. That kind of confidence is resilient enough to keep you going through all the bumps, curves, and fads that the business inevitably throws in your path.

Stage Movement 101: A Primer

All stage movement can be reduced to a simple pattern, and when you know how to use it, you can simply and effectively maneuver in front of any audience anywhere. This basic format can be adapted to the biggest stage in town or the smallest coffee house in the world. Walk through the accompanying diagram with me and you'll have a reusable map that will guide you easily through any performance.

Point one. The beginning position, near the center of the stage, gives the audience its first chance to see and hear you. The moment you step up to the mike, it's important to establish a strong presence and command of the energy in the room. How do you do that? First, stand still. Many performers move around so much at the beginning of a song that the audience feels as though they're trying to catch a

STAGE MOVEMENT

glimpse of a UFO and get a look at the alien inside. Even if you're singing an up-tempo dance tune, you can still remain relatively stationary, with your feet in one area, while you move the rest of your body to the music. The goal here is to let the crowd make a few cognitive assessments. They deserve a moment or two to get a sense of who you are, what you're wearing, and what you look like. They also want to be able to figure out whether they know and like the song you're singing, how they feel about your voice and you, and whether they want to give you their attention. Ultimately they want to know: Can this performer and performance make me happy?

As you're looking down from the stage, if you've got an audience that's small enough for eye contact, direct your gaze just above their heads. You'll give the illusion of contact without the discomfort. Keep in mind that many songs are intense and emotionally charged, and an audience member may feel uncomfortable if you stare into his or her eyes and profess undying love. You're trying to wrap people in the song's emotion without intimidating or embarrassing them, so use direct eye contact sparingly as you move to each of your positions on the stage.

At point one on the stage, you're saying to the audience: "This is me. Give me a few minutes of your time and I know I can make you smile, or cry, or laugh, or feel what I feel."

When you've established yourself, the music will tell you when it's time to move to change position.

Point two. Every song has a story to tell. It offers a series of moments that unfurl like scenery out the window of a train, and as you listen, you'll notice that as it progresses, it moves in and out of a number of places and emotions. When you detect the first mood shift in the song—it may be the change from the intro to the verse, or verse to chorus, or it may simply be a new emotion bubbling up—it's time to move toward point two. (I've chosen to move to stage right on the diagram, but you can move toward either side of the stage.) As the music and lyrics make that first slight change, walk toward the right and focus your attention on the audience sitting on that side. You will be turning your body only slightly, so people sitting in the center and left will still see a part of your face and won't feel excluded.

Point three. As the song makes its next significant shift, change direction and walk toward the left side of the stage. Again, make sure that everyone in the room can still see a part of your face.

Point four. With the next shift, move back to center stage. You're now directly aligned with point one, but you're closer to the audience. They know you a bit better now and are ready to have you come closer, with no feeling of discomfort or threat. At this juncture, the song is probably near its conclusion.

Point five. Most songs will end at the fifth position, directly in line with points one and four but still closer to the crowd. This is the power position. You own the stage. You've conquered the back, the left, the right, and the front, and you've connected fully with the audience. Congratulations.

Points six through eight. Some songs are simply longer than others and require more movement. If you've covered the stage once and you still have more song to go, proceed to point six, a slight move to the right. From there, point seven once more addresses the left side. And point eight brings you back to center for a conclusion.

Does this seem too simple? Good! It's supposed to be, and the surprising thing is that all stage movements are loosely based on these directions. When you go to a huge rock concert and see Bruce Springsteen run to one side of the stage and jump up on a mammoth speaker to play and sing, he is at point two. As the music swells and he runs to the other side of the stage and throws himself out into the audience, he is simply at point three.

This plan will still work even if there is limited or no space at all to move. If you are performing in a space the size of a shoe box and you can hardly take a single step, you can still go through all of the points listed by moving your head in the correct directions or shifting your body toward the desired marks.

Because it's not always easy to figure out how to time your moves, let me take you through a simple song to illustrate how this timing works. Please sing along with me and walk through the steps on the diagram.

JINGLE BELLS

- **Point 1:** The song starts and we remain quite still to let the audience get to know us as we sing:
    Jingle bells! Jingle bells! Jingle all the way!
    Oh what fun it is to ride in a one-horse open sleigh.
    Oh! Jingle bells! Jingle bells! Jingle all the way!
    Oh what fun it is to ride in a one-horse open sleigh.
- **Point 2:** The song changes now to a different melody and feel, so we acknowledge that by moving:
    Dashing through the snow in a one-horse open sleigh,
    O'er the fields we go, laughing all the way;
- **Point 3:** The melody stays the same, so we decide to move a little to keep it interesting:
    Bells on bob-tail ring, making spirits bright;
    What fun it is to ride and sing a sleighing song tonight!
- **Point 4:** The melody returns to the place it started, so we move again:
    Jingle bells! Jingle bells! Jingle all the way!
    Oh what fun it is to ride in a one-horse open sleigh.
- **Point 5:** As the song concludes, we move to our last position:
    Oh! Jingle bells! Jingle bells! Jingle all the way!
    Oh what fun it is to ride in a one-horse open sleigh.

I didn't invent those changes in the music. They're built into the structure of the song, and you can hear distinctive shifts in any piece of music. All you need to do is pay attention to the natural points where the melody and lyrics move from place to place. Try singing any of your favorite tunes and mentally walk through the five or eight steps I've described. There are really no horribly wrong places to move. Just have fun and play with the pattern until you get the hang of it.

The Applause Is Not Just for You

When you perform or speak in front of a crowd, your singing or speaking is the gift you bring to the audience. At the end of the song or the performance or the speech, the audience's applause is its gift to you. So don't waste that moment or make your audience feel like you won't receive its gratitude. Many times, as soon as a singer finishes a song, and the last syllable of the last word comes out, he breaks out of character and disconnects from the audience by losing eye contact and moving offstage fast. Please don't do that. After you perform, stand still, look at the audience, and take in its applause. Some of you might be uncomfortable with this, but you must get over it. It insults your listeners when you won't accept their thanks.

Who Me, on a Stage?

It's one thing to sing in your room or map out your Temptations choreography in the garage, but I'm sure that more than a few of you felt a little chill every time I used the words *onstage* or *your audience* to help you imagine how to move while performing. It's scary for most of us to get up in front of people, lay our talent on the line, and hope that someone likes it. In fact, stage fright dogs even the most seasoned performers.

Most of my students are surprised to learn that I've never looked at stage fright as a negative. I see it as a natural part of performing— even a necessity. When you're afraid, your autonomic nervous systems flips a switch that sends a burst of turbo energy to your body to help you cope with the danger you feel. Yes, your heart pounds and your palms sweat. But the shot of adrenaline boosts your energy, and if you let it, it'll carry you to new levels of creative expression.

Many top performers have wrestled publicly with stage fright. Bruce Springsteen says he still feels nauseated before going on. Most performers have the same feelings you do about stepping into the spotlight, but where some have at times turned their fears into a debilitating negative, Bruce has embraced the positive. As far as he's concerned, until he's sweating, sick to his stomach, and nervous as hell, he's not ready to go out and give a true superstar performance. He sees his stage fright as preparing him for possible greatness.

Worry if you don't have it, and if you do, try to walk through it and let it take you higher than you imagined you could go.

One technique that may help, if positive thinking doesn't, is a breathing exercise I've developed. It will not only calm you, it will ground you in the diaphragmatic breathing that will make your singing fly.

Color Breathing

Sit comfortably and close your eyes. Rest your hands on your stomach, between your ribs and your belly button, and inhale deeply. Fill up your lungs while keeping your shoulders down and relaxed and your chest quiet. As you exhale, listen to the sound of the breath leaving your body. Concentrate on that sound and allow yourself to imagine that the air you're breathing out has a color. You might want to make it red, the color of fear. Keep inhaling deeply and exhaling fully, and every time you exhale, as you listen to the sound of your breath, imagine a red cloud of fear and tension and anxiety leaving your body. Do this for a minute or two, until you begin to feel calm. As you begin to relax, imagine that the red of fear is gradually turning blue, and continue to breathe in and out, listening to your breath, until you can imagine that every breath you exhale has become a deep, rich blue. When there's no red left, open your eyes. You're ready to go on. Blue is the color of peace. Take it with you when you step onstage.

Happy Trails

What's your dream? Is it to sing the lead in a musical? Front a band? Knock 'em out in the church choir? I can't promise that you'll hit the jackpot or stumble onto the elusive combination of traits and talents that make people into recording stars. But if you build on the basics I've taught you, it's almost certain that you will connect with the richest, most powerful sounds you're capable of making and that you will find yourself delivering your music in a way that is truly your own. Whatever your goal, keep going for a style that expresses who you are and what you feel. It's your unique contribution to the world, and I know it will bring you joy.

· II ·

Standing Out in a World Shaped by *American Idol*

NOTHING CHANGED the singing world, and our idea of the power of the voice, more than three now-iconic television shows: *American Idol, Glee,* and *The Voice.* There had always been singing competitions and star-making talent shows. But these shows mapped a route to stardom that made winning the prize as much about the work (and drama) that went on behind the scenes as the polished performance.

Once we saw people like us line up for those *American Idol* auditions in cities across the country and got pulled into the story lines, real or fictional, of "nobodies," or even misfits and social outcasts, who stepped into the spotlight and proved themselves to be potential stars, it seemed possible to make the leap from couch karaoke to a real career in music—and thousands of people went for it. That trajectory, along with the conventions of the reality competition, is part of our cultural DNA now. It's behind a million YouTube videos by a million kids working to be discovered, and it will no doubt power the next incarnation of the viral singing competition, whatever form it takes.

When you decide to jump into the pool and compete, or when fate knocks on your door and offers you an opportunity to participate in the hardest, most exciting vocal work of your life—a part in a demanding production, a reality competition, a singing gig that puts you onstage night after night—I want you to be ready. So in this chapter I'd like to show you what my work with reality competitions, and the phenomenon that was *Glee,* taught me about how you can thrive in front of the TV cameras, on the road, and every time you need to step into life with confidence.

This I know: The scripts and formats will change, but the demands of working on high-pressure productions won't. You can walk in ready to shine, and *triumph,* if you pay attention to what I'm about to share with you. All the daily work you've done with the exercises to strengthen your voice is giving you a strong instrument, and with the basic stagecraft I've taught you, you can hold your own with a compelling physical presence. The strategies in this chapter will help you keep rising, and making the cut.

Acing the Audition

Many people think that getting attention in an audition is about proving that you can sing like the star of the moment, or the people who are winning on other shows. But in reality competitions—and in every other audition, to tell you the truth—the goal is to find the song that showcases what's unique about you. Say you're a woman and you've got a low voice like Toni Braxton, but you're watching shows or contests on which the people who are winning are full of gospel style, strong and high and overflowing with the vocal acrobatics you'd hear from Jessie J or Jennifer Hudson.

Your job is not to join the rush to be the next Jessie J. It's to find a song that goes really low, so people will say, "Wow. I haven't heard that today. I love it when she sings down there."

Try to become aware of the parts of your voice that are rare and different. You may think of those parts as imperfections, but they're your secret strengths. I recently worked with a woman who shone at the bottom of the range. She spoke with a husky voice that was clearly strongest on the low notes. But when she started singing me a new song she'd written, it was airy, pretty, and light.

"What happened to that husky voice?" I asked.

"I wouldn't want to sing down there," she said. "That's ugly."

"But that's how your speaking voice sounds, which is great," I told her. So we worked on emphasizing the huskiness of her singing voice to match exactly what was going on when she spoke. I had her say the lyrics to parts of the songs, and then sing them. We would flip back and forth between saying them without pitch and then singing them the same way on the right notes. Within a few minutes she realized that she could easily add the huskiness of her speaking voice to her singing.

Fact is, she just had never thought about doing that before. She and a lot of other aspiring singers get locked up in the idea of a style that they think is working for them but that is actually holding them back from showcasing their originality. I often mention that everyone's speaking voice is different. That's why if your best friend calls you later today, he or she doesn't have to start by saying, "Hi, this is Roger Love, your best friend." You recognize the voice because everyone sounds different to some degree. Your speaking voice is a great place to start looking for sounds that are special to you. Once you've found those distinctive sounds, then think about adding them into your singing. The results can be wonderful and surprising.

When you have a sound that makes you a little different, you'll find that you're recognizable above all the other voices in the crowd. Audiences, and contest judges, will remember you. This is a *good* thing, not a reason to be embarrassed.

Homing In on What's Original about You

It's not easy to be objective about your own voice without a lot of practice, so as you're trying to figure out where you shine, ask other people, and pay attention to their responses when you perform. When you're singing to friends, what do they like? Where do they start smiling, or even breaking into applause? Ask people you trust for feedback— "Hey, Dad/boyfriend/work colleague, what part of the song made my voice sound the best? Was there something you particularly liked?" As you begin to do this, don't ask strangers. Start with people who are positive, people who can be both honest and supportive.

Next, identify a style that suits you. Again, pay attention to people's genuine responses. When you sing a rock song, how many people offer to buy you a soda? When you try out your new EDM number, do people look up from their pizza and pay attention? Ask your trusted friends: "I'm singing a rock song and a country song, guys. Which do you like better?"

When you've zeroed in on what's unique about your voice and have decided that jazz, say, is what gets the room interested when you sing, look for the right song. Maybe you need a jazz standard that showcases your beautiful low range. Great.

Choosing the Song That's Perfect for You

Now get more specific: It has to be a song you can sing. That sounds painfully obvious, but every day I see people who choose songs that are too hard for them; it's happened in every competition I've been involved with. Singers come in with audition pieces that are all over the range, songs that they struggle to get through. And their strains and stumbles blow them out of the water. Your audition pieces aren't rated on their degree of difficulty like balance beam routines. You don't pick the hardest song to get extra points. Just choose something that emphasizes the part of your voice that sounds the best and the style of music that makes your sound shine. The ideal song will smoothly fall into your range, stylistically and in all other ways.

It will also call attention to *you,* and not to itself. You don't want to pick a song that is so new and unfamiliar that the people judging are going, "Wow! What's that from? I've never heard it before and it's great." At that point, they are not thinking about you and your singing. They are thinking about the song you picked. That's why you don't always want to be the hippest person in the room. You're not showcasing the talents of the songwriter. You want *all* the attention to be on your voice and how you're making people *feel* when you sing.

One exception: If you're a singer-songwriter and you only want to sing original songs, that's fine. But once more, choose songs that fit the part of your voice where you like to sing and sound best, pieces with words that feel comfortable in your mouth and are tailored to your style and special sound.

The magic, "just right" audition song is not so current that people don't know it or have someone else's voice in their ear when they hear the tune. Ariana Grande has had a couple of songs on the top of the charts, and obviously her interpretations have killed it. You don't want to show up with one of those unless you know you can do it better, or pull it off in a significantly different way than she can.

There's a reason you see so many of the same songs popping up on the reality singing competitions—songs from the '90s and early 2000s. They're pop hits people know but have forgotten enough that they can appreciate new interpretations.

Choose a song like that, then put your spin on it. Rearrange it. Make it your own. If you're a great rapper, add some rap. If the song originally had riffs and runs but that's not your thing, go in the opposite direction and sustain the notes in a way that suits your voice.

In the end, judges and the public are looking for singers who remind them of someone they love, with the new twist *you* offer that they haven't experienced before. Bruno Mars reminds his audiences of Michael Jackson and James Brown. He's easy for people to like, because we have a frame of reference for him.

Standing out is not about reinventing the musical wheel. It's more about making current and classic styles of music sound original because of what *you* bring to the music.

Let Me Say It Again: There's Gold in Those "Flaws"

Some people strive forever to find that new element that will make people notice them, and I see again and again that often it's right there in their speaking voice, or something they think is a flaw.

Bruno Mars has a voice that's husky, not clean. And if he'd cleaned it up to sound like an angel because he thought he needed to "perfect" it, he might not have become so popular. Tipping his hat to James Brown, he went for a sound that was scratchy, edgy, and even a little hoarse-seeming. It's full of passion, and it plays to his strengths and the image he's building.

If you're always trying to downplay your "imperfections," think about Nicki Minaj. Her nasal voice and New York accent could seem like a liability, but they're an essential part of the way she sings and speaks, and she wouldn't be Nicki without them. She's one of many rockers and pop stars who have interesting voices that some people might consider flawed. When I coach them, I'm not set on changing what's unique to them, but on providing them with the technique to showcase their own tonal qualities—as well as to access the whole range of other sounds. It's like giving them more keys on the piano.

That's what I want you to do. Embrace your imperfections—and never stop working on your technique. Really listen to the qualities of your voice, including those quirky sounds in your speaking voice, and get good at listening to other successful artists and pinpointing the imperfections and stylistic abnormalities in their voices. There are always sounds to hear, learn, and perhaps borrow.

If you're a guy who sounds airy and high, Chris Martin of Coldplay is a model of someone who's parlayed those attributes into hits. One of his songs might suit you perfectly. Whenever you identify people who've got voices similar to yours, work up songs from their catalog. If you sound great, you may have landed not just on a "mentor" to emulate but also on an audition song. And if their songs don't work for you, pick singers who sound nothing like you and see how well you can imitate them. You can never have too many sounds in the grab bag of sonic choices you fill by imitating other artists.

A Reality Show Will Hand You an Identity, But You'll Also Need Your Own

Competition contestants often have to make temporary decisions about their image, and about who they want to be. When a singer comes on who sounds like Carrie Underwood, the producer and musical director may coach her in a particular direction. They may listen past the country and hear the pop sounds in her voice, or push her to go more jazzy, more gospel. And if she's smart, the contestant will follow their advice. When you're in that environment and make it to the next round of a competition with a particular kind of song, you add more songs like it to your repertoire. The audience likes it, the pros like it—you're on your way. Maybe our Carrie

Underwood sound-alike gets encouraged to go toward rock, so now she's a rocker, simply by virtue of trying to survive in that medium.

Will that make her a better artist, or the artist she wants to be? Not really. In truth, these shows are not about turning people into artists, they're more like elevated karaoke competitions. A reality contest doesn't always end with the winner realizing what she or he is best at. The winning sound only reflects what happened during the process of the show. If you fit easily into a particular model and the viewers like that model at the moment, you can be swept up in the tide of being a rock singer or a dance artist or an R&B vocalist. Young singers get pigeonholed easily into one category or another in competition shows. It's not good or bad, it's just a normal occurrence. Later on, after you win the show, you'll have the rest of your life to become a varied artist, free to change, adapt, grow, and mature into many different areas of song, music, emotion, and image. Until then, you'll have to master the balancing act of the reality TV process: to be in the moment, helping to deliver familiarity to the viewers, while keeping a part of your heart looking toward the time when you can have more stylistic and creative freedom.

Judges are looking for original artists, not copycats. If you're not working hard to develop your own style in the way I've been describing, and if you're not writing your own songs (see chapter 13), winning a contest might be fun, but it won't allow you to take advantage of all the public exposure you received by being on television. The dream goal is to make it through the competition showcasing that you have unbelievable *promise,* win, and go about designing a long-lasting career that brings happiness to you and your fans.

You Can Be Your Own Best Judge and Teacher

If you're going to put yourself out there, maybe even on camera, to compete and be judged, you have to spend a lot of time recording yourself. Because before you can sell your sound to someone else, *you* have to like it first.

There's an enormous difference between singing a song and liking it, and *recording* a song and liking it. As you know by now, music sounds very different from the inside than from the outside. When you're listening to a recording, the sound is coming toward you, rather than moving away from you. When you are the sound-making chamber, your body is vibrating, you're feeling tension and relaxation, and you might be swept up in the emotion of the song. You're so far inside it you can't always judge or separate the feelings from what you hear. It's difficult to distinguish your experience and memory of singing from the sound itself—unless you record.

Recording lets you step out of your body and ask: How does the sound make you feel as you *listen*? If I heard this song, would it make me want to kiss the singer on the mouth (or whatever the song suggested)?

To be good at judging your sound when it's coming out, you first have to be good at judging it afterward. When you can really hear yourself, you can get much better and faster at self-correcting. You can sing version after version of a song and, listening back, you can pinpoint what's not working and shift it. Surprisingly, most singers never really record and listen back to themselves enough to figure out what changes they need to make. Even many of the pros I've worked with listen back only when they are recording vocals for an upcoming album, and don't bother to record and listen much when they're not in the studio, or getting ready to go in. But I think all singers, no matter how good, benefit when they take the time to analyze what they're doing and make changes until they love the sound.

I recommend doing this not as your harshest critic but as a curious, interested listener. In the end, it doesn't matter what other people say, or how much applause you get. Ultimately, you're singing for yourself and hoping other people enjoy it. Singing is supposed to make you feel good, and that's going to happen only if you like the sounds, and the feelings you get, when you hear your own voice coming through the air into your listening ears.

Do You Want It Enough to Do the Work?

Making it to the top of a reality competition has a lot to do with being smart enough to follow the lead of the producer and other people who are there to help you—the coaches, mentors, and judges who want to root for you. When I worked on a show called *Rock Star: INXS*, the winner of which would tour as the lead singer of the Australian band INXS, I was a vocal coach for the contestants and helped decide who would stay and who would go in each round.

I'd listen to the voices each week, of course, but I'd also pay close attention to each singer's attitude. Was he following my advice? Taking my suggestions and those of the musical director? Some people come in with attitude and resist the input of the people who are there to give them support. If you're putting up a fight, and you're difficult to work with in a business that involves a *lot* of collaboration, you're throwing roadblocks in your own way.

In the first round of the show, there was a singer we thought would be perfect. He was the right age, had the right look, and radiated charisma. He came in singing Elvis songs, and I knew that with the right material, he could be the one. I told him, "If you follow our instructions, you'll have a much better chance of going from living in your car to having a recording contract, touring with a huge band, and being a celebrity."

You'd think at that point a person would do anything for the opportunity. But our guy didn't practice and would arrive at show tapings without having memorized the lyrics. His poor attitude and work habits eventually led him to throw his big chance away.

It's easy to get distracted by the interviews, photo shoots, and other assignments that go with the star-making machinery, but no one wins without being able to demonstrate that she'll work her butt off to do great work.

That's because once you make it and the opportunities start flowing, the challenges grow exponentially, and the work is constant. You don't get the fame without the work, and the pressure to keep being your best persists. So you have to have the right reason for wanting to become a singer. The right reason, which audition judges and producers and fans are always looking for, isn't "I want to be famous" or "I'm tired of living in my car" or "I thought this would be a nice change." Every major singer with a career that has lasted more than a minute has had just one reason for trying to make it in the music business: They do it because they have to. "I didn't have a backup plan," they'll tell you. "If I had another choice, I would've taken it, but this is what I do. I just had to keep moving forward."

The devotion that builds as you follow the only path that calls to you is powerful. I've made a little study. Anytime I work with a superstar singer, I ask, "What's the main reason you succeeded?" And it's always the same: "I practiced. I stayed in my room and practiced and practiced, and I kept writing. I practiced until I was as good as everybody else, then better, and I kept practicing." Sure, good genes help, or coming from a musical family, but even if Mother Nature gave someone attributes that make him sound better than the next person, he will die in obscurity if he doesn't nurture them. The big thing that separates superstars from other singers isn't their gifts. It's what they make of their gifts with their deep, unstoppable work ethic.

The Real-Life Race to Create

When an artist's star is rising, or a show's popularity takes it into the stratosphere, the demands can be intense. Anyone who ever hopes to take that ride needs to be prepared for the hardest, most exhilarating work of his life. It's difficult to imagine the pace and pressure when you're sitting on the outside, enjoying the show. So I'd like to offer a glimpse of what it was like to ride the juggernaut that was *Glee* to show you what to expect if—or *when*—you wind up on the hard-chugging train to fame.

From day one, *Glee* was an insanely demanding concept, each week filled with production numbers. For the singer/actors, long days bled into long nights. There were so many songs per episode that it could've been a full-time job just to master them, except that there were also all the spoken lines to memorize, as well as choreography. All the singing was recorded in advance, so *Glee*'s stars had to find time to be in the recording studio when they weren't filming. Typically, the actors would show up and add their vocals to pre-recorded musical tracks. If they were lucky, they'd receive the track the night before. But it was common to get a song in the middle of the night, or to have to learn it on the spot in the studio. Then the actors would go home and try to learn whatever they needed to ace the next day.

I got involved with the cast when Cory Monteith, who played the role of the football-quarterback-turned-singer Finn Hudson, asked me to help him work on his singing. He was just a young actor who liked to play the drums, and he was no lead singer. But now he was performing opposite Lea Michele, the greatest new singer on TV, a Broadway star. Cory's goal was simply to sing well enough to keep from embarrassing himself on the show, so we set to work practicing technique.

When Cory's voice changed dramatically for the better, the producers asked me to work with the whole cast, and to prepare them for a summer concert series that would give avid fans around the world a taste of the show live.

I set up shop in a trailer on the Paramount lot with a keyboard and a CD recorder, and whenever the *Glee* cast members had a break, they'd drop by for a lesson, moving from breathing through chest, middle, and head voice and on to the songs they'd sing that week for the show and the songs they might have to sing on the summer tour.

The tour would take the cast to huge venues — Radio City Music Hall in New York, the Staples Center in Los Angeles — and needed to be impressive. But the stars filmed night and day and didn't have time to hunker down in a rehearsal space to get the show ready. So the production company had to rehearse the show and get it ready before the cast arrived. Dancers learned every move the performers would do onstage, and worked out their numbers wearing T-shirts that had the dancer's name on one side and the character's name on the other.

For a show that would play to thousands of people on a Saturday night, the cast flew in on a Wednesday night or Thursday morning, after long weeks of filming in Los Angeles, and got their first look at the show they would be performing. After watching the lip-synching dancers go through the numbers, they stood behind them and followed along. The entire floor of the huge venue was divided into spaces where the stars paired up with the dancers to learn each bit.

By Thursday night, the stars were by themselves, running through the show. They were at it again early Friday morning, rehearsing into the night. By early Saturday, they were timing their acts to the elaborate lights and effects. And at the end of that day, it was showtime.

The cast was exhausted, and though the stars were clearly enjoying every minute of the work, it was a grueling pace. As they tried to remember moves and the lyrics to songs they might've sung months earlier in the season, they were playing catch-up, and beat the clock, every day. The show ended up being fantastic, and I could not have been prouder of each of the cast members.

How did they do it?

A step at a time. And if you're ever faced with this kind of monumental challenge, that's what you'll do too.

Winning the Race for Time

Your job in a situation like the *Glee* summer tour is, first, not to get sick. So you're eating well. Drinking lots of water. Resting your voice whenever you can. Washing your hands.

Then you simply stay focused on the very next task in front of you. Mere mortals would be falling asleep or collapsing, but you have to stay focused, asking, Okay, what's next? What can I do right now?

The *Glee* cast couldn't think of the sixteen hours in front of them. They had to keep asking: What do I have to do *now*? Learn dance moves. Learn lines. Practice my song and scene. The only thing to do is go from task to task to task, giving it your all.

Without fail, you need to build a foundation through practice, always warming up your voice. Do whatever exercise you need to be in good physical shape, which will keep you in good mental shape. Practice until it's a given that when you speak and sing you'll sound good, then take your polished craft into the art you need to make today.

There's always a race for time. I've never been hired to work on a movie when I thought I had enough time to make a singer as good as

I wanted, and I've never been brought into a project with a singer where there was enough time to heal a voice before a singer with a cold or laryngitis had to go back on the road.

Yet we always manage to do good work, because we're pros, which just might be another word for *practice addicts*. We pull out our tools and use them in the time allotted. And just like those phenomenal singers in *Glee,* we turn our exhausted, time-crunched efforts into shows the audience will never forget.

That's what you're signing up for if you're aiming for the top: the hardest, best, most impossibly beautiful work of your life. Is it worth it? If this is your passion, there's only one answer: Of course.

· 12 ·

Going Big When You Sing

OVER THE past few years, movies with singing at their core have gained popularity and prestige. These aren't the "Hey, kids, let's put on a show" vehicles of the past. Though there are still musicals out there (*Frozen*, anyone?), the best of these films have been character studies of people whose lives revolve around music.

Because the character's the thing, directors have looked for top-notch actors who can also sing—or, more likely, actors willing to learn to sing. As a result, I've had the opportunity to work with brilliant performers with little or no singing experience playing musicians whose vocals and stage presence are crucial to making a film believable.

You may never be in the position of Joaquin Phoenix or Reese Witherspoon, nonprofessional singers who had to step up to play the country music icons Johnny Cash and June Carter Cash in *Walk the Line*. But the same insights I shared with them about working in front of a band, and the process we used to go from zero to "legend," can give you big advantages when you step into a challenging singing opportunity or need to be larger than life to stand out.

The Basics

The first time I meet a nonsinger who's preparing for a musical role, we don't go near the songs that person will be working on. If I have access to the actor for several weeks, we'll spend the first week on technique, beginning with breathing, then mastering chest, middle, and head voice and vibrato.

When actors walk in to learn to sing, like everyone, they have all the sounds they've made and heard in their lives stored in their memories. They're used to the sounds they make all the time, and they tend to stick to them. So the first thing I do is give them vocal exercises they've never done before. The patterns of the exercises are varied and jump all over the piano, and I always choose one that's far out of the range of the sounds they usually make. Soon they're out of their comfort zone, and they have their first glimpse of a whole new universe. I most often start with the octave jump exercise (refer to audio 22 for men and 23 for women on the website). It forces them to go very low and high in a short time and requires them to sustain (hold out) the top note. This not only requires a good ear, but also takes stamina, breath control, and a great deal of focus.

As these actors learn to breathe differently and handle volume differently, the way you've done by working through the exercises in this book, they can create a whole new set of sounds, and their brains begin to see that their voices are much "bigger" than what they thought was possible—louder, higher, and way more varied. Even if I have very limited time with my actors, I always show them how to lower the larynx. This, as you've experienced, opens up the back part of the throat, which helps them produce sounds with less tension, so their voices become thicker and stronger. (If you're inspired to try it again, go to audio 8 on the website.)

Joaquin had already spent hundreds of hours listening to Johnny Cash and watching videos of his performances. He had a solid imitation of Cash's speaking voice before we started working, and he knew what kind of facial contortions made his face resemble the Man in Black. But he'd spent very little time trying to figure out what notes he could or couldn't sing—that kind of analyzing wasn't part of his skill set. He was a true beginner. People who grow up singing pick up at least some technique by imitating other singers. But if, like Joaquin, you haven't done that, you've got a lot to learn.

So keep in mind that every time you hear Joaquin Phoenix sing in the film, you're listening to the result of a recently learned technique. I'd say that's pretty heartening to anyone who feels as though he or she is starting from scratch.

Taking a Higher Voice Low

Once we found Joaquin's voice, we realized he was more of a tenor, born with a high instrument—which is not what Johnny Cash is known for (just listen to "Daddy Sang Bass"). Joaquin would have to learn to get past the obstacles standing between him and the deeper sounds he needed. Like most people, he tended to go airy when he tried to go low because he literally ran out of vocal cord length, like a guitar player who runs out of string. To sing super-low notes, you need the vocal cords to go to a very long and thick position. Remember, the main job of the cords is to act like a gate and hold back excess air. In the low part of the range, there is a lot of air coming through the cords, and if you weren't born with a low voice, or haven't practiced for years to deal with all of that extra air, the cords simply can't stop enough of it from getting out to make a rich sound. As a result, your sound peters out down at the bottom of your range, because you're all air and no cord.

To perfect the Cash voice and get strong low notes, I had to teach Joaquin how to engage more cord. The trick we used was to go from the airy sound to an edgy one (listen to audio 33 on the website to hear this), which makes the cord vibrate more and also makes the cord longer.

Then we had to approach the many songs in the movie, which was a two-step process. When I'm teaching actors to sing, I first get them proficient at doing my vocal exercises, because that's how I can control the vocal cords and sounds. Then I help them make the transition from exercise sounds to the actual words they need to sing for the song, project, or film. This two-step idea is not just for actors. Everyone I teach has to be guided through moving from exercises to actual words and songs. It's the difference between understanding something and applying it.

If Joaquin has to sing the part of the song that goes, "Because you're mine, I walk the line," I give him the exact melody to sing, but I have him do it with an exercise sound like gug. So just as the original melody goes, "Because you're mine, I walk the line," I have him sing:

"Gug (be) gug (cause) gug (you're) gug (mine)...gug (I) gug (walk) gug (the) gug (line)."

When I do this, I control the position of the vocal cords and the way the air moves through them. When Joaquin tried the actual lyrics first, he couldn't hit all the low notes because there was just too much air coming out that low in the range. I chose the gug sound because the g acts as what's called a glottal stop, momentarily sending less air to the cords, so they can come together and make the low pitches louder and stronger.

When Joaquin sounded good with the exercise sound, we would flip-flop back and forth between the real words and the exercise ones. After some practice, he could substitute the lyrics of the songs for the gugs and make them sound low and powerful.

We didn't turn Joaquin into a singer as good as Johnny, exactly. He gained greater access to more of his voice, but it was still hard for him to cover the entire range that Johnny could. So we used another tool available to us: We changed some of the keys, making the notes higher than some of the ones that Cash had used, and the lows less low. Adjusting as we needed to, we got enough solid sounds on tape that we could piece together all the songs for the soundtrack, sung proudly, competently, and convincingly by Joaquin, who walked away with a Golden Globe and a Best Actor Oscar nomination, among many other honors, for his performance.

The Making of a Belter

Reese Witherspoon, who won a Best Actress Oscar for her role in *Walk the Line,* had been a bit of a casual singer in her school days. She didn't sing that much, but when she did, she would always stay quite high, in a pretty head voice, perhaps believing that all young girls in the South should first be sopranos.

But June Carter Cash, the singer Reese needed to become, was a belter, which means that she stayed at the top part of her chest voice and pushed all the notes out with power to underline the drama of her songs. It wasn't crucial for Reese to imitate her precisely, because the director realized that people were less familiar with June's voice than Johnny's. Our job was to deliver June's essence—the accent, the feeling of her singing—and especially that belting. For that, we had to focus on training Reese's chest voice, along with a bit of her middle voice.

Remember, the chest voice is the lower part of the range where most men and women speak. The head voice is the area much higher than where people speak normally, and the middle voice sits right in between those other two. Reese had to learn to hold on to chest voice even as the melody climbed higher. When we began, she was fine as she started singing low notes, but as soon as the notes began ascending, she would surrender her power and go light, airy, and pretty. Sometimes that works if the song, lyrics, attitude, and emotion of the piece call for it. But if the song calls for passion and power, and a more commanding sound, the lighter head voice just doesn't cut it.

When I first got Reese to sing higher notes in chest voice, she thought she sounded harsh and ugly, in comparison to her pretty head voice. So we had to work to make the chest voice bigger and also pretty. To do that, I added more air to her voice and lowered her Adam's apple a little more. That helped me open up the back part of her throat, taking away the pushed, tight, strained sound that she was getting too close to. With the throat open, the sound could pour out and actually sound strong and pretty. We did all that, and the results spoke for themselves.

Fans adored Reese as June and loved her voice. Next time you watch the film, listen to how high Reese goes while still keeping her voice powerful and strong. Some of her singing in the film actually goes high enough to be in the middle voice, but we made sure it had enough strength and connection so that there were no breaks or cracks where you hear the voice changing from chest to middle. All of that came with dedication, practice, and learning the right techniques.

Connecting Acting to Singing

One thing that shocks all the actors I train to sing on film is the fact that good "singing acting" is often bad, over-the-top "acting acting." Actors who are great on camera convey their emotions with a glance, a subtle expression. Acting on camera is all about the visuals and the ability of the camera to pick up changes in the voice and body the way someone lying next to you in bed might. It's intimate.

But actors forget that singing is about sound first. In a movie like *Walk the Line* or *Crazy Heart*, the Jeff Bridges film about a washed-up country singer, all the subtleties actors count on being able to convey to the camera are swallowed up onstage by the guitars, keyboards, drums, horns, and background vocalists—the swirl of sound and activity in a live performance. Each musician is trying to stand out, lead vocals compete for attention with that dazzling backup singer, and eyes and ears wander to the guitarist who's just out of the spotlight but laying down catchy lines. Guitar players can just turn up the knob on their amp if they want to be louder, but a singer has to make volume from the inside, while competing with all the electronics and noise on the stage.

You have to be BIG to hold your own. So I train my actor/singers—and anyone fronting a band—to pretend they're doing Shakespeare in the Park and trying to send their voice to the back row. Small, subtle vocal sounds and changes do not really reach big audiences. Singers need to accentuate the words, go way over-the-top in volume and variety, and make huge acting choices. When the camera is a foot away from Jeff Bridges, or from Keira Knightley in the film *Begin Again*, it can catch a tiny movement of one eyebrow and viewers think, "She's up to something, feeling something." They notice the change and react to it. But if Keira makes a tiny vocal change trying to show sadness, happiness, anger, or any other emotion, 99 percent of the listeners won't catch it. So I teach my actors that to emphasize emotions while they sing, they have to overact to a degree that most of them feel is silly.

Keira and Jeff both responded to my idea cautiously at first, having spent so many years learning how to create realism on-screen.

But I kept explaining, demonstrating and also recording them so that they could listen back and judge for themselves. You can do the same thing.

Keira wasn't a singer when she walked in, and didn't have to sound like a polished pro, but she was playing a singer-songwriter whose music gave someone a reason to live. She had to have real presence on the stage. To give her a taste of what that takes, I asked her to record a verse and chorus of a song and pretend she was a little kid standing up on her parents' coffee table belting out the song to entertain the guests at a party. I asked her to forget realism and think big, making broad, bold choices. I asked her to:

- Get really loud and soft.
- Go fast and then super-slow, go high and then suddenly low.

Try to emphasize the important words. If the song says, "Tell me if you want to go home," make the word *home* bigger than all the other words in the line.

Keira would experiment, and then we would listen back to hear if her rendition was as ridiculous as she thought it would be. Guess what? When she listened, expecting that the word *home* would stick out like that kid on the coffee table, she was shocked and pleasantly surprised to hear that the word sounded pretty normal. This happens to all of my actors. They begin to see, hear, and understand that the music surrounding their singing is so big and emotional that they have to make the singing a LOT BIGGER than they ever could have imagined.

You do too. So when you sing, accentuate the important words, do something special with them. Don't sing all the words with the same flat emotion you get when you send out a monotone: "I love my dog I hate my dog." If you say or sing all of those words with the same sounds and volume, it's hard to tell whether you love your dog or you don't. Choose key words and emphasize them. Make exaggerated acting choices that help you take your place alongside all of the other instruments that are producing noise while you are singing. Be a big, bold actor/singer and your audiences will love you for it.

The Mike Won't Save You

You'd think the invention of the microphone would've solved any volume issues for a lead singer, but here's the problem: The only thing the microphone amplifies is the sound coming out of the singer's mouth. The guitar and keyboard player both have pedals, keys, and electronics amplifying and drawing attention to their sounds. And as loud as drums are, they still get miked for many live gigs. That's formidable competition for a singer, considering that even without a mike you can hit a drum with a stick and create way more volume than a voice can.

At the same time you're being drowned out by sheer volume, some of the sounds in your vocal frequency range may get eaten up by those loud instruments, if they're making the same frequencies you're producing. If the guitar is playing the same notes the singer is singing, the sound waves can cancel each other out, and while people will hear sound, it'll be a blend of voice and guitar that doesn't let the voice stand out and get enough attention.

Your two friends in this competitive atmosphere are arrangements and, as usual, great technique. Ensuring that your musical arrangements don't have the band playing exactly the same melody as the singer keeps them from competing. And having great technique lets you create volume that's thick and strong, not airy sounds that dissipate before they reach the audience. This should be apparent, but I point it out to all the singers I work with: The amplifier's job is not to create resonance and substance in your voice. It's just to pump up whatever you put into it. If your voice is airy and nasal, the amp will give you a roomful of airy, nasal sounds.

As a lead singer, or as a speaker, you're competing with the band, street noise, helicopters and sirens in the background, people talking in the audience, clanking forks, papers—no setting is safe from sound distractions. Your first job is to create a voice that sounds the way you want and need it to sound, and then, if you have a mike, the great voice that you already feel comfortable with and in control of will simply be louder so that more people can hear how impressive you sound.

Making Them Believe You

Great singers learn that conveying emotion isn't about actually getting themselves to feel the emotions in the lyrics. The point is not to sing a sad song and make yourself cry, but rather to make the audience believe you are sad and to win their empathy—to make them feel emotions by triggering their own unique memories. Can you make someone remember the first time she had her heart broken, or the first time she broke someone else's heart? That's what's important if you want to be a successful singer. You need to touch others' emotions. Have you ever tried to cry or laugh while you are singing? It's not easy. When a singer cries, his or her throat starts to close up. Do you really want that to happen while you're performing? I don't. But I do want you to have the ability to move people at will through any number of emotions. That is a wonderful skill for a singer to have.

Emphasizing particular sounds will help you convey specific emotions. In anger, for example, consonants become stronger, so you hit them harder. And to sing anger to the back row means hitting those consonants hard multiple times. Anger also has sudden volume changes that are designed to shock the listener into being less dominant and more afraid.

Sadness sounds slower, and the words move with more deliberation and effort from one to the next. Because sad people have less energy, sadness also sounds softer, almost too afraid to be heard from such a vulnerable state of mind.

Happiness is certainly louder—it's a sudden infusion of joy and energy. It's also faster, as you want to share all of your newfound jewels with everyone around you. You're so excited about your good fortune, you let the words spill out.

This is key: You have to visualize and exaggerate any emotion you want people to feel. Exaggerating means adding more extremes of volume to your songs (or speeches). More melody extremes. More emphasis on certain words and on consonants. I could take the lyric "I lost my right shoe" and sing it in a way that's nonchalant, like I've got five hundred pairs of shoes and it's no big deal. Or I could sing it as though I were in the middle of the desert, with days to go before I found water, and this shoe, which my dead mother gave me, were the only thing keeping me going.

An Exercise for Exaggerating

As we saw in my work with Keira Knightley, it's almost impossible to get a sense from the inside of how your exaggerations are coming across, so I recommend this: Listen to a favorite song and then record yourself singing it with the emotion turned up to 10. When the line seems sad, go way over-the-top and see if you can showcase that. Anger, same way. And if there's hope, joy, or pleading, make that as huge as you can. If you're a speaker and want to try this, go way, way past what you think you need in volume, speaking from loud to soft, really fast and really slowly to absurdity, and pumping in melody. Listen back, then cut the emotion and variations in half as you record again.

What you hear is probably not that absurd at this point. The idea is to overact until you are believable. No one ever steps onstage or in front of a camera to underwhelm the viewer. Relaxed and casual doesn't work. Give your audience more energy, more excitement, more emotion, more entertainment than they bargained for.

The other key piece is matching your physiology to your song and, once more, doing it in a big way. When you're singing about something happy, it has to show on your face. Your eyes have to smile, your cheeks rise. If you're sad, the, eyebrows come down. If you're Eminem angry, the movements of your hands will be faster and stronger and end with something hard, like a karate chop. And if you're singing about sweetness and beauty, the motion of hands and body should be more fluid, flowing from one gesture to another and using the whole body.

The Power of "Big"

Astonishing things can happen when you go big and match your physiology to the music you're making. The indie band Future Islands got career-making attention during its first appearance on

The Late Show with David Letterman in March 2014 (you can look for a clip on YouTube). Lead singer Sam Herring performed the band's soon-to-be hit "Seasons (Waiting on You)" by doing what *Pitchfork* described as "wilding out and owning the stage with some seriously goofy and committed dancing." It was weird. It was compelling. It was definitely over-the-top. I'd taught Sam, and even I thought so. But if you look at his eyes and listen to the lyrics, he's angry and directing the feeling of the song through his body. He was authentic, he stood out, and, perhaps not entirely by chance, "Seasons" wound up as *Pitchfork*'s top song of the year.

You may still doubt that exaggeration is any way to get an audience to believe you. But did you believe Elvis? Did you believe Prince? Did you believe Tina Turner? Michael Jackson? Go back to their videos and watch what they are doing onstage with their bodies and emotions. There's nothing small about that. Did you believe Bono? Beyoncé? Pink hanging from silks? The megawatt stars want audiences with their mouths open saying, "I love this." And for them, there's almost no such thing as over-the-top. Big is believable. How many hours can Bruce Springsteen deliver "the Boss" onstage? Four? Six? He never stops. He gives 1000 percent every second to his fans. But YOU won't know what "big" feels like until you give it a try. I guarantee that you'll start getting bigger results.

Why Singers Need a Great *Speaking* Voice Too

Even when you perfect the way you sing and have a charismatic stage presence, you can spoil the magic when you open your mouth to speak. Some of the most powerful performers I've worked with drain away all the excitement they've built with their songs by speaking in between songs in a voice that is disappointingly unsexy and uninteresting, without a spark of power.

Audiences are yearning to connect with the person, or persona, they see commanding the stage, and speaking is so important that I now tell singers I'll work with them only if they'll let me work on their speaking voices too. We put too much time and effort into creating a real flow of emotion between the song and the audience to throw it away. Which is exactly what happens when the person who just sang the power ballad that had people up and cheering suddenly sounds as exciting as an accountant when he tries to do more than yell, "Are you ready to rock?"

If you can't maintain the same level of interest, mystery, and surprise when you're speaking from the stage that you had when you were singing, you ruin the experience for the audience. You don't have to be spontaneous—you can practice and refine your comments the way you did your songs. I work with singers all the time to help them figure out what they need to say between songs and in interviews, staying focused on what maintains the mood of the show.

More often than not, we'll rehearse a song, and then we'll think about what kind of emotion the singer needs to keep alive afterward. If Eminem is rapping about how ticked off he is, he can't finish a rant and then say, "Hey, I had the most amazing banana split for lunch. Anyone like banana splits?" The Eminem character talking about banana splits might have a story about seeing someone get run over in front of an ice cream parlor and pulling her into the backseat of his Bentley to drive her to the hospital. And if he does, he needs a voice with the same kind of "seen it all, survived it all" edge that runs through the rest of his work.

Every moment you speak onstage, your voice needs to enhance the character you've taken pains to create with your performance. If Beyoncé is full of sexy moves but stops to chat with the audience in a really nasal voice, or sounds like Nicki Minaj, the illusion is broken, and people will think she was faking it when she put so much sensual power across in her singing and dancing. They might even laugh, for all the wrong reasons.

I insist on working with singers' speaking voices because I know the sobering statistic that says about 85 percent of all professional SINGERS who damage their voices do so because of the way they SPEAK. Isn't that interesting? No matter how much singing you do during the day and night, you always speak more. If you are producing any sounds like the squeaky hinge, or the airy Marilyn Monroe voice, you are drying up your cords and making them red and swollen. That will take its toll on the cords fast and create hoarseness. So be sure you study the parts of this book that will help you keep your speaking voice healthy.

And if you skipped the speaking and presentation chapters of this book, singers, go back and take a look. They'll be your secret weapon when you grab the mike to chat with your fans. Then, when you reach the level of a Bono, you'll be ready to use your voice for good. One of the best results that comes from working to build a voice people love and trust is that they'll listen to you when you step off the stage. If you choose, you can use your voice to make the world a better place by becoming an advocate for people and issues you believe in. And on the most personal level, you'll have the power to use your beautiful voice to show your compassion and love to the people closest to you — the "audience" that means the most.

· 13 ·

Creating Your Own
Material: Yes You Can

I N EVERYTHING you do as a performer, it's your originality that will
set you apart from the sea of gifted singers who want to sound
just like someone else. It's thrilling to develop the chops to sing like
Sia or The Weeknd, but the next step is to incorporate some of their
sounds into yours to create something that's uniquely your own.
That's what I hope you've been working on. If you have, and if you
keep practicing your technique until you can count on your voice to
express exactly the emotions you want to convey, you can command
attention with your distinctive style.

But there's one more element to consider if you want to be in control of your own destiny as a singer or a band: You need to write or
cowrite your own material.

I know that may sound daunting. Not every singer wants to be a
singer-songwriter, and I'm not saying you need to be. But everyone
who wants to feel comfortable with the material she's becoming
known for needs to at least try to shape her own message. That
doesn't mean you have to be a super-gifted lyricist or a have a talent
for writing catchy musical hooks. Sometimes it just means you have
to come to the table knowing what you want to say so you can be
part of the process of creating the songs you sing.

The way to do that, even if you're a singer who's always been more
interested in the melody than the words, is to start writing.

Anyone, and I mean anyone, can do this. I helped my son, Colin, and his bandmates get started when they were barely out of kindergarten, and what I taught them consists of the basics I suggest to all my singers.

The project started when Colin was six, and two of his friends, brothers named Oliver and Eliot, decided to form a band. Colin came home from school one day and told me that the band was called the Negotiators, "because every time it's time to practice, they have to negotiate."

"Great," I said.

"They need a bass player," Colin added, "and I said I'd be in the band."

Colin had never mentioned being interested in the bass, or in music, for that matter. I'd certainly noticed that he had a beautiful voice and could sing on pitch, but I hadn't pushed him to do anything specific with it. He didn't want piano lessons when I brought those up, and he didn't want to try guitar.

But now he wanted to make some noise.

Colin began taking bass lessons with Greg, the person who was teaching Oliver and Eliot the guitar, and rehearsing with them twice a week. Soon they were talking about performing in public, and they did. They started with the school fair, and then a few local parties, and by the time Colin was eight, they'd jumped right up to doing gigs at the famed Whisky a Go Go on the Sunset Strip. They suddenly blossomed into a band that wanted to get somewhere fast. Like a lot of kids with bands, they were thinking bigger venues and record contracts and tours. But I advised them that it wasn't going to happen if they stuck to their covers of "Wild Thing" and Machine Head. So I told them what I'm telling you: You're going to need some original material.

It may sound impossible to do that if you're assuming that you need to provide all the elements to finish a song. But you don't. Anytime I work with someone who's not ready to write all the music and all the lyrics for a song, we start with ideas. And we all have them.

Step One: Start Listening to the People around You, and Make Notes

With the kids, our starting point was: What do you want to sing about? What have you been talking about? What's on your mind? Our songwriting sessions began with questions tailored to the minds and hearts of first, second, and third graders: What's happening in school? What's upsetting you or getting you excited? What do you want to say to your parents or your teachers?

We began making notes, and I gave each of the kids a little notebook to carry around. Every time they heard a phrase that sounded interesting—something a school friend might say, an expression that made them smile—they wrote it down as the potential title for a song. The notebooks began to fill up with lines like "Stop copying me," "Hit the beach," and "Your shoes are cool." If you don't have an idea for a title, I told them, write down ideas for songs that come from what's happening in your life. "If a friend is texting a girl he's interested in at school, and she's getting excited, you can write a song about texting to get a date," I said. "It's wide open."

If you think this is crazy, consider this famous line from my client Carly Rae Jepsen: "Call me maybe," a casual phrase that was waiting for someone to hear it. She turned that little phrase into one of the most popular songs of the decade, and a full-blown superstar career for herself.

Step Two: Do Some Stream-of-Consciousness Writing in Your Notebook

Once the kids had gotten into the habit of collecting titles and phrases, I asked them to write poems, or just some stream-of-consciousness thoughts, in their notebooks. Your assignment, if you're following along, is to tell yourself, "Today, and X number of times a week, I'm going to take out my notebook and write about a subject I choose." Start anywhere. You want to wind up with a page or two of sentences about mermaids, or basketball shoes, or your car, or your friends, or your feelings.

If you're writing a free-form poem, don't worry if it doesn't rhyme. Just write. Get out of your own self-conscious "I'm not good enough" way. Write like you used to draw with crayons as a little kid, not caring if you stayed between the lines. You were creating and could not be held back by borders—you just felt free.

When I encouraged the kids to write about their parents, they came up with statements like "I hate it when my parents don't let me stay up late at night or try to feed me protein shakes in the morning." "They won't let me play video games twenty-four seven." "I like going bowling." The point was to come up with as many such statements as they could think of, and not judge them.

For our songwriting sessions, we'd go through the notebooks. I'd look at the titles and phrases and say, "This is a great idea. Let's start here. Let's take this one line and see what we can do with it." It might be a line like "I woke up in slow motion," which we'd turn into a song called, you guessed it, "Slow Motion," which ended up being about a future girlfriend, and wanting to hold on to every second they would be together.

We talked as a group, with each of the kids contributing ideas. One would throw out an idea or line, and the guitar teacher, Greg, and I would encourage him to elaborate on it, something you can do with your own bandmates or friends or kids.

The boys' actual lines developed through this process into lyrics such as:
"I will hold you
Till you scream out
Enough, in slow motion
I will capture
Like a steel frame
Our love
In slow motion."
At the same time, Oliver, the guitar player, was learning chords and had ideas for music. We'd say things like "Try to come up with something like Machine Head, but different. Maybe the same kind

of rhythm." The result might become the verse. Then he'd noodle out another pattern that could be a chorus. We'd help the boys sew it all together.

It's a great advantage to have musicians in the family, and if you do, call on them. But don't worry if you don't. The important part, the key to honing your message, is to start listening to the world around you, and to carry a notebook to write things down. You know you've always got your phone with you. Use a notepad app that lets you keep your song/lyric ideas together and start writing. My daughter, Madison, has been doing this all her life, and as I write this, she's a professional singer-songwriter with three songs on the charts, including the Jason Derulo single "Kiss the Sky," which she cowrote. Yes, she's talented. But it wouldn't make any difference if she didn't write *all the time*.

Going Deeper: Making a Good Idea a Better Song

Bob Dylan said you have to write about a hundred bad songs before you come up with something good. In other words, very few people can just put their pen to paper or their hand on the piano and automatically produce something great. When I have a multiplatinum-selling songwriter in my studio showing me a new song, sometimes it sounds great, and other times it sounds like something the cat dragged in. I'm serious. The best of the best make magic only every so many tries.

So if you want to be a great songwriter, you need to practice every day. Keep capturing ideas for lyrics on your journal or notepad or smartphone, and get used to writing them down or singing them into your phone recorder. Whether you have a title or a line for the verse or the chorus, just get it down. Capturing your ideas is the first step.

Many new writers go for the obvious lyrics and themes: You broke my heart. I'm leaving you. You ran off with my best friend. Those *do* have the virtue of getting people to write, and we've got millions of songs to prove it. But if you want your song to stand out, the challenge is to describe emotions, situations, and thoughts that all of us have had, but find a new way to evoke them.

It might seem impossible to write a song about having your heart broken, for example, without making it trite, predictable, and boring. But a songwriter named Diane Warren started imagining her way into what it feels like to be in the middle of heartbreak and found the words that would speak to what everyone really wants to say after a breakup: Fix this. Make me not hurt anymore. *Un-break my heart.*

So simple and so brilliant. People related in a huge way, and "Un-break My Heart" became a monster hit, a classic, and won a Grammy in 1997. You find words like "un-break my heart" by writing, letting your mind wander, playing with phrases, plugging in the words you hear your friends say that have never made it into songs. Warren says she wasn't heartbroken at the time, but playing the part of someone who was, the way an actor plays a character, feeling everything, remembering her own experiences. You can try that too.

You can often find your way to what's memorable simply by digging a little deeper, being more specific. When I was in my early twenties I wrote a song called "What Do You See in Him?" It was about a guy who lost his girl to another guy, something I thought a big chunk of the audience could relate to. But I was too on the nose. At that time I was coaching a legend in the rock 'n' roll world, Robbie Robertson. (You might've seen him in *The Last Waltz,* the movie Martin Scorsese directed about him and his band.)

I asked Robbie to look at my lyrics, and after he did, he said that everything was all too predicable, except one line: "Does he sing you to sleep like I did?" He loved that line. Why? Because it focused on something so particular—a person who used to sing his lover to sleep, and no matter what some new guy had to offer, he probably couldn't do that.

Robbie made sense—that line was just so much better than the rest of the song. "Does he sing you to sleep" pointed to the one thing the singer did that his girlfriend couldn't help remembering—and held out the hope that if she did, maybe she'd realize she still loved him and would come back. I rewrote the song, and it became many times better and more real. *That's* what you need to do to start writing great lyrics.

If you want to watch someone playing with words and thinking out loud about it, take a look at Lorde's Twitter feed, @lordemusic. Sometimes you'll see her spinning out lines in real time. Experimenting. Just like you.

A Secret to Help You Come Up with Better Melodies

It's beyond the scope of this book to go into detail about composing music for your songs, but I can give you one tip that has opened up the world of melody for the people I work with: Be sure you start by being able to access the entire range of your voice—chest, middle, and head.

Most singers hang out in the vocal range they feel most comfortable in. If you're a Broadway-type belter, or a budding rock star who likes to shout a bit, you probably sing a lot of notes at the top part of your chest voice, like Florence Welch of Florence + the Machine. If you're a woman who sounds more classical, or a man who sings super-high, you probably spend a lot of time in your head voice, like Adam Levine.

So when you're playing around, trying to come up with melodies for a new song, you probably go to that "home base" part of your voice and stay there, where the singing is easy—and ignore the whole world of notes you can't hit. But you're severely limiting your melody writing if you can't sing every note easily. If you can move seamlessly through chest, middle, and head voice, though, you will feel no boundaries or constraints. That's the best starting point for creating—the land of no vocal limits.

You Don't Have to Do It All Yourself, but You Do Have to Be a Good Collaborator

As I mentioned at the outset, you don't have to be a great lyricist or musician to make a significant contribution to the creation of a song. The important thing is to develop ideas to add to the process.

If you're paralyzed by the thought of coming up with a melody, just pay attention to the words and remember that there's no need to do everything alone. Reach into your community and make friends with people who have the skills you lack. Look for people who are further along the curve, and learn from them. If you play an instrument and are comfortable doodling with songwriting, connect with a word person. If you've got a notebook full of lyrics and need tunes, get to know the person who's sitting in the corner with a guitar at a party or family gathering.

I can promise you that every band that's popular right now started with people who went to their communities to find the skills they didn't have.

Collaboration is what makes songs today, and being signed as an artist opens the door to a new level of development — the chance to work with people who have top-notch skills and much to teach if you pay attention. A sixteen-year-old artist I work with flew in from New York recently. His manager had him holed up with three people he didn't know, producers and writers. They had ideas for him, he brought in his own, and they stirred them together in search of a hit. That's a very common way for artists to create songs. They hook up with other writers and producers and put together something on the spot, hoping to spark some magic that turns into a hit.

A Cautionary Tale: Here's What Happens if You *Don't* Write

There's just one big drawback to this system. The producers and songwriters who team with new artists are great. But they're not *you.* And there lies the problem if you have not started writing and coming up with song ideas.

I describe this scenario to all my clients who want to make it in the music business but don't think they need to bring in material: Say you go to meet with someone who owns a record company, and the person with your fate in his hands says, "I like your voice, I like your vibe. Do you write?"

"No, not really," you say.

"Well, I think what's going to be popular right now are disco songs about Jell-O. You can handle that, right? I have this whole bunch of songs that would be great for you."

"That's not really my style," you say. "I don't know if I can do that."

"Too bad," says the mogul. "You don't have any songs of our own, and Jell-O is what I've got."

You're not ready to walk away from the deal you've always wanted, so you go with it. You record a disco Jell-O song, and suddenly you've got a hit on your hands. The public loves it. It's viral. They want to use it for commercials. And you can't stand it.

This is your biggest nightmare. Your name is out there, just as you'd dreamed, but you're singing about Jell-O, or oatmeal, or stuffed animals. And you hate yourself.

I know that's a silly example, but believe me, it's not far off the mark.

If you want to have a say in what you sing, you have to show up with a message. You have to keep writing—even if you don't think of yourself as a songwriter. Every real artist has a message. Taylor Swift became known for a message along the lines of "We're all princesses. Our princes will come, and we'll all live happily ever after." And as her life has changed, her message has changed. It's real for her, and it's real to her enormous audience. Beyoncé's unmissable message is "Women are incredible and powerful, and we can do anything."

Neither of these women is trapped in someone else's soulless idea of what will sell. What's your message? Find it by writing.

· 14 ·

Essential Extras for Speakers

TRUE ARTISTRY in speaking comes from creating a convincing blend of three elements: what you say, the way you say it, and who you are. When these pieces come together, you'll find that your voice becomes a vehicle that moves people to listen and take you and your words seriously, whether you're in the office, at home, or onstage.

The vocal exercises and the work you've done to bring varied new sounds into your voice have given you strength, stamina, and technique. You now have a great sense of just how broad a reach your instrument has, and you know how to tune it up to correct sound qualities you don't like. What's left? The only thing standing between you and great speaking—if you're not comfortably there by now—is probably habit. Sometimes, even when your singing voice is thick, strong, and full of color and variety, habit can throw you back into the narrow confines of your old way of speaking. You may be used to talking so fast that you don't give your body a chance to let the new sounds out. You may be caught in a monotone that you hardly notice, clinging to the idea that there's a difference between the way you sing and the way you speak. But if you're bold enough to experiment and to tear down the wall between singing and speaking, you'll find the speaking voice that's awake, vibrant, and *uniquely yours*.

In this chapter I'll give you some techniques that will help you consciously shake up your old voice and incorporate new sounds. I'll also ask you to turn your attention to how a number of factors shape the particular message you want to deliver. Vocal dynamics—your speed, pitch, and volume; the way you stretch particular sounds; and the way you use silence—deeply influence the way people hear and respond to you. It's as though your message were pure water, and dynamics create the container. The same words can take on the glistening clarity of crystal, the warmth of a diner coffee mug, or the shock value of a blast from the nozzle of a fire hose. I can assure you that what you say will have impact in any context if you wrap it in sounds that emphasize, rather than detract from, your meaning.

As you'll see in this chapter, a voice that's effective and powerful may not necessarily be one that people say they love. It may not be a voice that they admire for its flawlessness. But because there's a strong synergy between the message and the messenger, both are memorable.

By taking the time to match the music of your speech with the "lyrics" of your thoughts, emotions, and desires, you can connect with any listener, from a boss to a lover. And you'll feel the unmistakable power that comes from removing vocal roadblocks and setting your voice free.

Finding a Pace That Works

Have you ever bought a car? Every time I've gone to a dealership, I've been struck by the vocal dance of the car salesman. It's his job to make a wall-of-sound pitch for the vehicle you're interested in, squeezing in as many extras as he can and confidently running down the specifics of the deal in language that keeps things legal by fully disclosing fees and charges. The experience is a little like being run over by a steamroller. The salesman's voice is relentless, and after a while it's hard to break in and ask questions. You might feel a little slow on the uptake if you interrupted with a "What was that? I didn't get what you meant." So, perhaps against your better judgment, you let him keep going, though you may have to step outside when he's finished to let your head stop spinning. You hear the extremes of this kind of professional speed-speech in television commercials that rattle off the "fine print" details so fast that even an auctioneer couldn't keep up.

What do you think when you hear this kind of fast-talking? In the case of salesmen, I think most of us assume that the speaker's trying to create a sense of urgency (and thus pressure), or even that he's nervous or has something to hide. The very pace of the delivery gives the interaction a tone that's as clear as if it were marked on sheet music by a composer.

So what is your tempo saying about you? And how is it affecting what your listeners hear?

First, keep in mind that every body runs at a different pace. If you're high-strung and restless, your metabolism is probably naturally set on high. You walk fast, eat fast, and talk fast. On the other hand, you may be a low-key, centered, and grounded person who rarely seems rushed. Your heartbeat is probably slower, along with your breathing. Tune in to your natural speed. Do you talk faster than the people around you? More slowly? Spend some time asking your friends and paying attention to how your pace compares with others'. There's no essentially good or bad speed, but I'd like you to be aware of what happens when your natural tendencies are accentuated—which often happens when we're under stress.

If your natural speed is medium to fast. Nerves or excitement can easily push the pedal to the metal and accelerate your speech to a pounding pace. You might be fine one-on-one or in familiar situations, but when you step in front of an audience or prepare to confront a spouse with some bad news, adrenaline kicks in, increasing your pulse rate and releasing energy to prepare for the coming stress. If you don't tune in to your body at this point, a number of things start to happen. Your voice, mirroring your body's "tempo change," rushes out. As your mouth, throat, and tongue work feverishly to articulate the words, you can fall into a dronelike monotone because there's simply not enough time or breath to allow the voice to move around freely and produce varied pitches. In all likelihood, your breathing rate has increased and you've lost touch with diaphragmatic breathing altogether, which means the resonances of middle and head voice are less available to you, and chest voice is thin instead of thick. This is *not* the voice you want to use to tell your employees that layoffs are coming, or your spouse that there's a huge new dent in the car—yet it may seem to be the only one available.

Worse for the listener at times like this, your words and breath are probably not connected in any meaningful way. Pauses are important in speech because when they're used effectively, they break information into units based on sense. They're aural punctuation. If you give in to the tendency to talk nonstop until the breath gives out and pause only when you're gasping for air, it's as though you're throwing periods and commas in at random. Where you pause has nothing to do with where thoughts begin and end. The only message that's absolutely clear is the one you really don't want to send: "Get me out of here! I'm scared!" You may also give the impression that you're on autopilot. If you've ever visited a tourist attraction at the end of the summer and wound up on a tour with a guide who's given the spiel a thousand times, you know how lifeless rushed, "canned" words can sound. You assume the speaker is bored and definitely not interested in either the topic or you. What gives the warmed-over effect? Generally, it's uninflected, monotone speed.

If you're like most people, and nerves are the big problem that throws you into unwanted overdrive, the first thing I'd like you to do is go back to the basics of diaphragmatic breathing, which will slow your body down with its gentle, regular pattern. Focusing on your breath is a well-known and effective technique for pulling you back to the present and grounding you in your body when you've been caught up in racing, worried thoughts. If you establish correct breathing, you lay the foundation for proper sound production and allow your body to remember and make the sounds it's learned in your singing exercises.

I'd also like you to play with your pacing when you talk. You might start by recording yourself as you read the newspaper or a book aloud. Read a sentence or two at your normal speed, then change the pace. Slow down for a sentence or two, then speed up. What speed gives you the best sound? What makes you sound energetic or authoritative or loving? You might notice that different content seems to be more effective at different speeds. Play with this. If you're a fast talker normally, try slowing your pace on every other phone call at work. How do people respond to you? When you're face-to-face with a friend, watch for cues. Are you connecting better when you slow down? Or does a certain amount of speed buff up your message? If you're delivering a speech, you might want to play with speed for emphasis. Slowing down at difficult or key points might draw attention to places you'd like to underline.

A lesson I'd like you to take from performers is to learn to read your audience. Are you reaching them? Are they looking at you? Are they fidgeting? Nodding? If you're talking to your child, is she listening? What does it take to break through to the other person? Speed is just one variable, but it has a big effect on how understandable and approachable you seem to be, so it's a great place to begin to work with this kind of experimentation. If you think of speech as music, and give yourself license to play it like a jazz musician until you find the effect you want, you'll dissolve your limiting vocal habits permanently.

If you're incredibly slow-talking by nature. When you speak very slowly, you run the risk of distorting the sound of your voice by causing it to waver just slightly. There's a certain laxness to the sound that you can hear if you listen to audio 34 on the website. To my mind this speech pattern sounds weak and frail, and more than a touch seasick.

In pressure situations you may tend to pause too often to make it easy for your listener to catch your meaning. (Just read a sentence, pausing after every word or two, and you'll see what I mean. The individual words seem to be disconnected, and it's easy to lose track of how they're related.) You may also start to articulate your pauses, filling them in with an *ah* or an *um*, which is like adding a layer of static to the sound of your voice.

I think that in many settings, listening to a slow speaker who frequently pauses makes you question the speaker's credibility. The pauses suggest hesitancy or lack of authority. The speaker may seem to be unprepared or inarticulate—though the impression may well be completely false.

To get a reading on your pace, record yourself speaking (not reading). Tell me about your favorite childhood memory, and reach in for as much detail as you can. Play back the recording, listening not for content but simply for speed and the way you use pauses. Are you pausing before you finish an idea? Do you hear yourself pausing to search for words? Did you fill in the pause with a sound?

Try it again, deliberately speaking faster. If you didn't like the pauses you heard the first time, concentrate on speaking complete thoughts. What happens to the sound of your voice? Does it gain color?

Spend a couple of days consciously matching the speed of your conversations to the pace of your companions. If they talk fast, talk fast. If they speak slowly, speak slowly. Do you feel any difference in the energy of your interactions?

There's no magic pill for fixing the pace of your speech, just listening and adjusting, listening and adjusting. Record yourself for feedback. Keep in mind that different situations require different paces. If you're a therapist, for example, you want to provide lots of space in your speech to encourage the other person to respond. Some comedians use extremely slow speech to set up jokes based on the conclusions their audience has jumped to while waiting for them to finish talking—and it's very effective. Slow is not inherently bad. Just be sure it's appropriate to your situation. Your audience will let you know.

Breaking Out of Monotone

I still remember when I took my son to his first day of preschool. In the middle of the session, a tall man entered the room and said, in a loud, bassy monotone: "Hello, I'm Ed, your coach. Please form one line and we will proceed outside to play." The kids just sat in their seats. Most three-year-olds love the word *play*, and they're easily excitable, but Coach Ed's message left them cold. He might have been the most energetic and fun guy in the world—but his voice gave no clue. Seventeen preschoolers heard the sound that came out of his mouth and had no desire to follow him anywhere.

The work we've done to this point has given you dozens of vocal tones and shadings to use, but like Coach Ed, you may not yet be incorporating them into the way you speak every day. I'd like you to tune in now to how much variation you're putting into your speaking voice. Pick up a book or paper and record your voice reading any passage you like. As you play back the recording, listen specifically for how high and low you go. Does your voice swoop and soar all over the keyboard, or does it remind you of my son's PE coach? You have almost three octaves of range to play with, so I encourage you to move the notes around.

Listen to audio 35 on the website and you'll hear an example of what I'm talking about. I'm emphasizing variety in my voice as I speak, giving it a lot of texture. As you experiment in this way, you'll no doubt come up with a lot of goofy sounds and voices that you may never use. But you'll also stumble upon qualities that you like and want to incorporate. You'll get the best results if you spend time consciously exaggerating the highs and lows and moving into areas you're not used to.

It might be easier for you to get an idea of how to do this if you try the following exercise: Write down ten or twelve lines of the next conversation you'll probably have. Maybe you'll be talking to your kids or asking someone for a date. Now take those lines and pretend they're the lines of a song. Forget that you're not a composer, and without worrying too much about your melody, go back and *sing* the whole conversation, everything from the "How's it going?" to the "Now can you take out the trash?" I know that you're probably muttering "No way," but I challenge you to try this. No matter how strange the "song," I know you'll hear more thickness, more energy, and more pitch variation than you generally put into your regular speech. Once you've sung the words of your planned conversation, go back and speak them and see if you can keep some of the same resonances and variations in your speech.

Here's one more experiment to try: Write out five or six lines of a talk or conversation and attach them to the melody of "Happy Birth-day." (Follow along with audio 36.) My sample conversation was something along the lines of: "I'm going to have lunch with Joe, then I'm getting a haircut. After that I'm going to get the laundry, pick up dinner, and go home." You can also try singing a more negative mes-sage: "Profits are down" or "I just crashed the car." Listen to what happens as your voice goes high and low. Notice that because of the turns, pauses, and longer notes in the music, you're stressing certain syllables, giving emphasis to particular words. This is no dull mono-tone, and you can let the variety and energy you just sang into the same words as you speak them. Try it.

If you get confused about how to put high and low sounds into speech, listen again to audio 35, and do some more improvised sing-ing followed by speaking.

Use the News

You can also practice varying the pitches and stresses of your voice by imitating the reporters and anchors on the evening news. I don't recommend this style of speaking as an ideal, but you can pick up a number of helpful strategies and techniques that may help you break out of a stubborn monotone.

Newscasters often aim to make negative information sound intriguing but not depressing. Rather than giving in to the emotions tied to news of death and devastation, they look for ways to keep a high-energy, positive sound in their voices. The feeling of energy is created in part by the way they "punch" particular words, making them louder, or lifting the pitch, for emphasis. These speakers also end nearly every sentence by either staying on the same note or going higher. In regular conversation, most of us drop the pitch at the end of a sentence, which releases tension and lowers the feeling of inten-sity we're creating. But by ending on the same pitch or going higher, news voices sustain the feeling of importance that they've built around what they're saying—and leave you wanting to hear what comes next. Experiment with both of these techniques. I know they feel a little artificial, but you can use them as a springboard to more natural ways of speaking with a lot of variety.

It's easy to turn this kind of variation into a parody, as performers like my student Jon Lovitz sometimes does. I know that those of you who make a lot of presentations or speak often in public are wary of the singsongy cadences of the "professional speakers' voice," or a stagey kind of broadcasters' voice in which inconsequential words get emphasized and every sentence is molded into the same roller-coaster format, whether it fits or not. Don't worry—I don't want you to wind up with a voice that's varied just for the sake of novelty. I've noticed that when speakers begin to sound that way, it's usually because they seem to be completely disconnected from their meaning. But you can begin to address that problem by focusing on phrasing.

Making Phrases Work for You

We think in phrases—groups of words. We learn that way too. If you recite the alphabet, you'll probably notice that you pause in the same places as you do when you sing the ABC song, and if you try to recite it to a different rhythm, it'll probably feel wrong to you. As a speaker you may not need to make a lifelong imprint on your audience, but you can ensure that your message stays easily in your listeners' minds by using phrasing as carefully as a singer might.

I've talked about Frank Sinatra and his masterly use of phrasing, but perhaps you didn't make a connection between Frank singing "My Way" and the most effective way of, say, delivering a report to a group of clients. Frank used pauses to group words by meaning and let them sink in. He connected every word to a note, the melody line, an emotion, and an idea, and you can do this when you speak.

Return to the speak-singing exercise we did earlier, your ten to twelve lines of written conversation, and this time break the sentences into phrases that each convey important parts of your message. For instance, if your thought is "Helen, I want to go out with you...," you might break it into "Helen / I want to go out with you /

we'll talk / we'll get to know each other / after all / it's you / you're the only one / the only one I want."

Before you can speak-sing it, you need to know what kind of song this is. If it's a love song, you'll deliver it differently than a children's song, emphasizing different words, and of course adding very different emotions. Often we don't stop to consider the emotional weight we want our words to carry because we're so focused on the words themselves. It's helpful to ask: If this speech/talk/conversation were a song, what kind of song would it be? That's the same as asking, "What kind of energy do I want this communication to have?" Is it a stirring inspirational hymn? Rousing march? If you liken your speech to the Michigan fight song instead of a folksy country tune, you'll help yourself produce a very specific effect. For right now, let's say we're working on a love song (and if you need to, you can change "Helen" to "Roger").

If you sing "Helen / I want / to go out / with you," you'll notice that instead of stopping short at each pause, you'll probably stretch some of the sounds first—for emphasis. Don't theorize about this—try it! The more time you spend on Helen's name, for example, the more you're celebrating Helen. Stretch out the word "want" and you emphasize desire. You can also emphasize "out" or "go out" and that last "you." The pause itself emphasizes the word that comes before it.

We're used to hearing singers do this, and what we often don't realize is that great speakers do this too. They work the words, letting them resonate into the pauses between phrases. They give words different lengths, and of course, different pitches.

Now try breaking the Helen lines in different places and sing them again. The less musical and rhythmic you make your pauses, the harder you'll be to understand. ("Helen I / want / to go out with / you.") It's the pauses that make the phrase, so use them consciously, not arbitrarily. Stay right in the moment. You don't have to pause a long time, but if you're delivering complicated information or asking people to visualize something new, give them a moment to digest what you've said. Break your message down subtly, by offering your listeners space to think or laugh.

Practice phrasing by singing your written conversation. Sing the same words as a children's teaching song, a torch song, and a dance tune, keeping in mind that your purpose changes each time: you're trying to teach something simply, tell a love story, or get your audience to get up and move. The rhythms, phrasings, and sounds that produce those effects can be part of your repertoire when you speak, if you're willing to try them. When you hit on a sound you like, repeat it. Don't forget to translate these sung sounds into speech. Read your "lyrics" and try to carry the same kinds of inflections, pitch variations, and meaningful pauses into the way you talk.

Pauses are, not incidentally, your chance to breathe. Many singers mark their music to indicate exactly where they want to breathe, and especially if you're giving a talk, I encourage you to do the same thing. Some very basic guidelines to keep in mind:

- Don't keep talking when you run out of breath!
- Allow yourself to talk to the end of a complete phrase.
- Let yourself be silent, instead of producing a filler sound, when you are thinking.

If you concentrate on speaking in phrases and using pauses thoughtfully, you'll automatically shift your focus, and your listeners', to the meaning of what you're saying. Filling in your pauses with *ums* and *ers* and "you know"s essentially erases your phrases, so if you've noticed that you tend to make sounds like this, spend time breaking the habit. Record yourself often and practice filtering out the filler.

A Reminder about Volume

Every time I've ever worked with a speaker who's trapped behind a small, closed-off voice and asked for more volume, the standard response has been: "No, no—I'm shouting." But the crowd listening inevitably goes wild as the decibel level increases. We can all hear that the speaker sounds a hundred times better with the thick, strong voice that proper volume makes possible. I know I've encouraged you more than once to stop rationing your voice and to let the sound and energy out. Please go with me on this. Phrasing, pitch variation, and singing your way into speech aren't going to help if people can't hear you!

Volume, volume, volume!

A Better Way to Practice a Speech

I recently listened to a scientist give a talk about changing the way we eat. He was speaking to a friendly audience that was interested in all facets of health and self-improvement, yet within just a few sentences, I knew that the people around me had almost completely tuned out. Why? I think it had a lot to do with the way he had practiced.

The man was speaking without notes, yet he seemed to be adhering to a set script, as though he had a TelePrompTer behind his forehead. His voice moved up and down, with lots of variation, but he certainly hadn't been thinking about phrasing his information in a meaningful way. He seemed mechanical, and after a while it was just annoying to listen to him. I sat, trying to pay attention, but I soon found myself imagining this person practicing the night before with a legal pad in his lap, reading and rereading and repeating this speech until he had every word memorized. Many speakers do this, but it inevitably makes for mechanical delivery.

What would I have suggested instead? You guessed it—singing. If the scientist were my client, I'd have advised him to take his notes and sing his way through them. When you do, you'll find yourself discovering interesting ways to emphasize words, you'll hear them a different way, and you'll begin to hear the real message shining through. The scientist might have discovered that the essential thing he wanted to communicate was his excitement about ways we can all live longer by eating differently. He may have found that he wanted most to encourage his listeners, or motivate them—and he may well have come up with new examples to help him do just that. Memorizing the text only gave the scientist access to words, not to the larger sense of what he wanted to say, and it made for a dry-as-dust presentation.

Singing gives you new perspective on your material because it's one of the only times both sides of your brain—the creative, imaginative side and the orderly, logical side—operate together. When you practice by singing a few phrases, then going back to speak them, you tap into the power of your whole brain, and when you're connected to both your logical mind and your imagination, you can't help but express yourself in a way that feels whole. You might even surprise yourself. Your delivery feels fresh, and people can't help but listen.

Basics for the Stage and Presentations

A great voice and wonderful delivery will go a long way toward communicating your message, but it will also help to have a basic familiarity with presentation skills as you take your new vocal strengths out into the world. I can't pretend to give you a comprehensive guide here, but I'd like to give you a few hints that I've found particularly useful.

Using a microphone. Hearing your own voice amplified can be a shock. We're familiar with the way we sound unplugged, but the voice that travels through a maze of electronic equipment and booms back at us through speakers can sound loud and affected. It does, in fact, change with every step it takes down the road of cables and amplifiers, and I tell my students that the only true sounds of the voice are what occurs in the space between our lips and the microphone. Don't change your sound or your technique for the sake of the mike! For most speakers, that translates: Don't speak more quietly when you hear your voice filling the room. Many people hush themselves as soon as they step in front of a mike, assuming that because it's doing all the work, they don't need to. But as you know by now, a soft airy voice can't provide the flow of air and cord vibration necessary for ideal sound production—microphone or not, you need to keep your own volume up. Does this mean you should blast directly into a microphone? Not exactly. You can adjust the volume coming through the sound system by changing your proximity to the mike.

You may find, if your technique is good, that you don't need a microphone at all. Most of the time when I lecture in a smallish space for fifty to seventy-five people, I'm fine without one. Quite often auditoriums and lecture halls have good acoustics, and the unamplified sound you generate bounces off the walls and ceiling to create positive reverberations that make your voice sound loud and thick enough to be heard unaided.

Don't change your voice for the microphone. Allow yourself to make the musical sounds you've worked so hard to develop, and look on the mike as a potential helper, not a reason for changing all the rules.

Eye contact. The goal of a great speaker is to communicate on a completely real, honest level with the listeners. The finest speakers I've ever heard made me feel as though they were talking to me alone—even in a room full of people. In fact, they made almost all the listeners feel as though they were part of an intimate exchange. How is this accomplished? The secret is brief eye contact. Direct eye contact for more than ten seconds can make a listener acutely uncomfortable and may make a person feel challenged or threatened. But brief contact can energize the listener—and you.

I gave a presentation to a small group of business executives recently and noticed a couple of smiling, energetic faces of people who seemed enthusiastic and happy to meet me. A couple of others were withdrawn and shy, as though they were apprehensive about what I might ask them to do. And the rest of the group fell somewhere in between. As I talked, I made frequent eye contact with the excited members of the group, which seemed to raise their level of interest and gave me positive feedback that was energizing. I also took care to look at the faces of the more reticent members of the group and made an effort to connect with eye contact. Small presentations like this are conversational—you have a chance to see your audience's reaction up close and to address questions and concerns as you see them flash across your listeners' faces.

It's a great opportunity, and you can grab it and use it if you reach out of yourself by using eye contact. You don't need to stare, but look. Be curious about how your message is being received. Open yourself up to others' feelings and the nonverbal messages they're sending. You'll gain valuable information.

Using your hands. You may have a great voice, and read your audience like a book, but still fall victim to a common habit that undermines your effectiveness. I call this problem "parallel gestures," and it involves using both hands in exactly the same way. Instead of slicing the air with one hand to emphasize a point, you slice with two. Everything one hand does, the other mirrors. The effect is extremely comical, though of course it's not intended to be. In the course of a normal conversation, our hands move independently. We might lift one hand, then let it drop, or point with one hand while the other rests. Observe yourself as you talk with your hands. Each side of the body is controlled by a different side of the brain, and our gestures reflect that.

When nerves enter the equation, however, it's as though you're standing outside your body and watching yourself, or choreographing your every movement. And the second you disconnect your body and your mind, you're in trouble. You begin to orchestrate your gestures, and instantly you create a barrier between yourself and your listeners.

If you tend to use parallel gestures, try this exercise. Stand in front of a mirror that allows you to see yourself from the waist up. Sing your favorite song or speak any passage of text you've memorized. Watch what your hands do. Are they mirroring each other? Make a mental note of what you see. Now go back and sing or say the same thing. Stop the moment you find yourself making a parallel gesture, and let one hand drop, or move one of them up or down. Change something. Continue speaking or singing until you find yourself making another parallel gesture. Stop again, reposition, and continue. This simple mirror work will increase your awareness and let your body know that you're onto its unconscious habit. Notice the gestures, then stop using them. It's really that simple and possible.

Voices That Work

In singing, the path to developing a distinctive personal style is to imitate a wide variety of vocalists and broaden the range of sounds you can use to create something original. In speaking, though, I recommend listening and analyzing instead of imitating. Many voices that we can recognize instantly—say, Larry King's rasp or Andy Rooney's amusing nasal whine—are memorable because they serve the persona of the speaker very well. But if you use them without the rest of the package—especially the matching personality and content—you run the risk of sounding like a cartoon. (It's also possible that you will pick up bad habits, as character voices often accentuate a quality that may not be attractive in another context.)

I'd like to help you begin the process of analyzing what makes speakers effective by spending time with a couple of my favorite clients, people whose voices do just what I'd like yours to do: they perfectly reflect the essence of the speaker's personality and message. Most people do, indeed, send out distinct messages about themselves: "I'm a funny guy—laugh with me" or "I'm a competent, caring professional—follow my advice" or "I'm the world's greatest lover—come closer." Our messages vary, and they change in different situations and at different times in our lives, but when the sound of our voice is in tune with that message, it's like having a transmitter that goes straight to the mind and heart of our audience, and that's the system I want you to start building.

Two Voices, Two Messages

For one of my favorite clients, Tony Robbins, the mission is motivation. Tony travels the world coaching presidents, star athletes, heads of companies, and celebrities. If I were to characterize his voice, I'd say he sounds like a schoolyard bully who's ready for a fight. Technically, he often creates a gravelly sound, and he has a tendency to overpower his cords with huge amounts of air. On the surface, it might seem like a voice that's ripe for a makeover, but it's helped him become one of the most successful men in his field because it lines up perfectly with his attitude and his message.

When Tony takes the stage, he challenges you, the audience, to a fight. The contenders in this battle are the old you and the person you want to be. Both opponents are tough, he says, and they are ready to fight to the death. He puts himself in the role not of an impartial referee but of a force that will not let the wrong man win. He will destroy the opponent for you if he has to. It's a challenging position for him to take, and it requires that his audiences believe he can deliver. What's one of the key components of his credibility? His voice.

Before he was on TV, and before you could see his tall, imposing figure in person at a seminar, he had a radio show. His only tool was sound, and he used to claim that he could fix any psychological problem in one hour—guaranteed. Never taking no for an answer, he powered his way into his listeners' minds and forced positive changes. He's not a hand-holder—he's more like an exorcist. And he reinforces his message by using a full gamut of vocal sounds. He may whisper or yell, caress or explode—whatever it takes to move his audience to action. Though some of his sounds are tough on his vocal cords and we're working to make them healthier, his voice is a perfect motivational steamroller. It's not always pretty, but it works.

On the other end of the vocal spectrum is John Gray, who has helped bridge the worlds of men and women with *Men Are from Mars, Women Are from Venus*. John has positioned himself as a mediator and translator, helping the sexes understand each other, and his voice is a gentle blending of male and female sounds. By filling his voice with the soft resonances of middle voice rather than always staying in chest, he successfully manages to create sounds that women feel are unthreatening, inviting, and compassionate—perfectly in line with his mission of helping people open up emotionally.

His soothing sound also reaches male listeners. Rather than challenging men to a confrontation, he invites them to get in touch with the female psyche and to understand that while it may seem foreign, it's not the inexplicable mystery it's always seemed to be. John doesn't drastically switch personas when working with women and men, swinging from gentle to macho. He carefully cultivates a sound that speaks to both sexes in a convincing, nonthreatening way. In incorporating male and female sounds, he never sets himself up as the "other" — so he allows himself to be an emissary to both. Would this technique work for a rugby coach? Probably not. But it's ideal for the fertile ground that John has chosen to walk as a teacher and healer.

Matching Your Voice to You

Do I think that the voice is the primary factor in a person's success? Of course not. I know, however, that the voice is very high on the list. Time and again I see that the people who make it to the top of their chosen field have created a vocal personality that helps them. They have mixed all of their sound possibilities into a big grab bag and continually learned to pull out the ones they need at will.

By now I hope you've accepted the idea that there is no one perfect voice. In some ways your voice is the soundtrack to the life you're creating. If your voice is doing ragtime and your life has the texture and content of an English costume drama, it's going to seem out of place and work against you. There's nothing wrong with ragtime per se, just as there's nothing inherently wrong or right about a voice that's macho and booming, sweet and feminine, or brusque and efficient—as long as the voice enriches the big picture instead of working to undermine it.

♦ When a stockbroker gets on the phone and tries to persuade his top client that he alone knows what the market will do tomorrow, his voice needs to be a blend of strength, knowledge, security, passion, and persuasion. If he sounds too airy, too hesitant, or too disconnected, the client will absolutely not have deep confidence in him.

♦ A Realtor showing a house needs to have a voice that conveys security, compassion, patience, understanding, loyalty, and insight. Can you imagine the effect on a potential home buyer if the broker's voice was nervous and fast-paced, or if she jumbled all of the words together in a mad rush? What if her breathing was so bad that she sounded desperate, always gasping for air. I can guarantee that it would be much harder for her to make the sale.

◆ A doctor's voice needs to be a blend of good bedside manner and cutting-edge technology. Each word needs to be compassionate, knowledgeable, and even technical at the same time. If your doctor were extremely nasal and sounded like he had a cold, would you allow him to get very close to you? If he blocked all of the natural resonances from going above the soft palate and sounded like Yogi Bear, would you perceive him to be incredibly intelligent? Maybe not.

Finding the voice that matches your message doesn't mean pretending to have something you lack—to be effective you need to be genuine. If you're a red-clown-nose kind of guy and you have to speak to a group of terminally ill patients and tell them that the cure they were hoping for isn't working out, use what is real. Make them laugh. Show them the strength of laughter instead of tears. I'm not saying make fun of your audience or make light of a serious situation. I just want to point out that you'll have the most to give if you use what you have and let your listeners share a moment with the real you—who cares enough to be with the real them, even at a terrible time.

Record your voice as you talk about your passion in life. When you listen to your own words, do you hear the enthusiasm, the clarity, the emotion that you feel for your subject? We spend a lot of time developing the expertise to be great parents or professionals or entrepreneurs or artists, and the fact is that if we want to put our talents into the world, we have to spend time developing the voices that will communicate what we know, instead of shortchanging our talents. I don't have any problem persuading singers to sing or to practice imitating sounds they admire. Singing is what they love. I hope you'll begin to look on speaking with that kind of passion.

When you begin to put yourself and your ideas clearly and thoughtfully into the world, with all the energy you feel, people will notice. Their new attention and interest may make you feel self-conscious, but keep using the techniques you've learned. You'll be a more active, influential player in your life, instead of being pushed to the sidelines. Use the exercises in this chapter to experiment with the way you sound. Especially, use the speak-singing technique. *Speak the way you sing.* I can't stress strongly enough just how much that will transform the way you talk—and your total way of thinking and communicating.

And don't be afraid to play. Talk like a broadcaster. Exaggerate the highs and lows in your voice. Spend some time carefully phrasing a snippet of conversation. Shut the door and try on voices until you arrive at something you like. I hope you'll let yourself get carried away with this project of refining your voice—and finding the precise sounds that express who you are. When you do, every conversation you have will be an opportunity to express the energy of your ideas.

· 15 ·

The New World of Presentation

I'VE SPENT my life honing and teaching the skills I've described so far in this book, and have polished thousands of voices. But in the past few years, I've gone beyond helping people make their voices stronger, more resonant, and more expressive. I've zeroed in on a particular set of sounds that have completely transformed my work with speakers: the sounds of emotion.

I'd like to give a taste now of what I've learned about the ways in which you can consciously adjust the variables of your voice—pitch, pace, tone, volume, and melody—to guide the emotional response of your listeners.

If you've ever teared up listening to a TED talk, heard a sermon that made you want to shout *Amen!,* or been charmed and dazzled by a super salesman, you know the power of sound to move you on a pure feeling level. Were you influenced by the words? Probably. But what grabbed you viscerally were the sonic qualities attached to the message. The sound *became* the message. Sound reaches straight into the emotions, and I believe that you can shape your voice in particular ways to evoke specific feelings in your audience.

I've shown thousands of people how to do this, and in the process, I've become known as an influence expert. Because *influence* is what you gain when you know how to tailor the sounds you make to shape the way people feel about you and what you have to say.

You don't want to leave your emotional "imprint" to chance. A recent study revealed that within one second of hearing your voice, people form a judgment about you. Researchers played recordings of the word *Hello* to a group of listeners, and found that they instantly decided how warm, trustworthy, likable, and strong the speaker probably was—an entire first impression. The good news is that you can learn to control what happens in that first second, and all that follow. The sounds of emotion open the door for you and close the deal, whether in a meeting, a webinar, a presentation, or a tête-à-tête—and they do the job almost independently of your words.

In this chapter I'll help you make the sound/emotion connection that can give you new power as a presenter and amplify your effectiveness in every part of your life.

To Master Emotions, You Need Your Entire Vocal Range—Just Like a Singer

When singers come to me and I show them the parts of the voice, the one piece of information that's the Holy Grail for them is middle voice. If they didn't understand it before, it's as though they just got a message from above that explains everything they've been doing wrong in their singing voices. When they can smoothly move from high to low, singers often cry tears of joy.

But when I show speakers middle voice, many of them are underwhelmed. "I get it that my voice is maybe interesting and higher when I use middle," they tell me, "but why do I need that for speaking? I'm not trying to sing opera. I've got no reason to cross that bridge from low to high."

They think all they need is chest voice, the place their voice usually occupies when they speak lower, and the rest of the range is for when they decide to sing karaoke or (rolling their eyes) try out for *The Voice* or some other singing competition.

But to be a master influencer, you need access to every part of your voice, because the sound waves you create enter the bodies of your listeners, triggering memories, feelings, and physical changes that determine how receptive they'll be to you and your message. Just as the melody of a song creates the emotional soundscape that determines whether an "I love you" is an excited discovery or a longing goodbye, the melodies of your speaking voice, shaped and supported by your breath and the other elements that create your sound, send an instant emotional message.

Each part of your vocal range produces sound waves that affect listeners differently. Remember the Three Tenors, the trio of opera greats— Luciano Pavarotti, Plácido Domingo, and José Carreras—who became a pop sensation in the 1990s? They famously gave a one-night show in Dodger Stadium that was seen by a billion people around the world. Notably, there was never a supergroup called the Three Baritones. Why? Because it's the higher tenor part of the range that makes the hair stand up on people's arms. It's full of frequencies that make people excited enough to fill a stadium and scream. Baritones have a certain gravitas, but they can't get a crowd on its feet with the same tidal wave of feeling.

To generalize in a very broad way:

◆ Chest voice is thick, strong, weighty, powerful, commanding. It puts across the feeling: I'm in control.

◆ Middle voice has an energetic quality that makes people pay attention and might just get them up and cheering you.

◆ Head voice is full of sounds that people experience as kind, loving, and compassionate.

When you know how to use all of those sounds, you can combine them in ways that make people want to agree with you, or believe you, or give you what you want, whether it's a deal, a date, or a Kickstarter investment.

I've become convinced that success is based on those sounds. If I want a smart and beautiful woman to kiss me on the mouth, I need to persuade her to do so. If I want a bank to give me a loan or people to do business with me, I have to break through the static and make them believe I'm not only a good risk but a good person. I can't do this with a text or an email or the perfect presentation I've written out. I have to do it with my voice.

The danger of having a limited palette of sounds is that you'll wind up coming across with far less nuance and range than you have in real life. Bosses who live in chest voice may be underlining their sense of control, but they struggle with inspiring, energizing, and connecting with their staff or audience—because no matter what they say, they don't sound energized. They don't sound like they care. They're not believable because their words say one thing and their voices say something completely different.

Four Emotions to Master First

In the first instants of any presentation you make, your audience, whether it's a single person or a crowd of thousands, wants to know one thing: Is this person likable? You have just a second or two—that might give you four to eight syllables—to convey that you're honest, you have charisma, and you're an upbeat and approachable human worth listening to.

1. Start with Happy

So the first emotion you want to master is Happy, because happiness is magnetic, and we tend to equate happiness with success. When people pick up the literal vibrations of happiness from your voice, and see that your physiology matches, they wonder what you're happy about. It might be because you're healthy, have money, or offer a cure for the problems of the world—and they're curious to find out more. This is a lightning-quick impression: We hear and see Happy, Happy feeds and radiates confidence, and confidence signals, "My life is great!" The brain of the listener decides, in that instant, to pay attention.

The basic elements of Happy are increased volume, wide-ranging melody, and a brisk pace. How does that add up to Happy? When you are happy your pulse increases. As your heart rate rises, your body is filled with a blood flow that creates more energy, awareness, and focused attention. As the energy in your body increases, your senses become heightened and you become more attentive to what you see, hear, touch, smell, and taste. Your brain kicks into a well-tuned gear that allows you to process information faster and more efficiently. Here's how sound relates to each of those changes. As your pulse increases you begin to speak more loudly, simply because your newfound happiness cannot be quieted. You want to tell the world what you just won or did or heard or saw. Happiness isn't soft! It wants to be shared with everyone around. You want to let the world know, and you can't do that without extra volume.

You speak more quickly because everything in your body is flowing freely, including the words that are suddenly running out of your mouth because of your excitement, and your desire not to contain them or your feelings. Next, as more blood flows, your senses heighten; you cannot be confined by one monotone note. You find yourself low and high in the range, one moment on the left side of the piano keyboard, the next moment veering to the right. So the intense, extra energy comes out in bigger intervals from the low notes to the high ones, instead of just deliberate, calculated, step-by-step melody swings.

People who hear these sounds register Happy, and the interesting thing is that if you're brimming with happiness but do not amplify the vocal signals enough to send them to your audience in a second or two, you can miss your opening to connect. To sound as happy as you feel, you need to practice Happy.

On audio 37 on the website you'll hear me deliver a typical opening line of a talk, first sticking to low volume and chest voice, then with the sounds of Happy. Same content, very different effects.

2. Immediately Move to Grateful

Happiness is a good start, but it's not enough. People know that you can be happy and still be a jerk. So you can reinforce your identity as a good person by using sounds in a way that communicates that you are honored your audience is listening to you, and lets them know that you sense their attention and appreciate it. Grateful, because it is a response to the audience, is slower and softer than Happy. It's a pause to say, "I noticed you, and I'm savoring our contact." Slightly drawing out the syllables of your words creates a subtle reason for the audience to lean in and feel the appreciation you're sending it. Grateful is gracious—it doesn't rush. Grateful is softer because it comes from a place of honor, a place that is noncompetitive. Too many conversations are like a boxing match—you punch, they punch. By lowering your volume you are saying, "I do not wish to overpower you, only hear you and show you how much I respect your presence."

On audio 38, you'll hear the sounds of Grateful.

3. Master Passionate

Presentation is an energy exchange, and audiences tend to match the level and flavor of the emotion you send out. Your passion for your ideas, your cause, or your product can be infectious when it's carried on the back of frequencies that say your belief in and enthusiasm for your message is genuine. Genuine passion is big enough to fill a room. Yet it's not bullying or coercive. This type of passion is not the same as romantic passion. I am specifically talking about passion as it relates to sharing your enthusiasm and excitement about someone or something.

To sound Passionate, start with consistent volume. When I mentioned Happy earlier, I told you to be louder, but Happy showcases a variable volume that rises with your building level of enthusiasm. Passionate needs a solid level of volume that's carried through most of the words in each sentence. It does not let up. It stays strong and consistent, giving people the subconscious feeling that you are not going to back down, that you are a force of good to be reckoned with and you cannot be silenced.

Melody also changes when you're Passionate. I often say that you should go up in melody when you get to a comma or a period, especially if you are demonstrating Happy. Now, for Passionate, I want you to work on staying higher in the range most of the time. Then, when you get to that comma or period, I want you to stay on the same note. I don't want the last note before a comma or a period to go up so much. Passion is long-lasting, and you can suggest that with your voice by keeping the notes more linear, like a timeline. You won't sound monotone, because you are already on the higher side of your vocal range, and you have a solid amount of volume that signals to people that you're serious.

Passion sounds more thoughtful than Happy, so the big jumps in melody for Happy are not needed here. We just need smaller steps up and down with the solid volume.

Tune in to audio 39 to hear the sounds that color you Passionate.

4. Let Them Know You're Confident

Confidence is currency for a presenter. When it flows through your voice, listeners experience your belief in yourself and your message, and give credibility to you and what you're saying. At the same time, they experience your belief that they can take your message and put it into action, your confidence in them. Confidence is built on the bedrock of your hard work and expertise, and it doesn't jump up and down begging for attention or respect. It walks into the room assuming both are there, and it returns both to the audience. So to sound Confident, you can have solid volume but never feel like you're raising your voice.

Confident doesn't go loud like anger or soft like timidity. It functions like the lead violin in the orchestra, happy and vibrant alone, but ready to play with others when the occasion arises. You should extend the syllables of your words to their longest possible lengths for a Confident sound. To create the sound of Grateful, you sustained syllables a small amount. As you hold out the vowels in Confident mode, you are saying: "Listen to me. Every word counts. Every thought matters. Each word is crafted to share a long-lasting bond that we are creating together." The Confident sound profile tells your audience: "My words are long and strong, and I am confident that you will be stronger by listening to and communicating with me."

Listen to audio 40 to hear my demonstration of what Confident sounds like.

Using Emotion Doesn't Mean Acting, or Going for the Depths

I've worked with hundreds of people in settings that allow me to call individuals up from the audience so I can help them improve their presentation skills. What I've often noticed is that the lovely people I sat next to at lunch, who were comfortable, entertaining, and candid as we got to know each other over a sandwich, get onstage and suddenly believe they have to act. For many people, that means telling the most dramatic stories they can and delivering them with what I think of as acted-out emotions.

I'm surprised at how often "dramatic" means negative. "Tell me about yourself," I'll say, and they'll go straight to the time their parents got sick, their wife left them, and their dog died.

I know we're all looking for a universal point of connection, something we've all been through, and it's true that everyone has faced hardship. But even so, your saddest story probably isn't your most inviting opener.

When you do decide to bring it out, though, here's the secret: You don't have to act sad as you tell it. A sad story, like every other story, is best told by a happy, grateful person—the person who made it to the other side, not the person who's still stuck and suffering.

When you share something tragic, make sure you go up in melody when you get to the last syllable before the commas and the periods. That gives people the impression that the story might have a happy ending. Also, don't take all the melody out of your voice and hold the lowest note in your range like you are Eeyore from *Winnie-the-Pooh*. The words you say are sad enough; you can add a little melody to be sure the listeners know they're not seated at a funeral.

And for goodness' sake, no fake tears. When you talk about your challenges and the moments that have tested you, you don't have to act out your emotions and pretend you're going to cry. I've been onstage with people who've told a story about some tragedy in their lives and punctuated it by falling to the ground. I don't know what effect they wanted, but they didn't get anything but shock and uncomfortable laughter. Even a Ben Kingsley or a Brad Pitt would have a hard time making that kind of drama seem close to genuine.

You don't have to learn to be a good actor to be a powerful presenter. You don't have to be an actor at all, because you're not acting—you're guiding listeners through a landscape full of ideas and emotions. Your job is to decide what you want your audience to know and feel, and to use your voice to help them experience it in the present.

You'll be off to a terrific start if you master Happy, Grateful, Passionate, and Confident, and incorporate those specific sounds where they're appropriate in your presentations. (In the next chapter, you can see how three very different influence experts tap the power of emotion with their voices and bodies to connect with audiences that number in the millions.)

The Sounds That Bring Men and Women Together: Overlapping Frequencies

We live in a mirroring culture. When you walk down the street and see someone coming toward you, if you say "Hey," they say "Hey." We look for signs of danger, and if we don't see them, we want to connect. We adopt the accents and tones of the people we're with, because we resonate with mirrored sounds—they make us feel safe and included. (That's another reason your sounds of Happy, Grateful, Passionate, and Confident draw the same sounds and emotions from your listeners.)

Until boys and girls hit puberty, they enjoy the powerful connection that comes with sharing precisely the same frequencies when they speak. Their vocal cords are about the same length and thickness, and their voices are in the same range. But at adolescence, their larynxes and cords grow at different rates, and boys wind up with the larger sound-making equipment. Their voices drop approximately an octave, and at that point, something fundamental shifts between the male and female of our species that stands in the way of our ability to communicate across gender boundaries. Our sounds are out of sync.

Lately I've been experimenting with a way to bring men and women back together sonically, and I've found a useful tool for reconnecting the genders and giving each side a new level of trust and influence with the other. There are parts of the range where our frequencies still overlap, and I believe that learning to use those frequencies in speaking to people of the opposite gender is a key to helping each side understand and be heard by the other. When we use our common frequencies, I believe we communicate with fewer barriers and gain greater closeness.

A man who can leave his chest voice to use middle and even head voice occasionally can enter the zone of overlapping frequencies, the sonic range that lets him approach women through the sounds of a trusted equal. It's not a foreign skill—men do this all the time when they talk to children and let their voices go lighter. It's almost reflexive, because they don't want to scare the kids. But interestingly, most men generally don't think to change frequencies, or at least let their voices enter the higher part of their range, when they speak to women.

I'm convinced that if they did, they'd find they could reach women in a way that they haven't been able to while locked in chest voice. Many men to whom I introduce this idea balk. They don't want to "sound like a girl." But they begin to entertain the possibility seriously when I point out that women are the number one buyers in the world. Women influence the purchases of their families, control much of their own spending, and shape markets around the world. The biggest mistake a businessman, or any man, can make is to fail to use all the tools he has to influence the women he deals with and wants as clients, customers, and partners. I'm not talking about manipulation. I'm encouraging all of us to enter our vocal common ground.

I remind men to talk UP to women, letting their voices rise into middle, which mirrors a part of women's range, and adding melody and the sound of Happy to neutralize the sometimes threatening tones of the deeper male voice. They can also limit sudden loud volume bursts. Men: Women do not like it when they perceive that you are trying to overpower them in conversations. By getting suddenly louder you not only scare them at a deep level, you also put them on the defensive, making them feel less than equal in the communication.

Women, conversely, can command attention in a group of men by learning to use more chest voice. Once again, I'm not suggesting that women try to sound like men. Rather, they can remind men with sound waves alone of their common humanity and intelligence when they incorporate elements of the male voice as they speak. Establishing that commonality, the "Hey, I'm just like you" connection that we all once had and now must work to build, is easy to do with the voice, even without words. Women can also stop trying to go super-airy and soft with men, thinking that those sounds always generate romantic attention and appeal. Quite often the airy, soft sounds just create more separation, making men feel as though there is no power or strength on the women's side that is worth engaging with. No one wants to have a long communication or relationship with a cotton ball. So, women, understand that if you try to sound airy and light, you can easily be dismissed as not special enough by the men you want to impress.

Listen to audio 41 to hear a man's voice and a woman's speaking in the golden zone where their frequencies overlap. Then try introducing those sounds into your conversations and presentations.

To Have Emotional Impact, You Have to Be Bigger Than You Think

As I've pointed out to many singers, to communicate all the emotion you want your audience to feel, you have to be larger than life. I repeat that often when I teach because in my experience almost everyone uses too little volume and melody, too few changes in pace. Especially as a presenter, you'll want to fill up the entire space in front of you with sound and engulf the people you're communicating with in a sound stream that's full of melody.

This may be uncomfortable at first, but you can grow into the voice that will have the emotion and influence you want by practicing. I know it'll take courage to try out your "new" voice and see how people react. But summon all you've got and start big. Don't judge yourself, just pay attention to how people respond to you differently.

People who know you well might be startled, and their immediate reaction may well be, "What happened to the quiet mumbling guy? Who the heck are you?"

So the best way of trying out all you've learned, and all the sounds and emotions you want to play with, is to take them out for a test drive in front of strangers or people who don't see you every day.

Communicate in a way that emphasizes the sounds of Happy and Passionate, and look for people to come back at you with the same qualities in their voices and communication.

You may think this is way too risky to try. But if you've been doing the exercises I've taught you, you already have a strong voice filled with melody and volume. You've weeded out the nasality, the squeaky hinge sound, and the airy sounds in your voice. You're entirely ready to present the new you to one new person—because you're already polished.

I'd also like to remind you that the vast majority of people you're likely to encounter have probably never thought about their voices, much less paid attention to using specific sounds to express and evoke emotion.

As you take your bigger, more expressive voice into the world, your goal is to stay engaged in what's going on at the moment. The best presenters have learned not to step outside themselves and judge what they're doing as they do it. They trust themselves to flow with what's in front of them—and that takes practice.

I practice at the dry cleaner and car wash, with the checkout people in the grocery store, at the coffee shop on the corner. I meet people with happiness and gratitude and passion, and I always have something to say, even if it's "I'm so glad it's not raining today." I'm out there with the intent of being sure there's volume and melody and controlled emotion coming out of me whenever I speak, so that when I need to step onstage, or be effective in a meeting, I'm ready.

No one is going to break into your cocoon and pull you out as a butterfly. But that's hardly a problem, because you can do it yourself. Go out and start practicing. Connecting. Influencing. You have nothing to lose.

· 16 ·

Secrets of the Internet Stars

SOME OF your most important audiences are people you may never be in the same room with. They're the potential fans, customers, and clients who hear you speak for the first time through the video on your website, or discover you in a YouTube clip on their phones. If you can send your energy, intelligence, and passion through the screen of your audience's phones and devices, it's possible to catch people's attention, make them believe in you, and build an enormous following that wants to spend time with you, and buy what you're selling.

Three of my students, Bethany Mota, Brendon Burchard, and Simon Sinek, have become some of the most influential people on the Internet, tapping into incredibly large—and very different— audiences by honing their presentation skills to take full advantage of the power of video and social media. I'd like to show you how each of them pours enthusiasm, relatability, confidence, and intelligence into what they create online, and how you can use the same skills to bring your own on-screen presence to life.

Bethany Mota: "I'm Your Best Friend"
Bethany is an energetic California girl who started making YouTube videos in her room by herself in 2009, when she was just thirteen. She became known for her "haul" videos, in which she'd bring shopping bags full of clothing home from the mall and pull out her purchases,

item by item, showing them to viewers and talking about them as if she were sitting in her room with her best friend—"This is such a cute skater skirt!" "I love this crop top with the little foxes on it."

Thousands, then millions of girls tuned in (at this writing, her YouTube channel has 10.3 million subscribers). Over time, she began talking about makeup, fashion, and food and offering do-it-yourself tips. Though she's out of her teens now, she may get upwards of 14 million views for a video on how to get ready for school in the morning or a tour of her bedroom. She's learned what her fans want, and she's more than willing to give it to them with the goal of inspiring them, and having fun.

To say that her fans love her is a gross understatement. They see her as a role model, and if they can't be just like her, they'll take the second-best choice: claiming her as their best friend. She makes it easy to believe she's speaking just to them.

What separated Bethany from so many other young women posting videos on YouTube? How did she rise so fast and far above the competition? I could talk about her business sense or her work ethic or her never-say-never attitude, all of which I've seen. But instead, I'll focus on the one thing you should focus on too: her ability to be liked and to create a character people want to be friends with.

How Bethany Uses Happy and Grateful

Watch any of Bethany's videos and you'll see her expertly showcasing the two "start here" elements of presentation I introduced in the previous chapter: Happy and Grateful. By exuding happiness, you make the audience feel your joy and energy and let people know that you are delighted to be sharing.

To tap the sound of Happy, you need to have more volume than usual, and a lot more melody. (Listen again to audio 37 if you'd like a refresher.) Bethany uses both volume and melody all the time to infuse her content with enthusiasm. Also, pay close attention to her physiology, what she's doing with her face. As she infuses her voice with Happy, her face lights up with a big smile that shows her teeth. Her cheeks are high, and her eyes are coming up at the corners because of it. Her whole face seems built around that smile. Notice also that when she gets a little more serious, mentioning any subject that might be less than fun, or something that didn't turn out so perfectly, she still seems to be fighting to keep a partial smile, as if to say to her fans, "Things don't always end up as you had hoped, but with a positive attitude, everything will still work out."

Some of you may remember that I've said going too wide with the corners of the mouth can make you sound nasal. So, you may be wondering, won't smiling send my voice to my nose? The quick answer: Yes, but it's a minor problem for speakers, and there's a quick fix. When singers' mouths go too wide, their vowels get distorted and they sound less focused and less beautiful. But speakers can keep nasal sounds at bay by continuing to drop their jaws as they talk, so nasal sounds won't take over. Smile, let your jaw drop naturally, and let the happiness flow to your listeners.

Bethany is also highly skilled at using her voice to convey to her audiences how grateful she is. She easily and naturally slips into the slower speech, lowered volume, and stretched-out words that comprise Grateful (compare what you see on Bethany's video with audio 38's Grateful demo). When she does that, and when you do it, audiences will feel as though you're appreciating every second you spend with them. Notice how elongating words, specifically the vowels, creates the sense that Bethany is savoring her every moment on-screen, because she appreciates your time, your patience, and the positive energy you're sending back to her.

Bethany is a breath of fresh air. She is not projecting any strong ego or overconfidence by suddenly getting very loud or reducing the amount of melody she normally uses. If she made either or both of those changes, people would think, "Wow, why is she mad? Who is she angry at?" By keeping her melody strong and varied, she keeps her listeners engaged.

The Body Reinforces the Message

Bethany makes people feel comfortable in subtle ways with her use of her body. She speaks directly to the camera and looks relaxed and comfortable. Part of that has to do with the position of her head.

Bethany seems to have zero tension as she tilts it left, right, and forward, her hair bouncing in rhythm with her movements. Many of us create tension in our neck and stomach areas. So when we watch someone who seems to have less tension there, because of the ease of her movements, we sense less pain and nervousness, and it makes us emotionally and physically relax a bit as well.

You can drain the tension from your neck by trying this: Let your head fall to your left shoulder, now your right one, then let it fall backward, then all the way forward. At each spot, hold yourself there for five to eight seconds before you move to the next position. Then try some very slow head rolls. Move counterclockwise for a few rotations and then clockwise. That will help relieve a bit of the pressure if done regularly. And as I've mentioned, you can relax your stomach by making sure that as you exhale you don't tighten the very top part of the stomach area where the ribs come close together. You need to exhale and keep that part moving in slowly and gently. If you are pushing that area out, and a lot of you probably are, that's the specific place you need to focus on: Allow it to come freely back in as the air and sound come out.

Now look at Bethany's hands and the way they seem to move freely, accentuating the words and sounds coming out of her mouth. She rarely uses parallel gestures, which look stiff and a little robotic. Instead, she mixes it up, with one hand moving this way, the other moving that way, in harmony with the rest of her body. You should be videoing yourself constantly to be sure you haven't fallen prey to the parallel-gesture monster. I know you've seen politicians and TV folks doing it, but you'll need to be more fluid to succeed as part of the new generation that comes across on the small screen as real, not fake or calculating.

Be careful about using too much movement if you're being videoed and watched on small screens; you want to stay within the area the camera lens can take in. I've seen too many people wander in and out of the frame, looking more like ponies on a carousel than Internet media stars. Stay right where the camera can see you, and don't move too far left or right. As you fill your defined space, you can still create excitement with sound and body movements. Look at the camera and keep your gestures close to your body. Don't extend your arms so far from your body that your hands go out of the camera frame. You'll often see Bethany bounce on her bed, seeming full of energy she can hardly contain.

A note on equipment: If you have a video camera, great. If not, feel free to use the camera built into your computer as you're starting out. Just be sure that the camera is no lower than your eye level. The view of your face is less flattering from a lower angle, making it look as though you have a double chin even when you don't. You'll need at least one good light. (Check out the Diva Ring Light. It's a good one.) And invest in an external USB mike so your sound is clear. Bethany is a pro at showcasing herself as an average kid with both joy and the feeling of being comfortable in her own skin, not trying to be a supermodel or a know-it-all. She laughs at her own mistakes and even edits in video clips where she messes up. All of that makes her more relatable. People don't follow those who lead from ego. Viewers want to follow those who lead from the heart, and Bethany is a master at that.

Her believability—the result of the way she uses her voice and body—has propelled her to Internet superstardom in just six years. Ever enthusiastic about the clothes she showed viewers, Bethany got the attention of clothing brands and signed a deal with the company Aeropostale to design a clothing line, which dramatically exceeded all sales expectations the first year. In 2014–2016 Bethany was voted the number one female Web Star at the Teen Choice Awards. Now she's singing, and the first song we worked on together went straight to number one on the *Billboard* charts.

That's where great presentation skills can lead.

Brendon Burchard: "I'm Just Like You. If I Could Do It, You Can Too."

Brendon Burchard, another client who's an Internet sensation, is one of the top ten most-watched people on the Web. Unlike Bethany, who's about half his age, Brendon is not trying to attract or engage millions of teens. His audience is an older group of men and women looking to achieve financial success and self-fulfillment by learning to market themselves and their unique abilities to the public.

Brendon's clients are entrepreneurs, presenters, and influencers — doctors who want to write books and become best-selling authors, or fitness experts who want to bring new exercise and health techniques to a mass market. Some of the people he attracts want to be motivational speakers or high-performance coaches, so he teaches them how to corner that particular part of the business world.

While Bethany is looking to help teens choose the right eye shadow for that night's date, Brendon is trying to help people sell books, products, and seminars, enrich their own lives, and, if possible, make the world a better place. His motto is Live, Love & Matter. He believes that if you embrace your passions, love intensely, and have a positive effect on the people around you, you'll be fulfilled financially and emotionally. With that much difference between Bethany and Brendon's branding and messaging, and the very different ages and interests of their viewers, you might assume they would need completely different voices, personality traits, and presentational styles. But you'd be wrong. Brendon and Bethany have a great deal in common, and it starts with the learned and practiced ability to engage people and to make them feel something.

Though Brendon is older, he's still filled with a childlike wonder and energy. Watching him is like seeing a kid open presents on Christmas morning. He has a wide-eyed joy and happiness that are both uplifting and infectious. How does he create that childlike, positive personality? He starts from the same place Bethany does: by delivering Happy and Grateful.

Brendon makes sure that his volume is strong to showcase how happy he really is, and that his melody takes a very specific "upturn" when he gets to commas or periods. This helps viewers stay connected and positive. At each pause, Brendon consciously makes his voice rise in pitch. I often talk about my distaste for the way kids learn the English language in school, specifically how they learn cadence and phrasing. We are taught that when we get to a comma or a period, we should make the last syllable go lower and softer.

The problem with this use of sound (audio 42 on the website) is that it sends a subconscious signal to the viewer or listener that the speaker is done after each pause. The voice goes down, it gets softer, and, essentially, it waves goodbye. If you were listening to an orchestra and the sound trailed off every five seconds or so, then jumped back to life and blasted out more music for another five to eight seconds, you would get up and leave. It would be hard to endure even the most exquisite sonata if the flow were broken and the energy drained away at annoyingly frequent intervals. Yet we're taught that it's fine to do something quite comparable when we give a talk or read aloud. Let me just say this: Don't do it. You're pushing your audience away.

Instead, use the commas and periods to put more melody into your voice and make people feel happy. It sounds like this (audio 43) when you use Brendon's technique and raise the pitch of your voice, or stay on the same note, when you get to a comma, a period, or the last part of a word.

This technique will keep your viewers excited, looking forward to your next words. You *have* to master this tip if you want people to think you are happy. And believe me, you DO want that. It's the best way to start communicating with someone you don't know yet. Brendon always leads with Happy.

But it's worth noting that the sounds of Happy for Brendon and Bethany are necessarily a bit different. Bethany can use a lot of extra melody, going high like a flute and jumping all over the melody scale. She is young and fun, and her viewers are wild and spirited, the kinds of kids who might suddenly get up and dance on a bed or eat a gallon of ice cream and squirt whipped cream from the can right into their mouths. That type of exuberance is filled with abandon — and it feels amazing. Bethany's audience knows that feeling, and they can handle much more melody from Bethany than Brendon's viewers want from him.

His fans are older, with more responsibilities. Brendon's peeps *do* get out of their chairs at his seminars, when he pumps up the music and runs around the stage, leading them in a brisk few minutes of clapping and jumping. But other than that, most of those people don't have a lot of that kind of action in their daily routines. If Brendon pumped up the happiness in his voice with the kind of vocal swoops Bethany makes, his audience would probably think he sounded fake or phony, or as though he were pretending to be someone he's not, at an age that he's not. So Happy for him needs to involve smaller melody jumps and less dramatic volume changes. His Happy needs to be real, and a good deal more subtle than Bethany's.

Listen to audio 44 on the website to hear what it might sound like if Brendon used Bethany's style of Happy, and get a sample of how I'd advise him to scale it down.

After Happy, Brendon moves into Grateful, sounds that are very similar to Bethany's. He, too, gets slower and softer and stretches out his words. The sounds of Grateful are less defined by age-appropriateness or attention than Happy is. I think that's because the whole concept of being grateful comes from a more adult perspective. A child is first happy to have a new toy, lost in the joy of playing with it. The idea of gratitude tends to come in only when a parent or gift-giver says, "Do you know how lucky you are to be the first one on your block with that toy?" or, "You'd better thank Nana right now for giving you such an awesome present."

In my mind, gratitude is a more mature concept, filled with self-awareness and perhaps a greater awareness of the outside world. So when Bethany sounds grateful, she sounds a little older, and when Brendon sounds grateful, he sounds his age. Do you follow?

Watch any of Brendon's videos and you will also see an impressive display of how to use your body properly. Brendon is the poster child for the word *energetic*. His arms, legs, and head are fluidly moving to accentuate every sound he speaks. When he gets serious and his pitch shifts to lower notes, his body comes to a noticeable halt. He might move only one arm, in a slow way that makes you feel how deliberate that gesture is.

When Brendon does that, shifting from big to smaller movements to denote seriousness, his face changes as well. His eyebrows come down from the Happy spot on his face, and he focuses his eyes very intently on one person at a time, as if to say, "Now I'm really talking to YOU alone, now I am coaching only YOU, and you are going to get my A material, the insights that will actually change your life."

If most people stared as intently as Brendon does, they might come across as angry, but because he softens his body movements, slows them down, and reins them in, viewers don't feel physically threatened. He also makes sure that his voice never loses its melody, because once you take melody out, people immediately think you are getting mad at them, and then they only want to avoid that feeling and YOU.

Both Bethany and Brendon use their voices and physiology to make you want to spend more time with them, learn from them, be friends with them, and feel good when you are watching them. Both make you feel as though you could be better, smarter, and more popular and successful, and could get more out of the life that is available to you right now.

When Brendon lowers his volume, tempers the melody, and slows his speech and movement — saying, "I'm just like you, and I built this big business, so you can do it too" — people believe him. When Bethany raises her volume, goes higher in pitch, speaks faster, and smiles more — saying, "I just made it to the finals of ABC's *Dancing With the Stars*, and I don't even dance that well, so you can do anything YOU want to do" — her fans believe her as well. The voice needs to match the message. You're not credible when your sounds don't match your words.

Positioning Yourself as an Expert

Bethany's and Brendon's love of sharing information and enthusiasm with their audiences created the kind of connection that's a foundation for selling products without being "salesy." Bethany's love for a pair of Forever 21 sweater shorts could send fans running to the store, and now she's bringing her own fashion line to them. And Brendon, who is selling ideas, has built a supremely successful business by enticing people to buy products, attend live events, and purchase services based on those ideas.

It takes an added skill set to do that: You have to know how to present yourself as an Expert.

Experts share insights about life, business, and strategies, and Brendon is a master at that, as well as being a motivator who makes people feel as though they can do anything they set their minds to. He doesn't come across as a teacher who is angry and demands respect. He's more like your best friend, who sees where you're missing the boat and then helps put you back on course.

So after Grateful, how does Brendon change his voice to get to Expert? First he gets louder again. Remember how Happy had volume and Grateful got a little softer? Well, Expert ranks just softer than the louder volume of Happy. Think about it. If you had just won the lottery, you would have moments of uncontrollable volume as joy poured in. But an Expert's volume is based on consistency, timelessness, confidence, and a solid background and foundation. It has to sound like trust.

So the Expert's volume is stable and even throughout each sentence, without sudden volume changes that catch listeners or viewers off guard. The goal is to make them feel comfortable with you, but also to make them see that you are a strong teacher who has their best interests at heart and is powerful enough to calm their fears.

Once an Expert has connected with an audience using Happy and Grateful, he or she needs to use melodies that make small jumps from low notes to highs. I call this Stair-Step Melody. On the stair steps, you are either walking up (going from low notes to higher ones), walking down (going from high notes to lower), or staying on the landing (making the same note repeatedly).

The Expert cannot miss any steps. He or she has to move deliberately from one small step to the next without trying to leap over any. This gradual movement of melody is what keeps the listener attentive and focused on you, without being pulled toward distractions like email messages or texts that pop up on their phones. Hear an example of this Stair-Step Melody on audio 45.

In my work with presentation students—and sometimes on the stages I share with Brendon—I teach not just Happy, Grateful, and the other emotions I've shown you, but a whole range of combinations of sound that help people emphasize the particular identity they want people to perceive. Practicing the sounds of the Expert can give you a taste of the way you can match your voice to your message and identity to reach through the screen and get an audience to respond.

The Sound of the TED Talk Guru

I'd like to give you one last example of what an Expert sounds like. Meet Simon Sinek, a very smart guy with a very fast brain. Simon is a leadership guru who was trained as an ethnographer, is on the staff of the RAND Corporation think tank, and teaches at Columbia University. One measure of his reach and influence: His 2009 TED Talk, "How great leaders inspire action," has been viewed more than 28 million times.

Simon's passion is teaching people and organizations how to inspire action so the world will have more fulfilled, effective people in it. Though he needs to connect with his audience on the same level of likability that Bethany and Brendon do, he also needs to establish himself as an expert whose credibility, effectiveness, and belief people will trust (as does Brendon). At the center of his message is that everyone needs to "start with their why," and communicate, from the very first moment, the "purpose, cause, or belief that inspires you to do what you do."

I got my first glimpse of Simon's intelligence when I heard him deliver a presentation at Zappos, where both of us had been asked to speak. I'd watched a video of him beforehand to familiarize myself with his work, and I realized as I saw him live that he was one of those rare people who can fully memorize every phrase, cadence, and comma of what they're going to say. That was all the more impressive because it's extremely difficult to deliver a memorized speech with empowered passion that feels alive in the room. Even the most practiced speakers can sound rote and distanced when they've memorized their material.

But Simon had mastered that art. His content was interesting, his presentation was genuine and entertaining, and he sounded as smart as he is. When I spoke to his head of operations afterward, praising what I'd seen, she said, "Really? He was all over the place today, taking chunks and moving them around." She sounded as though that had been a problem, but actually it's an effective way to stay in the moment. Even with every piece memorized, Simon still left room for his mind to jump to whatever he thought of next, just as people like me do when we speak from notes or an outline.

While I don't recommend that the vast majority of us try to memorize our presentations, Simon is proof that you can do it in a way that's so connected to the moment that you stay fully engaged in your own story, as though you're telling it for the first time—and that's what listeners hear.

Every teacher and Expert has to master the art of presenting very familiar material with the same excitement he or she wants his or her students and listeners to feel when they discover it. People often tell me, "You must have the patience of a saint to teach the same lessons, all these scales and warm-ups, day after day." But this is what I tell them:

Each time I'm in front of a new student or audience, I tell myself this is the first time I've ever been in this moment with you today, doing exactly this. It's a brand-new situation, and who knows what can happen?

The exercises become new information, and if you're my student, I'm listening to you, doing this for the first time. You are different, unique, and I have to think about what I'm hearing and watch for how you're responding so I'll know what I need to say next. Coming from that place, there's no such thing as rote or tedious. And I was very aware that Simon had found a way to let this attitude and approach shine through even a presentation he was delivering word for word, perhaps for the hundredth, or thousandth, time. That's the mind-set of the Expert. We did a lesson afterward, and as often happens when I work with a superstar singer or presenter, I wondered if I'd listen closely to what he was doing with his voice and wind up saying, "You know, I'll be honest: You're perfect and I have nothing to teach you." But the truth is, that never happens. Because there's always a way to make a voice and presentation run in a healthier, more powerful way. Even when someone's at the top of his or her game, we can raise the quality and take that person to a new peak. The people at the top know this, and they're the ones who always seem to work the hardest when they're with me.

It's OK to Sound Vulnerable, Even When You're the Expert

As we worked together, we realized that Simon was a tenor and had a high male voice. Yet every sound he made when he spoke was coming from the lower part of his chest voice. My theory about why he'd chosen to hang out in that range was that he'd been presenting material from his latest book, *Why Leaders Eat Last*, to a lot of heads of corporations. The lessons in that book were drawn from his work with officers in the Marines, and the stories seemed to call forth a low, "manly" voice.

One thing I pointed out to Simon, though, was that when I'd worked in the past with officers in the military, it always struck me that the highest-ranking generals were not the ones with the loudest, lowest voices. At those top levels, officers thought of themselves as strategists who led with compassion, organizational skills, and theories, not with brute force. It surprised me to see that many of them had high, airy voices.

Nothing in Simon's talk, and no point he was trying to make about leadership, was stopping him from also showing the higher parts of his voice, I told him. Just like the leaders he was describing, he needed to showcase a more vulnerable and gentle side of who he is. We worked on the whole top part of his voice, putting more middle voice into some of it to add another layer of compassion, and to let audiences experience a part of his personality and character that the generals expressed instinctively, and that he'd never allowed himself to show.

The Expert often thinks that he or she needs to be invulnerable, but the sound of leadership that an Expert wants to express is also the sound of compassion.

I'd noticed that Simon didn't have a lot of volume changes in his presentation. That, I guessed, probably had to do with the kind of seeking, introspective content he'd made his name explaining. He was an Expert in the "whys" of selling and motivation, and there's an almost meditative quality to looking inside yourself and your company to find the "why" at its core.

There is a calmness to this sort of inward-looking content, which so many Experts share. Yet they need to convey the excitement of discovering the content they're delivering. In Simon's case, that centered on pinpointing the purpose behind what you do—because that "why" inspires people to fall in love with what you do. It's compelling content, but there was another level of excitement he could bring to audiences by changing the volume of his voice, raising it to show excitement, then going softer to get listeners to lean in and listen harder. If he could go bigger with his voice after drawing listeners in, they'd feel more connected and feel as though they'd been on a journey with him. When Simon started soft and stayed there, he was muting the power of his material, but he quickly saw how playing with volume amplified the level of energy he could bring to his audiences.

That's a key tool for Experts. Your content is important. But the way you *sound* is what brings your audience to it and makes them want to stay. Practice and master the sounds of emotion. It's worked tremendously well for Bethany, Brendon, and Simon—and it will work for you, too.

· 17 ·

Breakthrough Techniques for Stuttering and Spasmodic Dysphonia

MORE THAN 70 million people worldwide stutter. That's about 1 percent of the entire population. In the United States alone, more than 3 million people cope with stuttering every day. Those of us without the condition can only imagine how frustrating it must be to know what you want to say but not be able to get the words out of your mouth—to be engaged in conversation, moving from word to word, vowel to consonant, not knowing which sound might get stuck.

Current research attributes stuttering to a mixture of causes—genetics, child development problems, disruptions in the way the brain processes speech and language, and even the pressure of a family's high expectations.

But although speech therapy has helped countless people to some extent, there's no cure. Over the years, a lot of people have sought me out, looking for an alternative therapy or cure, and I've been happy to help. My techniques have had a high success rate with many of my clients, and I love seeing the transformation they can bring to someone's life. One story in particular stays forever in my mind.

My kids have attended a wonderful nearby school in an unpretentious, charming community filled with great kids and with parents who are actively involved in supporting the students from the elementary grades through high school.

One day, the mother of one of the high school students called my office. Her son, Jeremy, had been stuttering since he began to speak. (About 5 percent of small children do, but three quarters of them stop by late childhood.) I could hear the pain in the woman's voice as she told me about the challenges Jeremy was having in school and in social situations. He'd been struggling for a long time with self-esteem issues, she said, and she blamed the stuttering for much of that.

She'd tried speech therapy with little success and didn't know where else to turn. She just wanted to help her son. So did I.

This is what I told her:

I'm not a doctor, merely a vocal coach who works intuitively with sounds, physiology, and mind-set. The theories and strategies I share to help people who stutter or have other voice-related problems stem from my experiences with clients. They're the results of experiments that we've done to see what variables bring relief.

As a voice coach, I have spent my life working on two key skill sets:

1. How to get the vocal cords to move in specific ways, and
2. How to control the way air comes through the cords.

If you can control the air and the movement of the vocal cords, you can sing or speak much better.

When I began working with clients who stutter, I used a lot of my standard vocal exercises to see what might work. I remembered that when I was little, my family used to watch a TV variety show where a country singer named Mel Tillis would come on as a guest. Before he sang, he would always tell a funny story and stutter his way through it, making fun of himself in a sweet, vulnerable way, and the audience would laugh with him and not at him.

The striking thing was that when Mel started to sing, he sounded completely normal. He never stuttered for a second. I stored that memory in my brain for many years, and I decided to focus on it when I started looking for a way to help people recover from stuttering. After a lot of experimentation and thought, I began to see stuttering as an airflow problem. When everything runs smoothly, the words are supposed to ride out of the mouth on a solid stream of air. If the air comes out of the mouth in small, disconnected bursts, the sound will follow that pattern and be broken up and disjointed. You can try this for yourself.

Hold up your hand about an inch from your mouth, palm facing toward you and fingers pressed together with no space between them. Remembering the diaphragmatic breathing you learned in chapter 3, take a nice breath in through your nose. Pretend you have a balloon in your stomach, fill up that balloon with air, letting your belly expand, and then exhale while you say and hold out the word "MEEEEEEEEEEEE."

You should feel a solid amount of air hitting your fingers, a stream that doesn't stop until the word stops. Now read the following sentence aloud, pausing each time you come to the dots: "Roger says... when I stop a lot...before I...get to a...comma or a period...it... sounds like this...and I don't feel a solid stream...of air...hitting my fingers. This is...what I mean by NOT having a...solid stream of air." (Listen to audio 46 to hear this pattern.)

When a person stutters, the basic instinct seems to be to look at what's happening in the individual's mouth, thinking that the tongue or the lips or the teeth are somehow getting in the way of the sound production. I thought that was a possibility as well.

But the more I played around with it, the more I realized that if the right amount of air were coming through the vocal cords and out of the mouth, the placement of the tongue, lips, or teeth would not be enough to make a person stutter. Instead, the right airflow would open up the back part of the throat and guide the words out regardless of what was happening in the mouth.

So today I always start by teaching clients who stutter how to do diaphragmatic breathing, the same way I've explained it in chapter 3. You inhale deeply, pretending to fill up a balloon in your abdomen, and then exhale and allow the belly to fall back to its normal position. With these clients, I emphasize focusing on the exhale, and learning to send air more evenly out of the mouth as they speak.

When you can breathe out in long, flowing lines, you can connect long, flowing lines of words.

We start with the sounds of the vocal exercises, then make the transition from singing "nonwords" to actual words. When they're comfortable with exercises, I ask people to sing phrases like "I CAN if I want," instead of gugs and googs and mums and nos. (Listen to my example on audio 47.) Other phrases that work well:

I MAKE my own way.

My TIME is at hand.

I GO where I want.

My NEIGHBOR is nice.

Next, say the following: If-I-connect-all-the-words-together-like-this, . . . and-only-stop-when-I-get-to-a-comma-or-a-period. . . . a-solid-amount-of-air-will-come-out, . . . keeping-the-words-attached.

When you sing a song, the words actually do connect to one another the way I just demonstrated. A song is not a random combination of unlinked words and notes. So when you sing, and when anyone who stutters sings, it's quite easy to connect the words and the air and have the words leave the mouth on a solid stream of air that doesn't stop until you get to a comma or a period.

Be Prepared for Success—a Cautionary Tale

I taught all these techniques to Jeremy, and after a one-hour session with me he was speaking like a professional orator. If you hadn't heard him before, you never would have guessed that he had a problem with stuttering. His mother cried when she heard the difference, and I felt like I had saved the world, or at least his part of it.

Before they left I asked Jeremy's mom to call me in a week and let me know how things were going. I was excited and anxious about Jeremy going back to school the next day and unveiling his new voice. I know how hard kids can be on other kids, and how some people react to change.

Many times over the years I have seen clients back down from using their new voices, just because someone else made them feel self-conscious or reacted in surprise to the new sounds coming out. The people who know you are used to your sounding a certain way, and if you make a change, no matter how positive, it can catch them off guard and they might say something that could make you retreat to old habits.

A week went by and I didn't hear from Jeremy's mom. At the end of the second week I called her, and once more she was in tears, not happy ones this time. Jeremy sounded great when we left your studio, she said, but the next day, one of the kids said to him, "Who are you trying to be? Who do you think you are now?" And almost instantly, Jeremy went back to the way he used to sound. His so-called friends didn't want Jeremy to be better, they just wanted him to be the same guy as the day before. And faced with that, Jeremy was afraid to change.

His mother was devastated, but there was nothing she could say or do to persuade her son to try again. I will never forget this story, and I wanted to share it with you because I want you to learn from it and not fall into the same trap.

Jeremy didn't do anything wrong—he was perfect. But he wasn't prepared to be challenged.

I want you to be prepared. In the quest to have speaking and singing voices that are healthy and life-changing, you will need to have the courage to stand behind your decision to be the best. You must focus on the prize and realize how precious it is. You will also need to explain to the people closest to you what you're doing. I now tell all of my students to let their friends and family know that they went to see a voice coach, that they may be making sounds that are a little different, and that they are asking for patience and acceptance as they try to make themselves better. Building this kind of support system works out a lot better than surprising people.

What I most want you to know is that you *can* succeed, just as Jeremy did before he was derailed—and that you need to prepare for success, then keep practicing what I teach you. You are not destined to stutter forever. You can change the way air moves in and out of your body, and the words will ride out the way they should.

Help for Spasmodic Dysphonia

Once I saw that this simple airflow technique worked, and that it seemed to be helping people more than conventional methods of treatment for stuttering, I was thrilled and happy to help people recover. My clients were very vocal within the social media community, posting their progress online and telling people about my effective stuttering therapy methods.

As a result, people began contacting me with other serious vocal issues for which they couldn't find solutions. One of those maladies is called spasmodic dysphonia, or SD. I'm sure many of you have never even heard that term. I'm a vocal coach and had never heard of it myself until relatively late in life. According to the National Spasmodic Dysphonia Association, www.dysphonia.org, SD is a vocal disorder—that's what dysphonia means—that results when the muscles of the larynx spasm, causing the voice to "break up, or sound strained, tight, strangled, breathy, or whispery. The spasms often interrupt the sound, squeezing the voice to nothing in the middle of a sentence, or dropping it to a whisper. However, during other activities, such as breathing and swallowing, the larynx functions normally."

The condition affects about 50,000 people in North America, the SD association says. It's more common in women than in men, it generally occurs in middle age, and there is no cure. The disease may go into remission, but remissions are rare and brief.

I am always up for a challenge, but honestly, when people started coming to me with SD, it was hard not to feel overwhelmed. They were understandably sad, frustrated, and confused. Can you imagine speaking normally your whole life, suddenly hitting middle age, and then having your words become strangled for no apparent reason?

There was some evidence to suggest that SD was brought on by an emotional crisis, like losing someone you love, but the statistics, and my own discussions with clients over the years, made me and others skeptical about that. Plenty of people had no specific emotional trauma and still had a sudden onset of SD.

One thing was clear: No matter what the cause, once you got SD, you could no longer trust your voice to be there for you. My career has been centered on helping people find their voices and communicate with the world around them, and when I became aware of this mysterious condition that was making so many people silent, I was passionate about trying to help.

In the beginning, I tried to use the same airflow techniques that had worked with stuttering patients, and had some success. Teaching someone how to get air in, and to effectively control how it comes back out of the mouth, carrying the words with it, is always helpful. But that wasn't enough to fix the SD problem.

I began to experiment with the pitch of SD patients' voices, how high or low in the range they were speaking. Many clients had lowered their voices, as if they were a piano with just the very bottom keys working. With those low notes, most were making the squeaky hinge sound I taught you about in chapter 2.

Others were adding a ton of air to their voices and sounding like Marilyn Monroe. They were simply trying to find any sound that could get the words out, and going to extremes in the process — eliminating the air, which creates the squeaky hinge, or exaggerating the air with the Marilyn voice. But neither was working.

In my trials, I started asking everyone to try to move closer to head voice, way above where they were normally speaking. That did help them get more sound out. The combination of speaking in head voice and speaking only while the stomach was coming back in from a diaphragmatic breath made things even better.

Then I asked people to connect their words as though they were singing, as I was doing for the stuttering patients, and that also seemed to help. The problem was, it would work for a short period, and then the person would spasm and the sound would disappear.

It was difficult to keep the air and the vocal cords working normally for any length of time, so I kept looking for what was missing.

I noticed that whenever the sound got strangled, I could see and feel clients creating pressure in two specific regions of their bodies. One was the upper part of the stomach area, and the second was the back of both sides of the neck. The fear of not being able to speak would make anyone tense. But the amount of tension I was noting in both of these spots was far greater than any I could attribute to nervousness, stage fright, or the fear of speaking poorly. The neck was filled with pressure and tightness.

In order to relieve the tension, I took the clients' heads in my hands and asked them to lend me control of the movement as they let their heads become free and heavy and allowed me to support the weight. Then I would gently roll the head in a small circular motion from front to back. It was hard for people to let me do this at first; they were tightening the muscles and trying to pull the head away from my hands. But I kept playing with it until they relaxed the neck enough for me to have some control.

You can play with this yourself by doing some small neck rolls in a circular motion, clockwise and then counterclockwise. Don't try to take your chin too close to your chest or too close to your back. Just make smaller circles, trying to release the excess tension in the back part of the neck. Once the client relaxed the neck, I was able to get more sound out, so that was very helpful.

My goal was to have clients use all the helpful elements we'd discovered at the same time:

1. Only speak while the stomach is coming in.
2. Speak much higher in the range, toward the head voice.
3. Relax the tension in the neck.
4. Connect all the words.

Those factors, used simultaneously, made the voice sound a lot less strangled.

I worked on the tension in the top part of the stomach by asking people to *allow* their stomachs to come back in *without* using the muscles to make that happen. Singers often tighten their stomachs on the exhale to "help" push the breath out, so I was familiar with the problem.

I used this analogy to help my SD clients understand why exhaling doesn't require any added effort from the muscles: When air goes into a balloon, the balloon gets bigger as the inside fills and the sides stretch out. When you want to release air from the balloon, all you have to do is open the top a little and the air happily rushes out of the hole. You certainly do not need to squeeze the balloon to get the air out. The same idea applies to the lungs. Air comes into the lungs and they expand, like the sides of the balloon. The lungs don't like that expanded feeling, so they want the air to come out. You don't need to pull your stomach in, any more than you need to push the sides of the balloon in. You need simply to relax your stomach as you exhale and let it gently fall back to its normal smaller position as air leaves your nose and mouth. (Review the discussion of breathing in chapter 3 for more details that might help you.)

Taking away tension in both the neck and the upper stomach area was a good step toward helping someone with SD relax and speak more easily. But it didn't solve my problem with consistency. Remember how the students would sound better for a few minutes or so and then go back to not being able to get the words out? Well, let me tell you what I've learned.

During my sessions with students, I continued to do all of the things I've mentioned to help eliminate the SD speaking problems, but I just couldn't crack the consistency issue. People would move in and out of making normal sounds, and I would do my best during the time I was teaching them, then send them away to work on the techniques I'd demonstrated. I also asked them to practice a daily warm-up set of vocal exercises, similar to the ones I use for all of my speaking and singing students. The results were spotty, but here is the amazing part of the story: The SD clients who kept trying the warm-ups anyway would contact me and report huge breakthroughs.

Some of these changes took only months, and some took as long as two years, but those who stayed with the program achieved striking improvements, even to the point of getting past SD altogether.

I came to understand that stutterers can see huge results quickly, but SD clients need a longer time to retrain the muscles and voice.

Though I love a quick fix, I am still very satisfied with any course of action that leads people to getting better, some faster than others.

If you are coping with SD or stuttering, remember: You *can* make things better. Just be patient and enjoy the process and improvements along the way, never stopping until you truly set your voice free.

· 18 ·

The Healing Power of Voice

Oᴎᴇ ᴏꜰ the things I enjoy most about my work is the opportunity it gives me to see the way singing changes people. A
session of vocal and breathing exercises might not sound like a ticket
to nirvana, yet day after day I notice that my students may walk into
the room feeling down or disconnected from themselves, but after a
half hour of vocalizing, they're calm and happy, even laughing. I'd
like to chalk that transformation up to my sparkling personality, but
I believe that what's happening is a daily demonstration of the healing power of sound.

For years I've been telling students that singing is good for the
body, and I've discovered that I'm not alone in that belief. Researchers and therapists are using sound to heal the body, mind, and spirit,
and are offering insights into why it feels so great to make those joy-
ful googs, gugs, and flights of notes. I've been dipping into some work
in the fields of sound healing, music therapy, and meditational
sound, and I'd like to share a bit of it with you. You may find the
ideas far-fetched, but if you're like me, perhaps they'll spark your
imagination and make you want to explore further and begin to play
with the healing possibilities of your own voice.

A Sound Path to Health

Webster's dictionary defines the verb *heal* as "to make sound," a
use of words that I find particularly apt. Webster wasn't talking about

making music — he was talking about making the body whole and healthy. But practitioners of two specialties, sound healing and vibrational medicine, believe that sound helps *make* the body sound.

I had an illuminating discussion about sound healing with David Gordon, an Oakland, California, sound healer who's been a singer and musician for many decades. David began his explorations of sound healing when, after a lifetime of singing, he found he could no longer connect with the joy of making sound. Searching for a way back to the power of music and song, he practiced yoga and meditation, finally discovering the work of sound healers, including the pioneering sound healer Don Campbell (author of *The Mozart Effect*). David combines these elements, along with his grounding in voice and music structure, in the program he teaches today.

Central to this work is the belief that the greatest healing comes from the work we do ourselves, from the inside. In a typical session, David observes his clients, paying attention to their breathing, the way they move their bodies, the tensions he notices in them. Then he gently guides them toward making whatever sounds come out of their bodies freely and easily. Though he's also a voice teacher, he chooses not to label this work as singing. He calls it "vibrating the breath"—which is actually a good technical description of what we're doing anytime we speak or sing. Any sounds the clients make are fine, and as David hears them, he "mirrors" them, repeating the sound back. In that process, a musical interplay develops between the student and the teacher.

The goal of this work is not to make the voice better. It's not about "How do I sound?" The focus is on "How do I feel?" And in the course of a session, clients are encouraged to make sounds that, pretty or ugly, they feel they need to make. There can be a wonderful sense of release in a sound-healing session, and when people work with sound in this way, the result can be a stronger sense of what's going on in their bodies and minds, as well as a shift in painful feelings and a greater understanding of how to relax and release pressure.

As well as sound work, David and other sound healers use a variety of techniques — breath work, movement, relaxation, exercises to center and clear the mind. They may work with something called toning, which involves singing prolonged vocal sounds on a single vowel. The sound-healing session becomes a safe, protected environment for the authentic, restorative sounds of the body and soul.

There are no extravagant claims in all of this. If you went to a sound healer with a stomachache, he or she would probably recommend that you see a doctor about the pain but would work with you to help put your body into a receptive state for healing. You might find, at the end of a session, that a stomachache that was sparked by unexpressed or unacknowledged fear or tension subsides when the work with sound allows you to relax. Or you might find that your stomach still hurts but you feel calmer about the pain and able to work more easily with your doctor to address it. Sound healing, David explains, is more about balancing your body and mind than curing anything.

I know this technique may sound a little abstract, but actually you've experienced something quite similar in doing the vocal exercises I've given you. When you're singing your googs and gugs and mums, in just a few seconds your brain puts the pronunciation of the words on autopilot and begins to home in on your overall sound and the feelings in your body. In a typical session, my students stop at least three or four times to ask, "What sound were we on?" It's not that they weren't concentrating. It's just that the mind and body have moved into a free place where they can make sounds and enjoy them without being encumbered by words.

That's the place that sound healers try to help their clients find.

Tuning In to the Body's Frequencies

Vibrational medicine practitioners believe that all parts of the body transmit and receive frequencies and are therefore influenced by them. (It's not as far-fetched as it may sound. Ear specialists have found that the ear, primarily thought of as an instrument of sound reception, is also a transmitter.) Different cells, bodily systems, and organs each vibrate at their own frequencies, these practitioners believe, and by learning the particular vibrational frequencies for specific body parts, we can learn to heal them with sounds.

The basic concept of vibrational medicine goes something like this: When we are in a state of perfect health, the parts of our body are like a great choir, each voice so finely tuned and in sync that it would make the angels smile. However, if a part of the body falls out of alignment and begins to vibrate incorrectly, we experience the discord as disease. It's as if one of the singers suddenly became tone deaf and were singing loudly, way off pitch. The aim of vibrational medicine is to get the "off-key" organ or system back to the right notes, restoring health to our bodies.

Vibrational medicine relies on the principle of resonance, which involves reinforcing or prolonging a particular vibration in one location by the use of a similar vibration in another location. You can see resonation in action if you turn up your stereo while playing, say, Beethoven's Fifth. Particular notes, passages, and frequencies make the lamps shake. Vibrational medicine practitioners might use a pair of tuning forks, or electrical instruments, or—most likely—the human voice to create certain sounds and set up particular frequencies in the body. And in doing so, they're trying to use sound to alter the shape, form, and function of cells in order to help them promote healing. The aim of research in this field is to develop ways to use resonance as a medical doctor uses antibiotics.

In my research, I kept running across references to the work of a doctor named Hans Jenny, a Swiss medical scientist who spent ten years of his life examining the effects that sound had on the shape and formation of substances. For his book *Cymatics*, Jenny photographed plastics, pastes, liquids, and powders, as they were being vibrated by sound. The results showed organic shapes being created from inorganic substances that were exposed to different sound frequencies—they look like starfish, human cells, and microscopic life. In vibrational medicine, these experiments are taken as evidence that sound has the ability to affect and change molecular structure.

There's no diagnostic manual yet that says, "To treat liver trouble, sing this note to create a vibration in the tissue at this frequency," but perhaps someday there will be. Researchers have found data that support the idea that particular sounds can change the shape and formation of white blood cells, and it's possible that such research will lead them to isolate sounds that can help enhance the immune system. Today's state of the art in the world of vibrational medicine is fairly intuitive. A practitioner most often uses a sense of guided direction, and experience, to determine what sounds a client should make or be exposed to—and many people have reported immediate therapeutic benefits. Other times, as with sound healing, the measurable effect of a treatment might simply be relaxation and a calm, receptive state that enhances healing. Or there may be effects that aren't quantifiable today but will be in years to come.

In both sound healing and vibrational medicine, there's frequent discussion of harmonics. No sound is made up of just one frequency. Instead, it's a mixture of a primary tone as well as overtones—harmonics—that create an entire spectrum of sound. Some believe that it's possible to use your voice to mold these harmonics into specific sound frequencies, and it's postulated that harmonics affect the nervous system and the brain, and that high-frequency sounds may actually charge the brain. Through the use of harmonics, it might someday be possible to open up new levels of sound awareness and to resonate portions of the body that have never been stimulated in this manner before. It may even be possible that vocal harmonics actually vibrate portions of the brain and create new neurological connections.

My sense of all this is that as long as you're not creating physical pressure or strain to produce sounds, it's safe and interesting to play with the way sound affects the way you feel. It may even be transformative. You may want to pay attention to places in your vocal exercises that seem to cheer you up, and repeat them. Or you may want to venture into your own exploration of sound healing and vibrational medicine. Maybe you'll want to expose yourself to harmonics and see what happens. If it makes you feel better, feel free to try it.

Meditational Sound

One of my students, a former monk, often broke into laughter during his lessons. He explained to me that the exercises somehow brought him to a very happy place and said he believed that the singing sounds we used were acting as a mantra—a trigger to bring him into a meditative state. When we combined particular sounds with diaphragmatic breathing, which is also used in meditation, his whole demeanor changed, becoming calm and centered.

Through the centuries, many people have been interested in calming the mind for various purposes. Chanting and singing have long been part of spiritual practice in a host of traditions, and in some systems the use of sound is central to achieving meditative states of consciousness. I was intrigued by the theories about sound and healing I encountered in the Ayurvedic tradition, which has been used in India for five thousand years. You may have run across some of these ideas in the work of Deepak Chopra, or through contact with the popular system of transcendental meditation, or TM, which has Indian roots.

In TM, you sit comfortably for fifteen or twenty minutes with the goal of allowing the body to relax and the mind to abandon its normal activity, experiencing deepened self-awareness. I have to admit that my basic mental picture of TM involved sitting on the floor in the lotus position chanting the sound *ommmm*. Actually, in this system practitioners are given a personal mantra, or chanting sound, but interestingly enough, that sound is not chanted aloud. It's invoked in thought—you "think the sound." And by doing so, one creates a state of restful alertness.

The idea of chanting silently is interesting because it's true, to some degree, that when you think of making a sound, your vocal cords vibrate—just as they do when you speak in your dreams. It seems reasonable to me, then, that internal sounds might work the same way external ones do.

Why allow—or encourage—sound to take you into a meditative state? By now it's widely accepted that meditation produces a wide range of benefits, including increased happiness; reduced stress; increased intelligence, creativity, memory, and health; lower blood pressure; better sleep; increased energy; and improved relationships. So every day, as you do your general warm-up, be open to the possibility that you're not only improving your voice but creating sounds that have the power to calm and heal. Any melody or sound that you sustain and repeat can be classified as a mantra—*om* is not

SET YOUR VOICE FREE

the only game in town. Gug or mum might just transport you into a quiet, meditative realm.

If you're interested in diving into a less well known use of sound, Gandharva Veda music, another Ayurvedic system, claims to be the ancient science of getting in tune with nature. Thousands of years ago, it's believed, seers capable of hearing and understanding the rhythms of nature played melodies at specific times of the day and night to invoke peace, harmony, and perfect health in the people. Every time of day, season, and event in nature has its own distinct sound or vibration, and Gandharva Veda melodies, experienced at the proper time, are supposed to bring your body into sync, harmony, and alignment with all of nature.

Making an Emotional Connection

A more down-to-earth method of healing with sound—music therapy—uses music to help people deal more effectively with disabilities, illnesses, and behavioral problems. It came to the public's attention after World War I and World War II when musicians went to veterans' hospitals around the country to play for patients suffering physical and emotional trauma from their experience in battle. Music seemed to reach and soothe these people in remarkable ways, and therapists began to investigate and develop techniques for using it with their clients.

Degrees in music therapy have been offered since 1944, and the American Music Therapy Association, which promotes research in the field, was founded in the late nineties. Today music therapy is used to reduce stress, elevate patients' moods and counteract depression, help promote movement for physical exercise rehabilitation, induce sleep, and reduce fear. Most of us, I think, use music for similar purposes almost without thinking. It's hard to imagine going to an aerobics class, or even doing yoga, and not having any music— we're accustomed to drawing on its power to get maximum energy from our bodies. Conversely, when my daughter, Madison, was younger, like many children and adults she would never think to go to sleep without calmly listening to her favorite relaxing music.

In music therapy, the driving, uplifting, soothing, and comforting properties of sound take fascinating forms. My friend and student Judy Nelson, a music therapist in southern California, described, for example, how autistic children who have become severely isolated can be reached by the simplest song. The therapist might sing "Row, row, row your boat, gently down the stream." Every time she sings the word "boat," she might point to a picture of a boat, and after a few times, the child might begin to make some specific nonword sound when the therapist sang and pointed. Instead of singing "boat," the child might make a sound like *ee*.

At that point, a good therapist might just change the song to "Row, row, row your *ee*, gently down the stream." Soon the child and therapist would be saying *ee* together regardless of the song. With a patient so lost in his or her own world, the therapist would consider this a real connection, and it could be the first of many building blocks that lead to more social interactions. It's part of the magic of music that children who might not communicate in any other circumstances often respond, eventually, to interactions that are built around songs.

With psychiatric disorders like schizophrenia and manic depression, often the goal of the music therapist is "reality orientation" — bringing a person into the present moment. Singing a song with positive sentiments, perhaps something like "You've Got a Friend," with lyrics such as "Just call out my name / And you know wherever I am / I'll come running to see you again / You've got a friend," can, therapists say, achieve dramatic results. Patients seem to be transported, if only for a few moments of the song, to a place where you can have and be a friend to someone who needs you.

This type of emotional connection to lyrics is no surprise to me. Over and over I've seen my students singing sad songs, only to break into tears. I've also seen them dance around the room and laugh during particularly high-energy songs. For my own part, I've noticed for years that whenever I am upset or angry in public and I can't just break into song, I start to whistle. It's instantaneous. I whistle and my mind immediately moves into a more peaceful place.

Music seems to reach a part of the brain that words alone can't, and as you engage your voice in exercises and songs, you have the opportunity to experiment with the way music affects you. It may be that you develop an emotional first-aid kit of songs that pick you up or calm you down. Or you may want to tap into the power of music and song to aid learning and concentration. Music therapists often set concepts to music to ease the learning process for children with learning disabilities (isn't that, after all, how you learned your ABCs?), and as you practice speak-singing, you might find that as well as improving your voice, singing a speech actually helps you remember it. Researchers have found, too, that baroque music (think J. S. Bach and the Brandenburg Concertos) seems to stimulate the logical, information-processing parts of the brain to aid concentration. Sound healer Don Campbell observes that such music played at a tempo of sixty beats per minute, the speed of a resting heartbeat, can create relaxation as well as produce mental and physical benefits. Skeptical? Try your own experiments. I know you'll benefit if you stay curious and observant about how sound and music affect you, and enjoy their positive effects.

Just Let It Happen

In this book I've walked you through the process of improving the sound of your voice and helped you bring your true character and emotions into the words you speak and sing. In changing the way you sound and letting it reflect exactly who you are, you're changing the way people perceive you and feeling the power and ease that come from a voice that flows freely and musically. I know that's a healing process in itself. I believe it's also possible—even likely—that the benefits of sound and music can penetrate your body and life in ways that are just beginning to be understood. Singing and speaking are good for you. Let it start by making you smile, then let it make you happy. Everything else will flow from that place.

Epilogue

As we come to the end of our time together, I hope you'll take a moment to think about how far you've come and what your next step will be. When we started our journey, we struggled through what probably seemed like an endless array of funny sounds, trusting that those sounds could ultimately create the voice you were meant to have. Whether or not you've fully uncovered that voice or are still working hard to develop it, you've most certainly started a course of action that can change your life for the better. You are infinitely more aware of the sounds you and others make. You have an understanding of how the vocal instrument actually works and how to make it work for instead of against you. You have seen, and experienced, the overlap between speaking and singing that enriches them both.

There's always more to learn—the process never stops. You practice, you see how your audience responds—whether it's one person or a thousand—and you learn the lesson of that experience, then take it into your next appearance. Along the way you keep returning to the basics. You always make sure that the chest voice is connected to the middle and then to the head voice. You daily reinforce your commitment to diaphragmatic breathing and drinking water every time you think of it. You stay sensitive to any physical straining or pressure and then relax your way out of trouble.

The road to mastery is lined with small setbacks. But each time you hit one, I hope you'll see it for what it is: a simple detour that gives you a chance to bring the most important lessons fully into your body and voice. The voice is one of the most difficult instruments to use well, and a quest for perfection will absolutely end in failure. But a sense of adventure will take you more deeply into the authentic sounds that will express what you want to say and sing.

I don't believe that being famous is the only way to measure success. The true goal of the work we've done is to make you feel gloriously comfortable in your own skin because you sound like who you really are. Of course, once the sounds you make match the person you are, no one is stopping you from seeking fame. If you have that calling—go for it. You've already learned more than most professional speakers and singers know about the voice, and that technical grounding will give you a tremendous head start. Remember, too, that you now have the tools to fix any vocal problems that arise along the way.

It's said that a teacher learns a certain amount from his teachers and then learns what he really needs to know from his students. I'm grateful to the students who have taught me so much—they're some of the most interesting people in the world and I'm blessed to know them. From now on, I count you among the growing family of students I hold dear. Thank you for your trust and your time.

I hope you'll continue to speak like you sing, sing like you speak, and enrich the world with the free, powerful, joyous, passionate, and completely individual sounds you were born to make.

A Glimpse into the Music Business

ECAUSE I know that some of you have dreams of using your vocal skills to make your way into the music business, I asked a couple of industry professionals—a music publisher and a manager—to talk a bit about what they do and to offer some basic advice about navigating through their corners of the music world. Whether you're a singer-songwriter, a parent with a talented band of kids in the garage, or a hip-hop artist with a hot tape, I think you'll find that their comments are a great starting point for thinking about how to take your work to a wider audience.

The Publisher

If you create a song, every time it's used by someone, you're entitled to payment. Music publishers, in exchange for a percentage of what your song earns, license your work to others and ensure that your money is collected properly around the world. But as Ben Maddahi, president of Unrestricted—a music consulting, publishing, and management company—explains, there's a lot more to the music publishing business than that basic relationship.

Q: Music publishing is unfamiliar to a lot of people. In your role as a music publisher, what do you do?

A: Someone described it in a very helpful way recently. I'm like a Match.com for writers, producers, and artists. As a publishing A&R [artists and repertoire person], I represent songwriters (both lyric and melody writers and musicians/composers), and it's my job to put the best writers, producers, and artists in the best possible combinations to yield songs that will be hits, or to create the most appropriate music for the projects I'm working on.

Q: How has the role of a publisher changed in recent years, with so many changes in the music business in general?

A: At the outset of my professional career (early 2006), I mainly saw the major publishers outbidding each other for songwriters who had hits climbing the charts, and trying to re-sign successful songwriters who had come to the end of their publishing deals. The most creative thing I had seen a major publisher do in those days was to make a call to get a great up-and-coming songwriter in the room with an artist or send out CDs of their favorite beats. Now, I see more and more A&Rs (both major and indie) taking a creative, hands-on, calculated approach to publishing. That's something we spearheaded at my boutique A&R group, APG.

Q: There seem to be publishers and managers who work with songwriters, and A&R people at publishing companies. How does that all fit together? What would be the perfect team a young writer or writer/artist would want to assemble, publishing-wise?

A: That's a tricky question because it really depends on the needs of each particular writer, and no two writers are alike. On the surface, a manager will be more responsible for handling a writer's schedule, and negotiating certain parts of a songwriter's business that the publisher doesn't handle (for instance, negotiating whether they get standard or full rate, or, if the writer is a producer, negotiating their production advance). It's more common for producer/writers to have both managers and publishers, since managing a producer yields more immediate income and is overall more lucrative for the manager. But certain songwriters have both managers and publishers because they may have different specialties/emphases that allow for every great opportunity to be capitalized upon. Some songwriters may not need managers, and some great ones crave them because they can help fill the gaps that the publisher leaves behind, or just add more value to the total equation.

Q: Have the relationships between publishers and record companies changed in recent years?

A: I see employees with dual A&R roles (working for both a label and a publisher) popping up more and more regularly. It's smart because parent companies like Warner/Chappell or Sony/ATV can split the cost of an employee, double down on acts by signing them to both records and publishing, and up the accountability of the person who signs the act, because they will be responsible for ensuring the act's success (from an A&R standpoint). I've seen great results with my colleagues Ryan Press at Warner/Chappell and Katie Welle at Sony/ATV.

Q: How do you find the people you sign?

A: It's a combination of blind submissions to my email, my A&R scouts bringing me their best material, meetings with creative partners I trust, and scouring online data.

Q: How elaborate should a demo be?

A: It depends on who you're sending it to. If it's a producer, the instrumental should be very polished and sonically and musically an 8.5 out of 10 or above if I'm looking to sign them. There is a world of a difference between an 8 and an 8.5, believe it or not. For a top-line writer, I'm satisfied with a piano or guitar and a vocal, as long as the lyrics and melodies are incredible. We can get the rest there; that's a big part of my job.

Q: What makes you pay attention to a song? What are you listening for? Would you only sign a mainstream, radio-friendly writer/artist? What if an artist does music that's really out of the mainstream?

A: If I'm listening for production, I want unique sounds and an incredible mix with earworm melodies and great drum programming. If I'm listening for a top-liner, I want clever lyrics and big melodies. I prefer to sign mainstream/radio-friendly songwriters and artists because I want the music that I work on to reach the biggest audience possible. That doesn't mean that I have anything against more left-of-center artists. I actually love that stuff too. It's my favorite thing to see an artist with a cult following or a left-of-center sound break into the mainstream. It means that they're moving the needle in popular music and not just trying to cater to what people want to hear. Although I didn't sign Sia, I did work with her on two big hits, and I was happy to see that happen with her.

Q: How much focus do you put into "sync licenses" — trying to get your writers' songs into films, TV shows, commercials, etc.? How important is that for a new writer?

A: We're putting more and more effort into sync nowadays because the power of sync has only increased. That means we're upping our sync staff and outreach regularly, as well as looking for projects like film and TV soundtracks. We saw some great success with this approach with Wiz Khalifa and Charlie Puth's smash "See You Again" when we were contracted to help create the soundtrack for the movie *Furious 7.* A sync, if properly placed, can be a day-and-night difference for a song, and ultimately the writers or artists attached to a song. While we always focused on sync, there's now a bigger effort to place songs in film and TV because the exposure and payoff is just that much bigger.

Q: What's your one best piece of advice for an artist who wants to build a long-term career in the music industry today?

A: Write, write, write. Keep writing for yourself and for others and keep yourself sharp. It's all about the music at the end of the day.

(Ben Maddahi began his career in the music industry as an intern at Atlantic Records in 2006, and rose to become president of the music publisher Artist Publishing Group (APG). He has played a key role in constructing hits like "Wild Ones" by Flo Rida featuring Sia, "Titanium" by David Guetta, "See You Again" by Wiz Khalifa featuring Charlie Puth, and many others that went on to sell a combined total of more than 100 million singles worldwide. In late 2015, Maddahi started Unrestricted, an A&R consulting and publishing company that also specializes in managing producers and songwriters. Unrestricted publishing is a joint venture with Songs Music Publishing (Diplo, Lorde, The Weeknd, DJ Mustard, Chromeo).

The Manager

Managers have traditionally been artists' career compass, steering them toward opportunities and helping them map strategies that will keep them in the game for the long run. Benjamin Rolnik, a new-generation manager, says the game's there for you to win—whether or not you've yet captured a manager's attention.

Q: In the new social media age, how has the role of an artist's manager changed?

A: The world of social media as we know it is largely less than a decade old, yet social media like YouTube, Facebook, Twitter, Instagram, Snapchat, and Vine have revolutionized not only how average people communicate, but how brands market to their consumers and how artists develop relationships with their fans.

Today, YouTube reaches more eighteen- to thirty-five-year-olds than any cable network in the world. It has more than one billion unique monthly visitors, with billions of hours of content being watched per month. YouTube is also the number two search engine in the world—and guess what the most popular search category is: music. Across every social platform, the statistics are staggering. The truth is that most managers are not equipped to deal with the changing tides of the media industry. It is just not enough to "break a single" today. If a release is not backed up by a strong social media plan that will grow a fan base, the opportunity is lost.

Managers used to have to fight just to get "earned media" (press, TV) and paid media (advertisements) for their artists. Now they have the opportunity to gain *owned* media by developing direct social media followers and reach, which corresponds to the longest career longevity and return for an artist.

A manager in the twenty-first century is akin to the CEO of a lean start-up company. Artists today can create their own future as never before, and with that power come tremendous opportunities for innovative business models and new ways of reaching fans.

I spend a lot of my time around influencers, social media, and developing artists, so I see the opportunities and the challenges. There has been more innovation in the last ten years than in the last hundred years, so 99 percent of the industry still has not caught up to the radical shifts that have already occurred. Those who "understand this stuff" today are like the people Peter Thiel, the PayPal founder, describes as able to capitalize on a great secret truth in an industry simply because the majority of people don't realize it is true yet.

Q: Now that artists are using the Internet to get their music to the public, how do you think about helping them plan a long-lasting career?

A: There is more content in the world today than ever before. One hundred hours of video are being uploaded to YouTube every minute. It's getting increasingly difficult for artists to stand out, and even if they do, it's much easier for them to be quickly drowned out and forgotten. Ultimately, lasting success comes down to the music.

Silentó, an independent rapper in Atlanta, broke through when he released a song that went viral on YouTube in the dance community, and his single "Watch Me" got to the top of the *Billboard* charts. There's no formula for this kind of trajectory, though, which is why there were so many one-hit wonders in the past, and so many more today. But if artists can capitalize on any of their current success to build a following, they will maintain a certain level of influence throughout their careers—meaning, before, you could have one hit and fall off the map. Today, you can have one hit and stay on the map forever (even if your brand flatlines).

Ed Sheeran recently sold out multiple nights at Madison Square Garden playing with just an acoustic guitar and a loop station. Cat Stevens had the world in the palm of his hand and then retired from music. The only truth is: Releasing amazing music that people love and connect with is really the only secret to building a lasting career with lasting relevance.

Q: What is the single most important piece of advice you could give a new artist who wants to succeed in the music business today?

A: Fight to be seen. Don't wait to be discovered. Record labels today function more like institutional investors who place safe bets on products (artists) who have already proven their worth in the market. This means: Forget the old days of artist development, writing a song and thinking that it's precious. There are only about forty number one songs per year (think: fifty-two weeks/year, and many songs stay number one for a few weeks). There are only about four hundred proven hit songwriters and producers in the world. And there are probably tens of thousands of wanna-be artists, producers, and songwriters who are competing with you trying to break into the game.

My biggest piece of advice is: Stop waiting. Put your song out. See what happens. If it's *that* good and that much of a hit, then you should see the market reacting to it. Is anyone sharing it on Facebook, Twitter, YouTube, Instagram? Are any blogs picking it up? No? Then write another song—and release it.

Keep trying. Keep building. We work our entire lives to become overnight successes. The biggest mistake I see new artists making is having a catalog of unreleased music. That's like trying to swim in a hurricane with your hands tied behind your back. Hozier released "Take Me to Church" independently with a very low-budget music video. It took them months to be signed by Sony. Then it took Sony almost a year to break the song. Imagine if they had thought: This is a great song, we better not release it!

Or take OMI. He released "Cheerleader" in 2012. Nothing happened. Fast-forward to 2015: Felix Jaehn finds the song, remixes it, and it goes on to be the number one hit of the summer. It's not possible to have a sleeper hit or even to be noticed if you're not out there with a foot in the game. With services like TuneCore, you can start distributing music almost instantly to every meaningful place music is listened to or purchased in the twenty-first century.

Then you can independently promote your own material with

social media. Your destiny is in your own hands. Stop acting like it isn't.

If people aren't reacting to your music, make a decision: Are you making music for yourself, or are you making music that millions of people will want to listen to? If you choose the former, keep doing what you're doing. If the latter, you have the freedom and flexibility to get instant and honest feedback about whether you're "in the pocket" or not. A musician today (especially without a good manager) has to think like a first-time entrepreneur: Focus and build on what's working until your product is a hit. And if you're afraid about releasing something and how people are going to judge you, just think: The *best*-case scenario here is that other people even hear your music.

Getting even three hundred views on a video for a new artist is a hurdle. If you start getting a thousand views, then ten thousand, then a hundred thousand, then a million, you know you're really onto something. And if all else fails, remember the good old Oscar Wilde adage: The only thing worse than people talking negatively about you is not being talked about at all.

(Benjamin Rolnik grew up on tour, traveling the world with superstars like the Rolling Stones, Michael Jackson, and Aerosmith. As an entrepreneur partnered at a major talent management firm, he specializes in management, touring, high-tech innovation/development, marketing, social media, and media production in both the new media and traditional media industries.)

Acknowledgments

I WOULD LIKE to acknowledge a few of the people who have been of great help to me during the writing of this book.

Donna Frazier. Thank you for your encouragement, your professionalism, and your uncompromising pursuit of semantic perfection.

B. J. Robbins. Thank you for continuing to guide me through the ever-changing tides of the literary business.

Terry Adams. Thank you for giving me a second chance to tell more of my story.

My LA family: Eiko, Jacques, Jim, Tina, and Alexa, I love you all.

Scott Alberts. Thank you for being such a loving friend and business partner.

Wendy Estrada

The Loves in Oregon

And a special thank-you to my brother, Philip.

I will sing for you now that your voice is silent.

Index

Note: Italic page numbers refer to illustrations.

A&R (artist and repertoire), in music business, 273–275
accessory breathing, 38, 92, 118
acid, and phlegm production, 134–135, 138
actors and acting
  and emotion in presentations, 233–235
  and singing voice, 190–191
  and voice lessons, 182–183, 185–191
Adam's apple. *See* larynx
airflow
  and exercise syllables, 61
  and husky voice, 108
  and low-larynx exercises, 62
  and middle voice, 90–91, 107
  and nasal voice, 106–108
  and octave jump exercise, 67
  and one-octave exercise, 58–59
  and singing songs, 121
  and spasmodic dysphonia, 259
  and stuttering, 254–257
  and vibrato, 152, 154
  and zipper effect, 55, 90
alcohol, 135–136
Alexander Technique, 37
American Idol (television show), 172
American Music Therapy Association, 268

amplification, 192, 219–220
amusement, and practicing, 76–77
Apartment Singing syndrome, 75–76
applause, accepting, 169–170
Armstrong, Louis, 29
auditions, 172–173, 175–176
author's story, 16–17
autism, and singing songs, 269
Azalea, Iggy, 159

bankers, pitch range of, 9–10
Beach Boys, 4, 17
Beauty and the Beast (film), 146
Beckham, David, 29
Bee Gees, 66
Begin Again (film), 190
belly dance exercise, 155
belt exercise, 46
bending over breathing exercise, 47–48
Bennett, Tony, 89
Bernoulli effect, 152
Beyoncé, 158, 195, 206
biological clock, 144–145
Blair, Linda, 127
blowing out candles exhalation exercise, 44
body language
  image conveyed by, 241–243

body language *(cont.)*
  and online creations, 241–243, 246–247
Bono, 195, 197
books
  as breathing visual aids, 47
  as underfoot posture aids, 45–46, 103
Boyz II Men, 162
brassy voice, 27–29, 99, 105–106, 139
Braxton, Toni, 173
breathing. *See also* diaphragmatic breathing
  accessory, 38, 92, 118
  anatomy of, 35–36
  color breathing for stage fright, 171
  deep, 43
  evaluation of, 34–36
  and gravelly voice, 25–26, 102–104
  natural, 36–43, 49
  and one-octave exercise, 58, 63
  and posture, 35–37, 45, 92, 109, 118
  and stuttering, 254–257
  and voice lessons for actors, 186
breathing exercises
  classic, 46–48
  for exhalation, 44–46
  and middle voice, 91
  and singing voice, 6–7
  for stage fright, 171
breathy voice
  appeal of, 26–27, 237
  and chest voice, 99
  effect on vocal cords, 11, 27, 100–102, 196–197
  and hoarseness, 139
  and husky voice, 29
  and singers, 10–11
  using gug and goog sounds, 100–102
  using nay and nah sounds, 101–102
Bridges, Jeff, 4, 190

Brightman, Sara, 152
Brown, James, 176
The Bucket List (film), 5
Burchard, Brendon, 4, 239, 243–249
Bush (rock group), 53

caffeine, 133–134, 138
"Call Me Maybe" (song), 136
cameras, 243
Campbell, Don, 263
carbonated beverages, 134–135, 138
Carey, Mariah, 117, 161–162
Carreras, José, 229
car salesman, rapid speech of, 208–209
Cash, Johnny, 185–189
Cash, June Carter, 185, 188–189
challenges, preparation for, 257
chanting, 267
"Cheerleader" (song), 279
chest voice
  and June Carter Cash, 189
  in children, 148
  emotional effect on listeners, 229
  and high larynx, 126–127
  in men, 56–57, 56
  as middle voice component, 51, 68, 84–85, 90, 93–95, 122, 271
  and one-octave exercise, 58–59, 62–63, 66
  and overlapping voice frequencies of men and women, 236
  and pace of speech, 210
  in popular singers, 87–89
  and singing songs, 114–124, 127–129
  and songwriting, 204
  and speaking voice, 99, 228
  straining at top of, 118, 126–128
  and voice lessons for actors, 186
  and zipper effect, 54, *54*
chewing gum, 141

Chicago (musical group), 4
children, voice lessons for, 130, 145–149
chlorine, 142
Chopra, Deepak, 267
Chromeo (musical duo), 277
citrus fruit, 135, 138
cocaine, 142–143
coffee, 133–134
Coldplay, 177
collaboration, and songwriting, 204–205
color breathing, 171
composers, songwriting criteria of,
    118–119
Confident, sound of, 233, 235
Crazy Heart (film), 190
cry sound (exercise), 60, 66–67, 92
Cymatics (Jenny), 265
Cyrus, Miley, 158

"Daddy Sang Bass" (song), 187
dairy products, 137–138, 148–149
deep breathing, 43
Def Leppard, 4, 135
Del Rey, Lana, 158
demo recordings, 275
diaphragmatic breathing. *See also*
    breathing exercises; natural
    breathing
  and deep breathing, 43
  early learning stages of, 39–40
  ease of, 35, 39, 46
  effect on vocal technique, 49–50,
    99, 104, 271
  exercises, 44–48
  exhalation, 40–44, 90
  and hoarseness, 139–140
  inhalation, 38–40
  and light-headedness, 108–110
  and meditational sound, 267
  and pace of speech, 209–210

and Luciano Pavarotti, 50
and spasmodic dysphonia, 259
and speaking voice, 102
and stuttering, 255
diction, 61–62. *See also* pronunciation
digestion, effect on voice, 137–138
Diplo, 277
Diva Light Ring, 243
DJ Mustard, 277
Domingo, Plácido, 229
Drake, 156, 162
Dylan, Bob, 202

Earth Wind & Fire, 4, 17
edema, 27, 139
Elliot, Joe, 135
embarrassment, and practice, 73–76
Eminem, 144, 194, 196
emotion
  conveying when singing, 193–195
  influencing through sound, 227–230,
    233–235
  and music therapy, 269–270
  and spasmodic dysphonia, 258
engineers, pitch range of, 9–10
eucalyptus, 135, 140–141
exaggeration, 193–194
exercises. *See also* breathing exercises;
    syllables for exercises
  contrasted with singing songs, 114,
    116–121, 125–127
  diaphragmatic breathing, 44–48
  to eliminate parallel gestures, 221
  and goog sound, 100–101, 108, 140
  and gug sound, 92, 100–102, 108,
    140, 188
  and hoarseness, 139
  larynx lowering, 5–6, 28–29, 62,
    66–67, 105, 107, 110, 118, 126–127,
    139–140, 186

exercises *(cont.)*
  mum sound in, 92, 120–121, 128
  and musical therapy, 270
  nah sound in, 101–102, 108, 140
  nay sound in, 101–102, 108, 140
  octave-and-a-half, 66–67, 108
  octave jump, 67, 104, 128, 186
  one-octave exercise, 58–66, 108, 139
  pitch range, 29–30
  and sound healing, 264
  and spasmodic dysphonia, 261
  and speaking voice, 6, 97–99, 104
  and stuttering, 255–257
  and voice lessons for actors, 186–187
exhalation
  breathing exercises for, 44–46
  in natural breathing, 40–43, 49
  and tension, 40–43, 45, 48–49,
    260–261
The Exorcist (film), 127
Expert
  positioning oneself as, 248–249
  Simon Sinek as, 249–252
eye contact, 167, 170, 220–221

Facebook, 277, 279
falsetto, 54–55, 65
fast talking, 207–211
flip-flopping syllables, 92, 101, 108, 188
Florence + the Machine (singing
    group), 88, 204
Flo Rida, 276
Franklin, Aretha, 88–89, 158, 161
Frozen (film), 185
Future Islands, 194–195

Gandharva Veda music, 268
gesturing, while speaking, 221, 242
Glee (television show), 172–173,
    181–184

glottal stops, 61, 108, 188
goals, for voice improvement, 13
Gomez, Selena, 4
goog sound
  and octave-and-a-half exercise,
    66–67
  and octave jump exercise, 67
  and one-octave exercise, 58, 61
  in vocal exercises, 100–101, 108, 140
Gordon, David, 263–264
Grande, Ariana, 176
Grateful, sound of, 231–232, 234–235,
    240–241, 244, 246, 248–249
gravelly voice, 25–26, 98–99, 102–104,
    139, 222
Gray, John, 4, 139–140, 223–224
Guetta, David, 276
gug sound
  and octave-and-a-half exercise, 67
  and octave jump exercise, 67
  and one-octave exercise, 58, 61
  in vocal exercises, 92, 100–102, 108,
    140, 188
guilt, and practice, 71

habits, 32–33, 207, 211, 217
hands, parallel gestures with, 221, 242
the handshake, vibrato production aid,
    154–155
Happy, sound of, 230–231, 234–235,
    236, 240–241, 244–249
harmonics, to promote healing, 266
head position, and middle voice, 91–92
head voice
  in children, 148
  described, 51
  emotional effect on listeners, 229
  and falsetto, 54–55, 65
  as middle voice component, 68,
    84–85, 90, 93–95, 122, 128, 271

and one-octave exercise, 65, 66

and overlapping voice frequencies of
men and women, 236

and pace of speech, 211

pitch ranges of, 56–57, *56, 57,* 65

and singing higher pitches, 94–95

and songwriting, 204

and spasmodic dysphonia, 259–260

and voice lessons for actors, 186

and zipper effect, 54–55, *54*

healing

meditational sound, 262, 266–268

music therapy, 268–270

sound healing, 15–16, 262–264, 266

vibrational medicine, 263, 264–266

Hercules breath, 38

Herring, Sam, 195

high larynx

and brassy voice, 28–29, 99, 105

and chest voice, 126–127

and middle voice, 62, 67, 99

and nasal voice, 107, 110

high notes. *See also* pitch

and airflow, 121

low-larynx exercises for, 5–6,
126–127

and singing in head voice, 94–95

hoarseness. *See also* laryngitis

and diaphragmatic breathing,
139–140

and edema, 139

and infection, 138

and middle voice, 52–53, 56

hot drinks, effect on voice, 137

Houston, Whitney, 88–89, 153

Hozier (singer), 279

Hudson, Jennifer, 117, 173

humidifiers, 141

husky voice, 29, 108, 173–174, 176

hyperventilation, 109

Idol, Billy, 165–166

"If I Were King of the Forest" (song),
147

image

and body language, 241–243

created by speaking voice, 8–11,
224–226, 228, 249

and reality competitions, 177–178

imitation

and listening, 77–78

of newscasters, 214–215

of other singers, 114, 123, 156–160,
177, 198

imperfections, as sources of originality,
173–174, 176–177

influence

of online creations, 239

and overlapping voice frequencies of
men and women, 236

of sound on emotion, 227–238

inhalation

in natural breathing, 38–40

and tension, 39, 48–49

Instagram, 277, 279

Internet. *See* online creations; social
media; websites; YouTube videos

in utero exposure to music, 146, 149

INXS (rock group), 180

Jackson, Michael, 10, 176, 195, 280

The Jacksons, 4, 17

Jaehn, Felix, 279

jaw position, 120, 126, 153, 241

Jenner, Caitlyn (formerly Bruce),
121–122

Jenny, Hans, 265

Jepsen, Carly Rae, 136

Jessie J, 89, 115, 158, 161, 173

"Jingle Bells" (song), stage movement
for, *166,* 169

Jolie, Angelina, 4, 40
Journey (rock group), 88
joy, singing for, 15–16

Keeping Up with the Kardashians
    (television show), 121
Kelly, Tori, 116
key, choosing a song's, 122–124, 188
keyboard, determining voice pitch
    with, 8–9
Khalifa, Wiz, 276
King, Larry, 222
King, Martin Luther, 52
Knightley, Keira, 4, 190–191, 194

Lady Gaga, 150
Lahr, Bert, 152
Lambert, Miranda, 158
laryngitis, 27. See also hoarseness
larynx. See also high larynx; low-larynx
    exercises
    function of, 19, 28
    and husky voice, 29
    and middle voice, 62
    and nasal voice, 107–108, 110
    and puberty, 235
    and spasmodic dysphonia, 258
    and vibrato, 153
The Last Waltz (film), 203
The Late Show with David Letterman
    (television show), 195
Lawrence, Jennifer, 4
Levine, Adam, 204
light-headedness, 108–109
lighting, for online creations, 243
listening
    and imitation, 77–78
    to your own voice, 90, 100, 115, 177,
        179
Lorde, 204, 277

Lovato, Demi, 162
low-larynx exercises
    and airflow, 62
    and brassy voice, 105
    and hitting high notes, 5–6, 126–127
    and nasal voice, 107, 110
    and one-octave exercise, 66–67
    and speaking voice, 28–29
    and trouble with vocal exercises, 118
    and vocal cords, 139–140
    and voice lessons for actors, 186
lozenges, 140–141

Maddahi, Ben, 273, 276–277
Madison (author's daughter), 146–148
Madonna, 152, 159
managers, 273–275, 277–278, 280
Manic depression, 269
mantra, 266–268
Mara, Rooney, 4
Maroon 5, 4
Mars, Bruno, 88, 176
Martin, Chris, 150, 177
Martin, Dean, 89
Matchbox Twenty, 4, 52
Mayer, John, 4–5
meditational sound, 262, 266–268
melody
    and online creations, 240, 244–245,
        248–249
    and songwriting, 204
    in speaking voice, 229
memorization, 218–219, 249–251
men
    average voice range of, 57–58, 58
    chest voice in, 56–57, 56
    overlapping voice frequencies with
        women, 235–237
    pitch ranges of songs for, 116–117, 117,
        119

Men Are from Mars, Women Are from Venus (Gray), 4, 139, 223
Menzel, Idina, 152
message
  in songwriting, 198, 205–206
  and speaking voice, 208, 222–225
Michele, Lea, 182
microphones, 192, 219–220, 243
middle voice
  and airflow, 90–91, 107
  in children, 148
  and the cry exercise, 60, 66–67, 92
  described, 51–52
  difficulty achieving, 97–98
  dissatisfaction with sound of, 86–87
  emotional effect on listeners, 229
  and John Gray, 223
  as head/chest voice combination, 58, 68–69, 84–85, 90, 93–95, 122, 271
  and high larynx conditions, 62, 67, 99
  and mouth position, 119–120
  and nasal voice, 107
  and one-octave exercise, 58–66
  and overlapping voice frequencies of men and women, 236
  and pace of speech, 210–211
  pitch ranges of, 56–58, 56, 57, 65
  and popular singers, 87–90
  and singing songs, 113–117, 119–124, 127–129
  and singing voice, 51–52, 228
  and songwriting, 204
  and speaking voice, 51–52, 99, 228
  and Gwen Stefani, 53–54, 56
  and Rob Thomas, 52–53, 55–56
  visualization aids for, 62–63
  and voice lessons for actors, 186
  and zipper effect, 54–56, 54, 90
Minaj, Nicki, 176–177, 196
minerals, and water consumption, 133

monotone, 8, 112, 115, 191, 207, 209–210, 212–215
Monroe, Marilyn, voice of, 26, 196, 259
Monteith, Cory, 182
moom sound, and one-octave exercise, 58, 61
morning, effect on voice, 143
Mota, Bethany, 239–247, 249, 252
mouth position
  and brassy voice, 105–106
  and middle voice, 119–120
  and nasal voice, 241
  and vibrato, 156
movies, singing and, 185
The Mozart Effect (Campbell), 263
mum sound
  and one-octave exercise, 58, 61
  in vocal exercises, 92, 120–121, 128
music business Q & A, 273–280
musicians, pitch range of, 9
music therapy, 262, 268–270
"My Way" (song), 118, 215

nah sound
  and one-octave exercise, 58, 61
  in vocal exercises, 101–102, 108, 140
nasal voice
  causes of, 23–24
  and chest voice, 99
  and high larynx, 107, 110
  and one-octave exercise, 108
  and smiling, 241
  and speaking voice, 106–108
National Spasmodic Dysphonia Association, 258
natural breathing. *See also* breathing; diaphragmatic breathing
  deep breaths, 43
  exhalation, 40–43, 49
  inhalation, 38–40

nay sound
  and one-octave exercise, 58, 61
  in vocal exercises, 101–102, 108, 140
neck, tension in, 259–260
Nelson, Judy, 269
newscasters, imitating, 214–215
Nicholson, Jack, 5
Nicks, Stevie, 152
nodes and nodules on vocal cords,
  131–132
"no" sound, and one-octave exercise,
  58, 61
notepads, and songwriting, 200–202,
  205

octave-and-a-half exercise, 66–67, 108
octave jump exercise, 67, 104, 128, 186
octave range, of normal voice, 12
OMI (singer), 279
one-octave exercise, 58–67, 108, 139
"One Sweet Day" (song), 162
online creations. *See also*
  presentations; social media;
  websites; YouTube videos
  and body language, 241–243,
  246–247
  and Brendon Burchard, 4, 239,
  243–249
  and Grateful element, 240–241, 244,
  246, 248–249
  and Happy element, 240–241,
  244–249
  influence of, 239
  and Bethany Mota, 239–247, 249,
  252
  and Simon Sinek, 249–252
  and stage movement, 241–243,
  246–247
"Open Arms" (song), 88
opera singing, and body size, 145

originality
  appropriate and inappropriate,
  164–165
  and singing style, 156, 158–160,
  163–165, 174–175, 178, 198–199
osteomyelitis, 16–17

pace of speech, 208–212, 247
Papa Roach, 144
parallel gestures, 221, 242
Passionate, sound of, 232–233, 235
pauses, in speaking, 210–212, 214–217,
  245
Pavarotti, Luciano, 50, 229
peer pressure, and stuttering, 256–257
performing
  eye contact, 167, 170, 220–221
  importance of sleep, 144–145
  and originality, 198–199
  and singing style, 165–166
  and stage fright, 170–171
  stage movements for, 150–151,
  165–169, *166*
Perry, Katy, 122
Perry, Steve, 88
personality, matched by speaking
  voice, 224–226
Phillips, Wilson, 4
Phish, 4
phlegm
  and caffeine, 133–134, 138
  and carbonated beverages, 134–135,
  138
  and dairy products, 137–138, 148–149
  excess, 63–64
  and husky voice, 29
  and sugar, 134
  and water consumption, 133, 138
  and zipper effect, 55, 64
Phoenix, Joaquin, 4, 185–188

phrasing, 160–161, 215–217

piano lessons, 147–148

Pink (singer), 195

pitch

  finding the appropriate, 29–30

  head voice pitch ranges, 56–57, 56, 57, 65

  middle voice pitch ranges, 56–58, 56, 57, 65

  perfect, 81

  pitch ranges of men's songs, 116–117, 117, 119

  pitch ranges of women's songs, 116–117, 116, 119

  singers' pitch ranges, 9, 51, 116–117, 116, 117

  singing higher pitches, 94–95, 121

  singing low pitches, 188

  and spasmodic dysphonia, 259

  and speaking voice, 8–10, 29–30, 213–214

  tone deafness and, 7, 12

  and vocal anatomy, 19–20

pizza, 137, 138

plateau stage in voice training, 79

popcorn breathing, 63

posture, and breathing, 35–37, 45, 92, 109, 118

practice

  and amusement, 76–77

  confusion about, 77–78

  difficulty of, 77

  and embarrassment, 73–76

  and finding middle voice, 68–69

  and perfect pitch, 81

  places to, 74–76, 238

  and rate of progress, 70–72, 74, 85–86, 93, 95–96

  and reading music, 81

  schedules, 70–72

  and stages of vocal improvement, 78–80

  times to, 74–76, 238

presentations. *See also* online creations

  eye contact, 170, 220–221

  and sound/emotion connection, 227–228

  and sound of Confident, 233, 235

  and sound of Grateful, 231–232, 234–235

  and sound of Happy, 230–231, 234–235, 236

  and sound of Passionate, 232–233, 235

  and use of entire vocal range, 228–230, 237–238

  using gestures, 221, 242

  using microphones, 192, 219–220, 243

Presley, Elvis, 89, 158, 195

Prince (singer), 66, 195

producers, 273–275, 277, 279

progress, stages of, 78–80

pronunciation, 61, 67, 264

psychiatric disorders, 269

puberty, 235

publishers, 273–277

"Push" (song), 52

Puth, Charlie, 276

reading music, 81

reality competitions

  choosing songs for, 176

  and decisions about image, 177–178

  demands of, 172–173, 180–184

  and work ethic, 179–181

recording your voice, 21–23, 86, 112, 122, 178–179, 194, 213, 225

red meat, effect on voice, 137–138

resonance, and vibrational medicine, 265
rhythm, following, 124–125
riffs, 161–163
Rihanna, 157
"Roar" (song), 122
Robbins, Tony, 4, 43–44, 49, 72, 222–223
Robertson, Robbie, 203
Rock Star (television show), 180
Rolnik, Benjamin, 280
Rooney, Andy, 222
Rossdale, Gavin, 53

salesman, rapid speech of, 208–209
saunas, 141
"Saving All My Love for You" (song), 87
"Say" (song), 4–5
schizophrenia, 269
Scorsese, Martin, 203
"Seasons (Waiting on You)" (song), 195
"See You Again" (song), 276
self-consciousness about practicing, 73–76
setbacks, in voice training, 79–80, 271
setyourvoicefree.com, 4, 13–14
"Shake It Off" (song), 157
Shakira, 156
Sheeran, Ed, 156, 278
Sia (singer), 114, 198, 276
Silentó, 278
Sinatra, Frank, 89, 142, 156, 160, 215
Sinek, Simon, 239, 249–252
singers
    and breathy voice, 10–11
    music business Q & A, 273–280
    pitch range of, 9, 116–117, *116*, *117*
    and speaking voice, 195–197
singing
    healing properties of, 262
    and joy, 15–16

singing songs. *See also* songs
    and chest voice, 114–124, 127–129
    contrasted with exercises, 114, 116–121, 125–127
    and conveying emotion, 193–195
    and eye contact, 167, 170
    following rhythm while, 124–125
    imitating other singers, 114, 123, 177, 198
    and middle voice, 113–117, 119–124, 127–129
    and music therapy, 269–270
    and recording, 178–179, 194
    stage movements for, 150–151, 165–169, *166*
    substituting exercise syllables for words, 120–121, 127, 188
    and voice roadblocks, 113–114
    as warm-up, 143–144
    working through difficult songs, 114–116
singing style
    and applause, 169–170
    choosing perfect song for your, 175–176
    conveying emotion with, 193–195
    developing through imitation, 156–160, 177, 198
    and originality, 156, 158–160, 163–165, 174–175, 178, 198–199
    and original music, 163
    and phrasing, 160–161
    and reinvented songs, 163–164, 176
    and riffs, 161–163
singing voice
    and acting, 190–191
    and breathing exercises, 6–7
    embracing imperfections, 173–174, 176–177
    evaluation exercise, 31–33

Madison (author's daughter),
   146–148
and middle voice, 51–52, 228
monotone, 115, 191
pitch range of, 51
relation of speaking voice to, 11,
   20–21, 31, 73, 81–82, 97–100,
   173–174, 195–197, 207–208,
   213–219, 225–226, 228–229
sleep, 144–145
slow leak exhalation exercise, 44, 45
slow talking, 211–212
smoking, 142–143
Snapchat, 277
social media, and music business,
   277–278, 280
songs. *See also* singing songs
   choosing for men and women,
      116–118
   choosing for reality competitions, 176
   choosing key of, 122–124, 188
   choosing stylistically perfect,
      175–176
   and music publishers, 273
   original material, 198–206
   pitch ranges of, 116–117, *116, 117*
   reinvention of, 163–164, 176
songwriting
   acquiring original music from, 163
   Colin (author's son), 199
   and collaboration, 204–205
   criteria for creating songs, 118–119
   developing ideas for songs, 200–204
   and message, 198, 205–206
   and music business, 273–277, 279
   writing songs yourself, 198
sound
   of Confident, 233, 235
   of Grateful, 231–232, 234–235,
      240–241, 244, 246, 248–249

of Happy, 230–231, 234–235, 236,
   240–241, 244–249
influence on emotion, 227–238
sound healing, 15–16, 262–264, 266
spasmodic dysphonia (SD), 258–261
speaking
   adjusting pace of, 208–212, 247
   using pauses, 210–212, 214–217, 245
speaking style
   of Brendon Burchard, 244–249
   and memorization, 218–219, 249–251
   monotone, 8, 112, 207, 209–210,
      212–215
   of Bethany Mota, 240–243
   and phrasing, 215–217
   of Simon Sinek, 249–252
   and singing, 160–161
speaking voice
   and amplification, 219–220
   brassiness of, 27–29, 105–106
   as expression of personality, 224–226
   gravelly sounds in, 25–26, 98–99,
      102–104, 222
   image created by, 8–11, 224–226,
      228, 249
   influence on others' emotions,
      227–238
   Michael Jackson's, 10
   and message, 208, 222–225
   and middle voice, 51–52, 99, 228
   nasal sound of, 106–108
   need for entire vocal range in,
      228–230, 237–238
   and octave jump exercise, 104
   pitches of, 8–10, 29–30, 213–214
   and practice, 72–73
   relation of singing voice to, 11, 20–21,
      31, 73, 81–82, 97–100, 173–174,
      195–197, 207–208, 213–219,
      225–226, 228–229

speaking voice *(cont.)*
  singing exercises to improve, 6
  and tongue position, 111
  volume of, 101–104, 109–110,
    217–218, 252
speak-singing, 82, 101, 213–219, 226,
  259
speeches. *See also* presentations
  eye contact during, 170, 220–221
speech therapy, 253–254
Springsteen, Bruce, 170, 195
stage fright, 170–171
stage movement, 150–151, 165–169, *166*,
  241–243, 246–247
stages of vocal improvement progress,
  78–80
Stair-Step Melody, 248–249
Stallone, Sylvester, Rocky character's
  nasal voice, 24, 106–107
Stefani, Gwen, 4, 53–54, 56
Stevens, Cat, 278
Sting (singer), 88
Streisand, Barbara, 50
stuttering, 253–259, 261
style. *See* singing style; speaking
  style
sugar, 134
swallowing
  and hoarseness, 138–139
  and larynx function, 28, 258
  and lubrication of vocal cords, 140
  and tongue position, 111
Swift, Taylor, 123, 156–157, 206
swimming, 142
syllables for exercises
  flip-flopping, 92, 101, 108, 188
  and octave jump exercise, 67
  in one-octave exercise, 58–62
  and sound healing, 264
  and stuttering, 256

substituting for words, 120–121, 127,
  188
sync licenses, 276

"Take Me to Church" (song), 279
talking. *See also* speaking
  fast, 207–211
  slowly, 211–212
tape recorders, 21–22
teeth, closing for vibrato, 156
tempo of speech
  medium to fast, 207–211
  slow, 211–212
tension
  effect on vocal cords, 48
  and exhalation, 40–43, 45, 48–49,
    260–261
  and inhalation, 39, 48–49
  and singing high pitches, 121
  and spasmodic dysphonia, 259–260
  and vocal exercises, 63
Thiel, Peter, 278
Thomas, Rob, 52–53, 55–56
Thriller (album), 10
throat sprays, 140–141
Timberlake, Justin, 114
"Titanium" (song), 276
tone deafness, 7, 12
tongue position
  and brassy voice, 105
  and speaking voice, 111
toning, 264
torso swing exhalation exercise, 45, *45*
transcendental meditation (TM), 267
TuneCore, 279–280
Turner, Tina, 195
Twitter, 277, 279

Ugly Duckling syndrome, 74
"Un-break My Heart" (song), 203

Underwood, Carrie, 158, 177
Urban, Keith, 158

Vandross, Luther, 17, 162
vibrational medicine, 263, 264–266
vibrato
   appropriate use of, 152–153
   belly dance exercise, 155
   and handshake point, 154–155
   how it works, 151–152
   Madison (author's daughter), 147
   shaking to produce, 153–154
   speed of, 155–156
   as vocal coloration, 150
   and voice lessons for actors, 186
video cameras, 243
Vine, 277
visualization, 62–63, 67
vitamins, and water consumption,
   133
vocal cords
   and breathy voice, 11, 27, 100–102,
     196–197
   in children, 148
   and edema, 139
   effect of brassy voice on, 28
   effect of gravelly voice on, 25
   effect of smoking on, 142–143
   and falsetto, 65
   function of, 19–20, 20
   and husky voice, 29, 108
   nodes and nodules on, 131–132
   and octave jump exercise, 67
   and puberty, 235
   and silent chanting, 267
   singing low pitches, 188
   and spasmodic dysphonia, 259
   and stuttering, 254–255
   and tension, 48
   and vibrato, 151–153

and water consumption, 110, 131–133,
   135, 140–141, 148, 183, 271
and zipper effect, 54–56, 54
voice. *See also* chest voice; head voice;
   middle voice; singing voice;
   speaking voice; *and other specific*
   types
   anatomy of, 18–20
   as component of credibility, 223
   continuous improvement of, 271–272
   and drinking water, 110, 131–133, 135,
     140–141, 148, 183, 271
   how yours' sounds to you and others,
     18, 20
   improvement of, 12–13
   listening to, 90, 100, 115, 177, 179
   potential harm to, 71, 90, 142–144,
     196
   and puberty, 235
   recording, 21–23, 86, 112, 122,
     178–179, 194, 213, 225
The Voice (television show), 172, 228
voice, truths about, 11–12
voice exercises. *See* exercises
voice lessons
   for actors, 182–183, 185–191
   author's, 17, 182
   for children, 130, 145–149
   at home, 14–15
   and stuttering, 254–258
   value of, 7–8
voice training, stages of, 78–80
volume
   and amplification, 192, 219–220
   and singing high pitches, 121
   of speaking voice, 101–104, 109–110,
     217–218, 252
   and vocal exercises, 93
vowels, focusing, 120
vulnerability, and Experts, 251–252

Walk the Line (film), 185, 188, 190
warm-up exercises. *See also* exercises
    and healing power of sound, 267
    and hoarseness, 139
    and practice, 71–73
    singing songs as, 143–144
    and spasmodic dysphonia, 261
Warren, Diane, 203
"Watch Me" (song), 278
water
    and phlegm, 133, 138
    and vocal cord lubrication, 110,
        131–133, 135, 140–141, 148, 183, 271
websites. *See also* online creations
    dysphonia.org, 258
    setyourvoicefree.com, 4, 13–14
    videos on, 239
The Weeknd (singer), 157, 198, 277
Welch, Florence, 88, 204
wet saunas, 141
"What Do You See in Him" (song), 203
Why Leaders Eat Last (Sinek), 251
Wilde, Oscar, 280
"Wild Ones" (song), 276

"Wild Thing" (song), 199
Winnie-the-Pooh (Milne), 234
Witherspoon, Reese, 4, 185, 188–189
The Wizard of Oz (film), 147
women
    average voice range of, 57, *57*
    and head voice, 94–96
    overlapping voice frequencies with
        men, 235–237
    pitch ranges of songs for, 116–117,
        116, 119
Wonder, Stevie, 17, 161
words, as obstructions while singing,
    120–122, 126

Xzibit (rapper), 144

Yogi Bear voice, 105, 126, 139
YouTube videos, 172, 195, 239–240,
    277–279
"You've Got a Friend" (song), 269

zipper effect (closing vocal cords),
    54–56, *54*, 64, 90

A Note About the Author

Roger Love is recognized as one of the world's leading authorities on voice. No other vocal coach has been more commercially successful in both the speaking and the singing fields. He has written three top-selling books, created original online and video programs, and appeared as a regular on four major network TV shows.

Roger was the voice coach for the megahit TV show *Glee*. He vocal-coached Reese Witherspoon and Joaquin Phoenix for the Oscar-winning film *Walk the Line,* Jeff Bridges and Colin Farrell for the hit movie *Crazy Heart,* Keira Knightley for the film *Begin Again,* and Quvenzhané Wallis for *Annie.*

Roger coaches singers such as John Mayer, Gwen Stefani, Selena Gomez, Demi Lovato, Nick Jonas, Maroon 5, Krewella, and Grouplove.

His acting clients are celebrities such as Angelina Jolie, Will Ferrell, and Rooney Mara. He coaches supermodels like Tyra Banks, as well as professional speakers such as Tony Robbins, John Gray, Brendon Burchard, and Suze Orman. Roger's work in corporate America has him coaching many executives of *Fortune* 100 companies.

Roger Love is the president of Voiceplace Inc., an interactive media company that specializes in the development, design, and fulfillment of vocal-related content for both educational and entertainment purposes.

You can find more information at www.rogerlove.com.

Tracks on the companion website to *Set Your Voice Free* by Roger Love, www.setyourvoicefreebook.com.

1. Welcome

Chapter Two:
2. Nasal Sound (1)
3. Nose-Pinch Test
4. Nasal Sound (2)
5. The Sound of Gravel
6. The Breathy Voice
7. Attaaaaaack of the Brassy Voice
8. Low-Larynx Sounds
9. The Husky Voice
10. Optimal Pitch Range
11. Diagnostic *Ah* Test (Male)
12. Diagnostic *Ah* Test (Female)

Chapter Three:
13. The Slow Leak

Chapter Four:
14. Chest-Middle-Head
15. The One-Octave Exercise (Male)
16. The One-Octave Exercise (Female)
17. The Cry (Male)
18. The Cry (Female)
19. More Low-Larynx Sounds
20. The Octave-and-a-Half Set (Male)
21. The Octave-and-a-Half Set (Female)
22. The Octave Jump (Male)
23. The Octave Jump (Female)

Chapter Six:
24. Too Much Chest
25. Flip-Flopping

Chapter Seven:
26. More Flip-Flopping
27. Soft but Connected
28. Speak-Singing

Chapter Eight:
29. Rhythm Nation

Chapter 10:
30. Vibrato (1)
31. Vibrato (2)
32. Vibrato (3)

Chapter 12:
33. Airy to Edgy

Chapter 14:
34. Slow-Talking
35. Monotone/Variety
36. Happy Birthday

Chapter 15:
37. Happy
38. Grateful
39. Passionate
40. Confident
41. Overlapping Frequencies

Chapter 16:

  42. Low and Soft at Pauses

  43. Raising Pitch at Pauses

  44. Scaling Down Happy

  45. Stair-Step Melody

Chapter 17:

  46. Small Bursts of Air

  47. Connected Words for Stuttering

Warm-ups:

  48. Daily Warm up (female-singing)

  49. Daily Warm up (male-singing)

  50. Daily Warm up (female-speaking)

  51. Daily Warm up (male-speaking)

  52. Goodbye